P9-DMA-250

STORM OVER TEXAS

Also by Joel H. Silbey

The Shrine of Party:
Congressional Voting Behavior, 1841–1852

A Respectable Minority:
The Democratic Party in the Civil War Era, 1860–1868

The Partisan Imperative:
The Dynamics of American Politics Before the Civil War

The American Political Nation, 1838–1893

Martin Van Buren and the Emergence of American Popular Politics

PIVOTAL MOMENTS
IN AMERICAN HISTORY

Series Editors
David Hackett Fischer
James M. McPherson

James T. Patterson
Brown v. Board of Education: A Civil Rights Milestone and Its Troubled Legacy

Maury Klein
Rainbow's End: The Crash of 1929

James M. McPherson
Crossroads of Freedom: The Battle of Antietam

Glenn C. Altschuler
All Shook Up: How Rock 'n' Roll Changed America

David Hackett Fischer
Washington's Crossing

John Ferling
Adams vs. Jefferson: The Tumultuous Election of 1800

STORM OVER TEXAS

THE ANNEXATION CONTROVERSY AND THE ROAD TO CIVIL WAR

JOEL H. SILBEY

OXFORD
UNIVERSITY PRESS
2005

OXFORD
UNIVERSITY PRESS

Oxford University Press, Inc., publishes works that further
Oxford University's objective of excellence
in research, scholarship, and education.

Oxford New York
Auckland Cape Town Dar es Salaam Hong Kong Karachi
Kuala Lumpur Madrid Melbourne Mexico City Nairobi
New Delhi Shanghai Taipei Toronto

With offices in
Argentina Austria Brazil Chile Czech Republic France Greece
Guatemala Hungary Italy Japan Poland Portugal Singapore
South Korea Switzerland Thailand Turkey Ukraine Vietnam

Published by Oxford University Press, Inc.
198 Madison Avenue, New York, NY 10016

ISBN-13: 978-0-19-513944-0
ISBN-10: 0-19-513944-5

Printed in the United States of America

To Abigail V. Hogan
and her brother, Thomas P. S.

CONTENTS

EDITOR'S NOTE

When Stephen Austin of Missouri settled the first of three hundred American families in the Mexican province of Texas in 1823–24 under a land grant from the Mexican government, no one foresaw the chain of events that would follow from this act and lead to the American Civil War four decades later. Yet that is precisely what happened, as Joel Silbey shows in this important new study of the Texas annexation controversy.

Achieving independence from Mexico in the revolution of 1836, Anglo-Texans petitioned for annexation to the United States. Expansionist Democrats, especially from the American South, eagerly supported acquisition of this huge new slave state, nearly half as large as the other fourteen slave states combined. Until 1844, however, Texas annexation was mainly a partisan rather than sectional issue, with Democrats from both North and South in favor and most Whigs in both sections against it. But in the presidential election campaign of that year, proslavery southerners added an ominous overlay of sectionalism to the issue. Secretary of State John C. Calhoun stated publicly that annexation was necessary to strengthen slavery, an institution "essential to the peace, safety, and prosperity" of the South. Calhoun's predecessor in the State Department, the Virginian Abel Upshur, had also insisted that southerners must "*demand* . . . the admission of Texas . . . as indispensable to their security. Both parties [in the South] may unite on that, for it is a *Southern* question, and not one of whiggism and democracy."

The election of Tennessee's pro-annexation Democrat James

K. Polk as president in 1844 settled the question. To balance Texas, Polk pledged to Northern Democrats the acquisition of Oregon territory all the way north to the latitude of 54° 40'. When Polk instead compromised with Britain on the 49th parallel but went to war with Mexico over the southern boundary of Texas, many northern Democrats felt they had been sold out. And when Pennsylvania Democrat David Wilmot introduced his famous "Proviso" prohibiting slavery in any territory acquired from Mexico, nearly all northern Democrats plus northern Whigs in the House voted for it while nearly all southern congressmen voted against it. As Silbey makes clear in one of the key themes of the book, this fateful wrenching of congressional voting patterns from partisan to sectional lines foreshadowed the crisis of secession and war fifteen years later.

That war was the consequence of cumulative events reaching back at least as far as the "firebell in the night" heard by Thomas Jefferson during the Missouri debates in 1820. But if there was a single pivotal moment in this series of events, it was surely the annexation of Texas in 1845. The Missouri Compromise had contained the genie of slavery expansion for a generation. Texas unstopped the bottle and let the genie out; all efforts during the next fifteen years to stuff him back in again failed. And the war came. This book tells the story of how that genie got out of the bottle.

James M. McPherson

"As certain as truth and God exist, the admission of Texas into this Union will prove, sooner or later, an element of overwhelming ruin to the Republic."

—*Congressman Daniel Barnard of New York*
on the floor of the House of Representatives,
January 1845

1844: Optimistic pro-annexationists believed that they were about to win their goal at last. LIBRARY OF CONGRESS.

Welcome Texas! welcome brothers.
Polk.
If we let go, we are ruined, and if we hold on— Oh! crackee!
Webster

PREFACE

THE MEXICAN PROVINCE OF TEXAS ATTRACTED much interest in the United States and drew many North American settlers to it in the early decades of the nineteenth century. That continuing interest and growing presence developed into a significant problem when the restive emigrants living in the province revolted against Mexican rule in the 1830s and successfully established an independent republic despite Mexico's bitter resistance to the separation. The new republic's leaders then pushed hard to be annexed to the United States. At first they were held at arm's length, by President Andrew Jackson and then by his successor, Martin Van Buren. But in the early 1840s a renewed and much stronger effort to bring Texas into the Union came to life and provoked a searing political controversy, which had profound long-term consequences for the nation.

A number of different dates—1819, 1832–33, 1846, 1854, 1856, among others—have been offered as the crucial moment when sectional momentum toward Civil War dramatically shifted into high gear in the United States. And it is not unusual for historians to focus much attention on the Texas annexation crisis in 1844 as having much the same impact as these moments: the opening up of deep, polarizing wounds in the American nation that seemed to decisively threaten the Union's well-being. But, as I argue here, the conflict over annexation *and*, most particularly, the political fallout from it, has fair claim to be considered as *the* critical base point on which the rest of the crisis of the Union grew. What began in the controversy over annexing Texas proved to be, I suggest, crucial in framing a long process that culminated, a decade later, in a profound reorganization of American politics and then in southern secession and Civil War—crucial in ways that earlier sectional crises had never reached.

Annexation may or may not have been, as one editor claimed, the "most disastrous event of our history for the last thirty years," but certainly the controversy that developed from it contributed significantly to the ultimate shifting of the dynamics of American politics away from its deeply imbedded partisan qualities by intensifying and crystallizing a sectional political dynamic.[1] That dynamic had always been present in American life. But it now became, for the first time, a major force in ways that had been strongly resisted, and not sustained, in earlier episodes of sectional sensitivity and anger. Rather, previous sectional passion, while often bitter and intense, was rarely widespread, always intermittent, and well contained by other forces on the political landscape. The controversy that erupted in the 1840s was made of sterner stuff as political realities began to shift in a profound way. Texas unleashed demons that, while restrained and apparently put back into the bottle after a short period, were never completely repressed. Whatever containment of these forces occurred lasted only for a time and ultimately gave way. A series of unexpected moves, some planned, some more inadvertent than not, created first a crisis over the area's admission and then a situation that forcefully contributed to the remaking of American politics into something overwhelmingly driven by implacable sectional confrontation.

No one event precipitated the descent into destructive and sustained sectional conflict, of course. Few Americans deliberately set out to split the Union. However, that possibility was certainly present in the minds of some political activists. And somewhere in the American soil the seeds that would develop into virulent and persistent sectional confrontation and then Civil War had long ago been planted and nurtured. In the 1840s, they began to come to fruition. New York congressman Daniel Barnard's warning that "as certain as truth and God exist, the admission of Texas into the Union will prove, sooner or later, an element of overwhelming ruin to the republic" expressed a prescient foreboding of what was to come.[2]

The full impact of Barnard's foreboding would not be realized for another decade. There was much more than a simple unbroken trajectory between Texas and secession. The process leading to "overwhelming ruin" was not the work of a moment. Rather, it was the result of a long period of recurring conflict that stretched back to its takeoff point in the early forties. The roadway proved to be often bumpy, the events that took place on it discontinuous and characterized by a pattern of fits and starts in their movement. But something clearly had begun to change in the Texas battle and its aftermath so that sectional confrontation became more and more regnant in American political life. By 1857, the United States was, as the historian Kenneth Stampp has described it, "a nation on the brink" of the final battle between the sections.[3] The process that led to that devastating moment began in, and then built on, the demands, claims, misunderstandings, and increasing sense of something going very wrong that originated in the Texas imbroglio and then led, ultimately, to the significant alteration of the prevailing template of American political life.

The crucial factor making Texas different from earlier crises is that what occurred as the battle over its accession to the Union developed created among those involved in American political life, both leaders and followers, an understanding, a mindset, and a way of looking at subsequent events that raised serious angst among them and, in consequence, unprecedented danger to the Union. In particular, that understanding became etched into political consciousness much more deeply and intensely than in earlier sectional uproars, and in ways that interacted with and sharply affected subsequent political events as they arose and were viewed through lenses originally fashioned in the battle over Texas. All that happened in the 1840s knitted together in a particular way that became a significant and particularly destructive precipitating force at subsequent moments, leading to the final crisis of the Union.

In tracing the story of these developments, while I have explored the role of all of the active players in the political controversy as it evolved, I have focused particular attention on the Van Buren bloc of the Democratic Party, dubbed radicals or Barnburners by their enemies, when not being given harsher names. Deeply loyal to partisan political norms, and initially extremely resistant to sectional political impulses, they were, I suggest, the fulcrum on which the annexation controversy turned, and their reactions to the events of the mid-1840s helped structure much of the framework on which all that followed rested.

I HAVE RELIED HEAVILY ON THE PREVIOUS WORK of many fine historians of annexation and the politics of the 1840s. From Justin Smith early in the twentieth century to Frederick Merk, Charles Sellers, and David Pletcher in the 1960s and 1970s and then, more recently, to Sellers again, Michael Holt, and Michael Morrison, among many others, scholars have thoughtfully examined what occurred in the Texas battle with subtlety, great care, and much imagination.[4] I have learned a great deal from the suggestions and insights they have offered even as I have cut my own pathway through the events they describe and perused the mass of primary material available about Texas annexation and the political fallout from it. I believe that much remains to be understood about these events and their consequences. In what follows, therefore, I am returning once more to this crucial moment and its aftermath, to rethink what occurred, to make what happened then clear, and, most pertinently, to explain why matters developed in the particular form that they did despite the original, and contrary, intentions, expectations, and desires of most of those who were involved in the blistering battle that erupted in the spring of 1844: why, in sum, the Texas controversy was more than a brief uproar but rather such a pivotal moment in the nation's history—why it became, in the words of an Alabama congressman, "the greatest question of the age."[5]

STORM OVER TEXAS

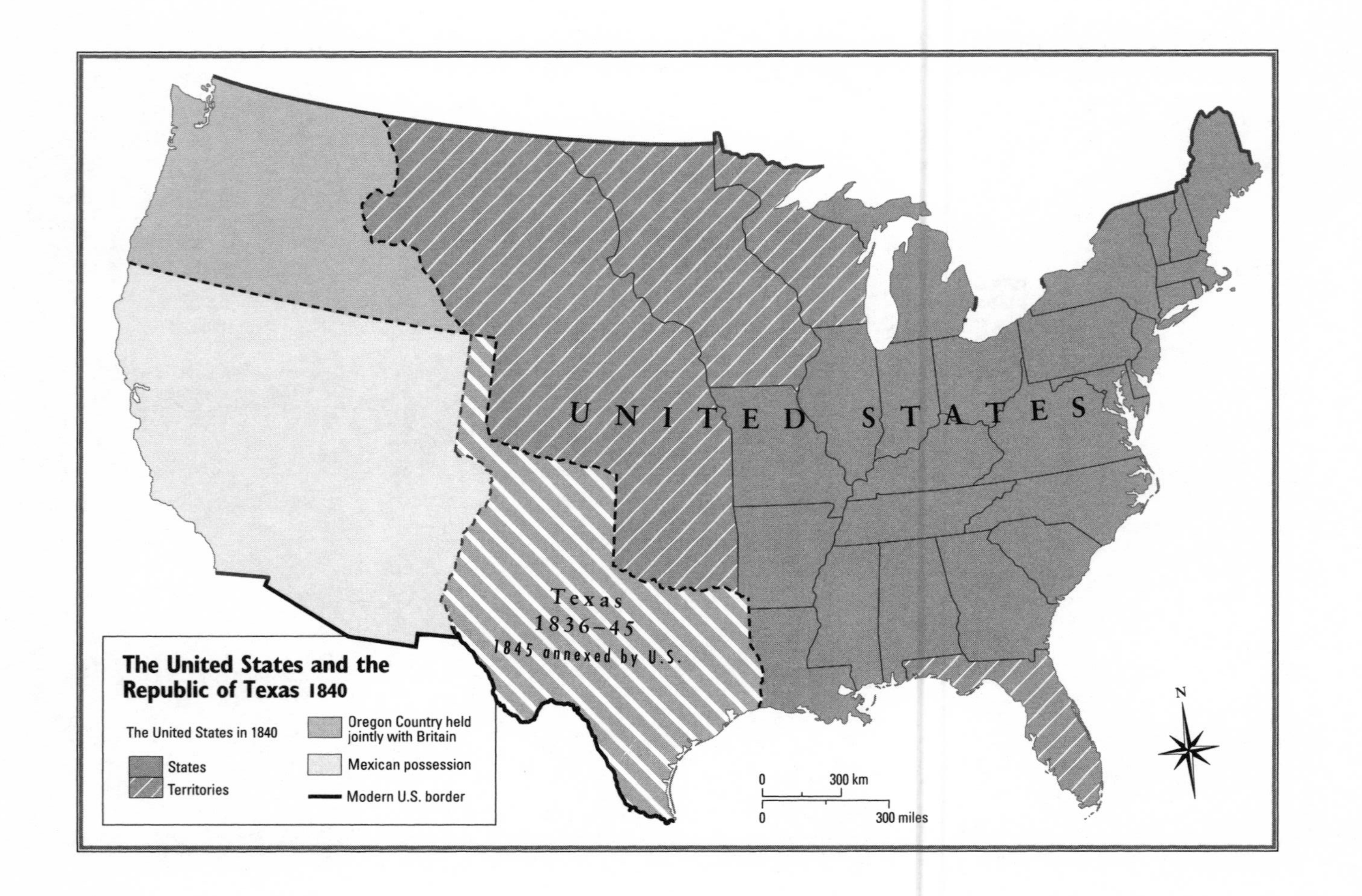
The United States and the Republic of Texas 1840
The United States in 1840
States
Territories
Oregon Country held jointly with Britain
Mexican possession
Modern U.S. border
UNITED STATES
Texas
1836–45
1845 annexed by U.S.
0
300 km
0
300 miles
N

PROLOGUE

"The Joint Resolution 'For Annexing Texas to the United States' Is Finally Passed"

THE TWENTY-EIGHTH CONGRESS of the United States was in its final hours in the last week of February 1845. In a few days its life would end, as the Constitution dictated, with the inauguration of a new administration and the official coming of its successor, the recently elected Twenty-ninth Congress. On February 27, the Senate met in an unusual evening session to complete work on a long-pending matter: the effort to make Texas part of the Union. The Senators had recessed their normal day session at 3:00 P.M. and reconvened at 6:00 P.M. When they did, the Capitol's usual atmosphere of overpowering noise, inadequate ventilation, and an excess of foul air was much in evidence. Conditions seemed even worse than usual that night. The Senate chamber was uncomfortably full. All fifty-two senators were present on the floor to hear the last arguments on the matter before them. Above them, the public galleries were similarly jammed with an excited crowd of government officials, senators' wives, and other citizens of Washington. As one historian has written, "all the learned and the beautiful seemed to be present." Many members of the House of Representatives had also come over from the other side of the Capitol to be present at this moment of high drama. The crowds spilled over onto the chamber's floor itself and into the corridors outside, filling nearby alcoves and stairways as well. They rubbed elbows with an array of food and drink purveyors diligently plying their trade at the back of the chamber, as they always did when Congress was in session. No one stayed still, adding to the din and contributing to a sense of great excitement and tension as the evening got under way.[1]

On the floor, the senators milled around, going to the back of the chamber to converse with their colleagues or the many onlookers, to smoke, drink, or eat pastries while waiting for the session to begin. The Senate was no longer led by the great leaders of the immediate past who had shaped so many events over the last two decades: Henry Clay, after bitterly tangling with President John Tyler over the Whig Party's legislative program, had resigned and gone home to Kentucky; Daniel Webster, after serving as secretary of state from 1841 to 1843, was in retirement in Massachusetts; John C. Calhoun had also resigned his Senate seat but had recently come back to Washington as the new secretary of state.

Despite their absence, some notable figures remained in the upper house, among them the mercurial but politically powerful Thomas Hart Benton of Missouri, Andrew Jackson's loyal lieutenant when the latter was president, and still high in the councils of the Democratic Party; Clay's close ally, the veteran Whig leader John J. Crittenden of Kentucky; Levi Woodbury of New Hampshire, who had served in the cabinets of Jackson and Martin Van Buren in the 1830s, a man often considered for his party's presidential nomination and who would end his career on the Supreme Court; and Webster's successor, Rufus Choate, who would become one of the nation's great jurists. Finally, there was the future president James Buchanan of Pennsylvania, an ardent expansionist, who, with Mississippi's Robert J. Walker, led the pro-Texas forces in the Senate. Walker, originally from Pennsylvania, had moved south and made a fortune as a cotton planter, slaveowner, and investor in western lands, among other things. These men, a fairly representative group of legislators for the period, were about to deal with a proposal that had simmered in national consciousness for a long time.

THE PARTICULAR ITEM in front of the senators that evening was a joint resolution of the two houses annexing the Republic of Texas to the United States. From the first, Congress had been sharply divided over the matter. The year before, senators had defeated a formal treaty of annexation that had been worked out between the two governments. But the issue had not died and came back before Congress when, in his annual message to the national legislature in December 1844, a determined President Tyler, the first vice president to succeed a president who had died in office, pressed the issue once again and called for an unusual tactic: a joint resolution of both houses to accomplish the same purpose as the defeated treaty. Such a resolution needed only a majority in each legislative chamber to pass, as against the two-thirds vote required under the Constitution for the Senate to ratify a formal treaty. Tyler's controversial maneuver underscored his adamant resolve to use his presidential powers to the full in order to bring Texas into the Union.[2]

Congressmen responded to the president's call by offering seventeen different bills and resolutions over the next several weeks to accomplish the acquisition of Texas. This outburst of legislative exuberance was followed by a great deal of bitter debate and much lobbying on the issue. "Don't let Texas slip from us" had been the annexationists' theme. "I regard the joint resolution as the apoplexy of the Constitution" was the unwavering counterview of former president and now Massachusetts representative John Quincy Adams, long one of Texas's leading opponents in the House.[3]

Now the issue had reached the last stages of its movement through Congress. The House of Representatives, firmly under the control of the pro-annexationists, had passed its version of the joint resolution several weeks before by a substantial margin, 120 to 98, but the Senate was known to be much more closely divided about Tyler's Texas initiative. The fate of the measure remained unclear as the members made their final speeches and moved toward a vote on the matter.[4]

The lateness of the hour, the full attendance, and the excited onlookers all testified to the importance of the moment. The bitter differences over means and ends that continued to be expressed in these last hours indicated how deep was the chasm separating senators from one another on the issue. The measure's opponents were led by the chair of the Foreign Relations Committee, William Archer of Virginia, serving his only term in the Senate, who was determined to block Tyler's cherished dream of annexation. Archer had used his committee chairmanship to hamstring the proposal for as long as he could, and on this night he sought to delay the final vote by offering time-consuming motions of various kinds. Nevertheless, after the summing-up speeches, most of which rehearsed the claims and warnings that had been heard throughout the session, voting on the measure began shortly before 9:00 P.M. After several preliminary roll calls, the Senate finally agreed to the joint resolution by a vote of 27 to 25.[5]

The roll call had been gone through in comparative silence despite the by now restless crowd and the inherent tension of the moment. That soon ended. Its passage was met with an explosion of shouts of approval, while outside on Capitol Hill cannon boomed to announce and celebrate the annexationists' victory. An important hurdle had been cleared, but the matter was not yet quite settled. After much sorting through the proposals before it, the Senate had focused on a measure spelling out its own version of how annexation was to be accomplished, a version quite different from the one previously passed by the House of Representatives. But the Senate's approach, as originally offered, had not survived the debates. Some hesitant senators had had to be placated, and were, by an amendment offered by Senator Walker. He moved to combine the House version of how to go about annexing Texas with the different method that had been the subject of the Senate debate and give the president of the United States the option to choose whichever of the two specified approaches he preferred. It was a clever compromise, and one that finally brought Senate passage. Now the House of Representatives, in its turn, had to agree to the amended resolution.[6]

It did so on Friday, February 28, the day after the Senate action, beginning when the secretary of the Senate appeared at the door of the House chamber to announce the upper house's passage of the amended joint resolution and to request the concurrence of the House of Representatives. There was an immediate uproar from those members who opposed annexation by any method, more foot-dragging motions offered by them, the raising of delaying points of order, and demands that the House recess or take up its regular order of business (which was not Texas). But the pro-annexation majority was in full control. The Speaker, John W. Jones, another of the Virginians so noticeable in the Texas debate from its inception, decisively ruled the opposition's various motions out of order. Then the many bills that were ahead of the Texas resolution on the House calendar were pushed aside, one by one, until the joint resolution was reached and offered for consideration as the House's pending order of business. After further debate, the vote in favor of passage, 132 to 76, was by an even larger margin than the representatives' original support of the earlier version of the resolution. A motion to reconsider the vote went down to defeat, and, as the reporter of the debate wrote, "*thus the joint resolution 'for annexing Texas to the United*

States' is finally passed and awaits only the signature of the President to become a law."[7]

PRESIDENT TYLER SIGNED THE JOINT RESOLUTION on March 1, three days before he left office. This "great and important national act," in former president Andrew Jackson's words, was, at last, the law of the land. Only a few steps remained to be taken to bring to a close the long-bubbling dispute: first, the necessary executive action called for in the document just passed to carry out the terms of the resolution, and then Texas's acceptance of the steps needed to finalize annexation as offered to it by the United States.[8]

The Richmond *Enquirer*'s headline, "Joy! Joy!! *The Last Stroke Struck*," expressed the enthusiasm and sense of accomplishment felt by the pro-annexationists. But, whatever closure that they and other observers thought had at last been realized on those final days of the Twenty-eighth Congress, the battle over annexation had not really ended. Texas would enter the Union as the twenty-eighth state, but the consequences of Congress's action were as yet neither fully elaborated nor clearly perceived in the enthusiasm—or anger—of the moment. A great deal was still to come.[9]

1

"GOIN' TO TEXAS"

Texas in the American Imagination and Politics, 1821–1841

Stephen Austin, originally from Virginia, came to Texas in late 1821, his mind filled with optimistic and expansive plans. His father, a longtime entrepreneur and promoter, had persuaded the Spanish government to grant him land there in order to establish a colony of North Americans in the province. Moses Austin died before the project got under way, and his son took over the scheme with the same lofty ambition. He was welcomed by the new reigning authorities in Texas. At the conclusion of their successful revolution against Spain, the newly established Mexican government followed the lead of its predecessor in encouraging Americans to come to Texas and settle there. They granted Austin, and a number of others, large blocks of territory. By the late twenties, Austin had bought many of the others out and amassed a personal holding of one hundred thousand acres of arable land. While doing so he advertised widely in American journals, promoting the attractiveness of his holdings and inviting settlers to come and buy up the fertile land he had to offer.[1]

His efforts paid off. There was an enthusiastic response from north of the border. The opening of new agricultural lands always attracted keen interest in the United States. Austin's depiction of a bountiful expanse seemed to offer great opportunities to a range of small farmers, adventurers, people on the make, and other would-be investors in the fertile lands and future prospects of the province. Throughout the 1820s, new settlers flocked in, bought land from Austin, and settled down to build a prosperous economy. Texas was soon dominated by these land-hungry and entrepreneurial arrivals from north of the border as more and more of them followed the earlier North American immigrants into the new republic. By the time of Austin's death in the mid-1830s, Texas's non-Indian population was 40,000 or so, and would reach about 150,000 by 1845.[2]

Much of that population growth came from settlers originally from Mississippi, Louisiana, Arkansas, and other southwestern states, many of whom were slaveholders who brought their slaves with them. There were emigrants from the nonslaveholding states as well, but not in the same numbers. Texas was destined to become dominated by those who believed in slave labor and utilized it in pursuit of their own economic well-being. (Mexico had abolished slavery in its territory in 1829, an action first opposed and then largely ignored by the Texans.) In the late 1830s, there were about five thousand slaves in the republic, with more being brought in every day.[3]

The momentum for "goin' to Texas," as newspapers dubbed the surging population movement, greatly increased when the American economy faltered and fell into a severe recession in 1837. The downturn was experienced everywhere, nowhere more so than in areas of recent economic expansion. Many western farmers, carrying heavy debt burdens due to their much too optimistic belief in the economy's continued boom, and overwhelmed by bank loans that they had taken out to increase their landholdings and were now unable to repay, lost or had to abandon their property. Some of them sought new opportunities in land-wealthy Texas.[4]

With so many Americans streaming in, by the late thirties the republic took on many of the attributes that suggested how much it had become an extension of the United States, whatever its current status as an independent entity. As President Andrew Jackson described Texas in a special message to Congress in 1836, "a large proportion of its civilized inhabitants are emigrants from the United States, speak the same language with ourselves, cherish the same principles, political and religious, and are bound to many of our citizens by ties of friendship and kindred blood; and, more than all, it is known that the people of that country have instituted the same form of government with our own."[5]

From the first, the Texas leaders who followed Austin believed that they could build on such attitudes and the realities underlying

Sam Houston was the Republic of Texas's pro-annexation hero and president.
LIBRARY OF CONGRESS.

them to achieve their ultimate goal. Led by Virginia-born Sam Houston, a former governor of Tennessee, hero of the Texas Revolution against Mexico, and now the republic's president, they began almost at once to explore, then energetically push for, annexation to their sister, and stronger, republic to the north. They sent agents to Washington who vigorously articulated their cause at every opportunity available to them, to newspaper editors, in the White House, and, at the other end of Pennsylvania Avenue, among congressmen on Capitol Hill. They described Texans and North Americans as "one people . . . united by all the sacred ties that can bind one people to another."[6]

They found much support in the United States. A powerful expansionist impulse existed among Americans all along the Mississippi Valley in the late 1820s and 1830s. Eight new states were admitted to the Union between 1815 and 1836, all but one of them (Maine) along the nation's western frontier. Many of these new states were carved out of the vast expanse of the Louisiana Territory acquired in 1803, but organizing and settling that area was not the end of the nation's ambitions. After a hiatus of twenty years, the United States was entering a period of renewed interest in further territorial aggrandizement.[7]

Texas was now caught up in this energetic expansionism. There had been a great deal of unofficial encouragement of the Texas Revolution emanating from various sectors of the American population. Public meetings were held in its support, primarily but not exclusively in the western states, and money for arms and supplies was raised on behalf of the Texans. Many American volunteers fought in the rebellion against Mexico. In its aftermath, there continued to be strong support for defending Texas from the ongoing threat from Mexican armed encroachment on its freedom—an encroachment that could be forestalled permanently by joining the nations together.[8]

What made annexation a popular cause among so many Americans was its connection to the nation's values and aspirations as well as the economic benefits promised in the uniting of the two republics. A reigning ideological perspective added to the mix that defined the annexationist outlook. Many proponents of adding Texas to the Union hoped to continue the extension of the republican sphere, and its values and institutions, across the continent, establishing political control over the land absorbed, promoting freedom, and increasing economic opportunity, all at the same time. As many saw it, the virtues and values of white Anglo-Saxon Protestantism should spread over an area that did not as yet enjoy such positive attributes. To these enthusiasts, the course of American freedom ran farther and farther westward across the vast land mass that was North America.[9]

Texas was part of the commitment to such feelings. From the first, the desire to replace what was widely viewed as a rotten, violence-ridden, tyrannical government, that is, Mexico, with a new nation espousing democratic republican values was palpable and widely voiced. To be sure, as one historian has noted, "public declamations about freedom and Mexican tyranny thinly concealed a mounting greed for the cheap, fertile Texan lands."[10] It was always clear that, besides simple farmers seeking new opportunities, those involved in the movement westward into Texas included land speculators who were already deeply involved in the area. Entrepreneurs had heavily invested in Texas land and the republic's bonds and other public debt and sought the security for their investments that they believed would come from formally tying Texas to the much stronger United States. Their agents were also hard at work in Washington on behalf of the annexation project and adding a great deal of political clout to the efforts underway.[11]

Nevertheless, they, and the specific interests they pushed, were never alone in constituting the impulse that worked so hard on behalf of annexation. The frenetic urge to expand the American nation drew on a constellation of motives—a constellation made up of the mixture of nationalist striving and economic opportunity—that influenced Americans and led so many of them to push settlement farther and farther into the nation's borderlands, and then beyond.[12]

At the same time, even as the expansionist urge continued to be widely expressed in the aftermath of Texas's successful revolt, there was also, from the outset, resistance within the United States to any further territorial growth at all, and particularly to adding Texas to the Union. Not everyone, policy makers, political leaders, or their constituents, welcomed the idea of additional territory being added to the Union, or agreed with the enthusistic hopes of the expansionists. In the first instance, there were those who feared the impact of more acquisitions to the already sprawling United States on the domestic tranquility of the American nation. They wanted a smaller republic, or at least one that was little larger than its present configuration. They argued that the nation could not readily absorb additional land without a significant negative impact on the economy and the further orderly internal development of the existing states. Are we "not large and unwieldy enough already?" one hostile congressman summed up the limited-size case against annexation.[13]

Texas raised additional concerns. Many opponents of the push to acquire it warned of the diplomatic consequences that would occur if the annexation project went through. The persistent and bitter post-rebellion Mexican-Texas tensions would inevitably draw the United States, anti-annexationists believed, into a confrontation with its southern neighbor. The danger of a war with Mexico was real in these men's minds. To them, it would be an unnecessary war provoked by rash American policies. The support of Americans for the Texas Revolution had provoked strong protests from the Mexican government and further exacerbated the existing bad feelings between the two countries—bad feelings that needed little, the anti-Texas argument went, to stoke them into something larger and more dangerous than they already were.[14]

Still other opponents of annexation argued against it by claiming that adding Texas to the Union would fundamentally and negatively threaten the character of the American republic. No one expressed this attitude about Texas more forcefully than the consummate and always intense political skeptic John Quincy Adams. Adams, nearing his seventieth year, had had a full public career, as a diplomat, senator, secretary of state, one-term president, and, in the 1830s, congressman from Massachusetts. During that long career he had won a deserved reputation as a highly moralistic and inflexible advocate of certain values including a great hostility to slavery. He suffered few fools gladly. He was quick to correct errors and condemn missteps. He made it clear that the country had been on a wrong course for some time. His contempt for the Jacksonians, running the country since the late 1820s—their values, intelligence, and policies—knew no bounds.

Adams had been suspicious from the first moments of the Texas Revolution. Once, when he was secretary of state in the years after 1815, he had been an ardent expansionist, even about Texas. He now reversed himself about that territory as he spied malignant forces at work in the annexationist impulse. As early as 1836 he was forcefully laying out to his fellow representatives in the House an anti-slavery case against acquiring the republic. Specifically, he saw in the current annexation agitation a conspiracy to extend slavery and further increase the overweening power of slaveholders within the United States. To him, the conspiracy was clear, as was the role played by the southern-dominated Jacksonian Democrats in pushing it forward—by both fair means and foul.[15]

Adams did not stop with one speech. ("Old Man Eloquent" rarely did on any matter.) "That mischievous bad old man," as the ardent defender of southern rights and interests John C. Calhoun described him, kept up his oratorical assaults on the proposal unrelentingly whenever he spied the annexationists at work—which was often—with all of his vituperative guns blazing. His pointed and accusatory sectional argument proved popular among some other northerners

John Adams was a fervent opponent of the Democrats' policies (including annexation) and of southern ambitions in the territories.
LIBRARY OF CONGRESS.

in the mid-1830s, particularly in his native Massachusetts and in other parts of New England and the region's diaspora across western New York and into Ohio.[16] In particular, committed anti-slavery reformers William Lloyd Garrison, Theodore Weld, Benjamin Lundy, Joshua Leavitt, and James Birney took the lead. They had long been critical of the institution's existence in the United States and demanded that it be ended. At first, they concentrated their efforts on persuading others to join with them. They founded the American Anti-Slavery Society in 1833 to rouse the American people against southern slaveholders and on behalf of black freedom. They took every opportunity from then on to inflame the public against slavery and challenge its continued existence. It was a foul institution that could no longer be tolerated in a free republic no matter what had been acceptable to earlier generations. It had to be erased from the national scene.[17]

In the mid-thirties, as the annexation issue unfolded, they continued their fierce assaults in in a flurry of speeches, editorials, and mass meetings and in the thousands of petitions they sent to

Congress against the institution. They assailed the placidity of most Americans on the matter and denounced the political leadership of their section for its failure to confront the issue. Their anger was tinged with intense conspiracy paranoia about the existence, reach, determination to have its own way, and growing appetite of the "slave power" in American life. Given the nation's basic ideological commitments and social values, which were, they passionately argued, clearly hostile to those of the slave power, Texas annexation was unacceptable.[18]

"We Should Still Stand Aloof"

The many speeches in the mid-thirties concerning Texas, from weighty political figures as well as from less renowned speakers, were not the only medium expressing what was at stake and what the United States should do. Petitions from organized public meetings in the countryside and from affected interest groups poured into Congress from all sides in 1836–37. Newspaper editors were fully aroused, and many congressmen added their voices to the clamor for and against Texas. A full-scale debate was under way, filled with expressions of intense anxiety, extraordinary hyperbole, and a range of controversial assertions, since the Texas matter touched on so many American values, interests, and fears about the future.[19]

Despite the rhetorical force of the anti-expansionists from 1836 on, those Americans who favored adding Texas to the Union when the issue first arose probably outnumbered those opposed to doing so. Nevertheless, there were complications and concerns imbedded in the issue that shrewd political leaders were quick to see and assess. Texas bred opportunity but also provoked difficulties that might be better evaded or postponed. As a result, neither President Jackson nor his successor, Martin Van Buren, gave the annexation movement the support expected by Texas's advocates in the United States or the republic's agents on the scene in Washington. Rather, both presidents followed a very cautious policy that went only a little bit of the way toward giving the Texans what they wanted.[20]

The two presidents offered many reasons for their hesitancy. As the pressure on behalf of Texas grew after 1836, political leaders were preoccupied with other policy matters to which they gave priority when they dealt with the forces working on them to bring

Texas into the Union. Among them, the diplomatic argument against annexation was certainly important, and probably persuasive, to both presidents. As noted, America's relations with Mexico were at the least difficult, and more often extremely hostile, in the 1830s, and both professional diplomats and political leaders hesitated about worsening those relationships by taking actions in Texas, an area that Mexicans heatedly claimed was part of their nation. (The United States once had some claim to Texas, but then–Secretary of State John Quincy Adams had ceded it in a treaty with Spain in 1819—although some expansionists continued to argue that our claims to the area remained valid.)[21]

The diplomatic problems present were real and certainly prompted Andrew Jackson's hesitancy when the matter came up, for he personally wanted Texas to become part of the United States. The first western president, he had expansionist fever in his blood as intense as anyone's, and he also expressed concern, from the first, for the nation's security against foreign threats—by which he meant the pernicious British presence on America's frontiers. He had tried to purchase the province from Mexico in the early days of his administration only to be rebuffed each time that he made the offer. That did not end his interest or his concern after the province's successful rebellion. Quite the contrary. As one historian has pungently summed up, "Texas existed as a ramshackle republic. . . . What was clear was that . . . [it] was too weak to stand alone for long." Jackson and his colleagues shared that assessment and greatly feared who might rush into the vacuum on America's southwestern border.[22]

Nevertheless, the situation was not yet settled enough for any untoward movements toward annexation. There were too many potential complications and dangers, the Jacksonians believed, too much controversy present that might interfere with their other domestic and foreign policy plans and activities. For one, Texas's boundaries remained uncertain and in dispute, with the Texans claiming more territory than the Mexicans accepted. "Prudence," President Jackson told Congress at the end of his administration, "therefore, seems to indicate that we should still stand aloof." All that he felt able to do, as a result of his fears, was to call official attention to the successful Texas Revolution and then, prodded by a congressional resolution that he do so, to extend formal diplomatic recognition to the new republic just before he left office in early 1837.[23]

Andrew Jackson wanted Texas for the Union but held back when he was president. LIBRARY OF CONGRESS.

DOMESTIC POLITICAL CONCERNS also influenced the way that the nation's leaders reacted to Texas's eagerness to become part of the United States. In particular, Jackson's successor and political disciple, the New York politician Van Buren, never an ardent expansionist, was always extremely sensitive to political currents that might affect the Jacksonian Democrats' control of the national government. After being the political "little magician," the astute party manager behind Jackson, he was now in command on his own. A cautious leader by training, temperament, and instinct, he had made few rash moves throughout his career, and when he made one he quickly regretted doing so. Now he saw good reasons to follow Jackson's lead and not become involved in Texas's push to become part of the United States. The assaults by those opposed to the annexation proposal raised issues that he did not want to confront. Among these, he was particularly sensitive to anything that might stir up angry debates between northerners and southerners. John Quincy Adams's repeated strong charges against the South and its alleged malign plotting were especially irritating since they provoked a quick and equally harsh southern response, all of which was, to Van Buren, beside the main point of American politics.[24]

Whatever the numbers of those involved in the sectionalist exchanges, or the accuracy of the charges and countercharges being made, they could have, Van Buren feared, some political consequences both at the polls and among Democrats in Congress. He had won the presidency in a troublingly close election in 1836 and wanted nothing to happen that might detach even a few voters or political activists from him and his party in the subsequent contests that were always on tap. Given the closeness of political divisions at election time, even the smallest dissenting minority, as he believed the ardent anti-slavery group to be, was troublesome to the Democratic cause. They were not numerous, but they were intense, loud, and persistent, able to roil the political waters in a number of crucial states and raise havoc with the plans and prospects of the majority. It was enough to make Van Buren wary. Why raise the Texas issue when there were so many other things that needed the president's attention and would not cause the disruptive fallout (no matter how small in scale it might be) that annexation threatened to provoke?[25]

Van Buren made it quite clear, therefore, that, whatever the virtues present in the annexation proposal, the time was not ripe for any action, nor did he give any indications when it would be. He resisted attempts by some congressmen and Texas's agent in Washington to raise the issue early in his administration and stuck to that policy thereafter. He said little about it in his annual messages even as he extensively discussed Mexican-American relations. Texas was not on his agenda. Throughout his term in office he focused instead on the many important matters, other than the new republic's situation, that filled up his very busy days.[26]

Most pertinently, from the opening weeks of his administration, Van Buren was overwhelmed by the severe economic crisis afflicting the nation. The Panic of 1837 occupied almost all of his attention as political battles over the appropriate domestic policies to deal with the downturn bitterly divided the parties in Congress. These disputes were not readily resolved and persisted throughout his administration, as did the economic crisis. As a result, the president found his attention continually focused on the economy as the primary matter before him.[27]

Nevertheless, Van Buren did have to deal with additional problems, outside of the economic realm, that could not be deferred. These included America's difficulties with the British Empire over the uncertain boundary lines that existed along the nation's northern border with Canada. In addition, many Americans along the northern frontier supported the Canadian rebellion against Great Britain, support that remained alive throughout much of Van Buren's term in office. The administration spent much of its time working out peaceful solutions that would be mutually acceptable to all those involved, calm everyone down, and—Van Buren hoped—hold together thereafter.[28]

FOR ALL OF THESE REASONS, therefore, Texas remained an independent republic at the end of the 1830s. So far as the United States was concerned, it was clear to everyone interested in its becoming part of the Union that something not yet in the mix was needed to jolt the issue out of its doldrums and bring it to the center of political attention in ways that would force the matter toward a resolution once and for all. But nothing was as yet in sight that could do so. The republic's leaders had certainly gotten the message from north of the border and formally withdrew their proposal for annexation in late 1838. That action solved little by itself. Some of them wanted to continue on their own as an independent republic, but most of the top leaders knew better. They needed assistance and protection. There continued to be serious difficulties between Texas and the Mexican government and the consequent need of Texas's leaders to look around for help to ensure the republic's survival. (Texas and Mexico remained technically at war and continued to engage in armed skirmishes with each other.) Since Jackson, Van Buren, and their associates in Congress were not interested in its fate enough to make the desired moves in their favor, Texas's leaders began to consider whether other nations, such as Great Britain, might be willing to do so. They began to meet with representatives of the British government about finding ways to bring the two nations into some kind of closer association. To be sure, Texans were not united on the wisdom of these overtures. There was a great deal of political brawling in the republic about what to do. Still, the crucial item for many Texans was that, as the 1830s ended, the United States remained distant and aloof from them and their problems.[29]

"The Shrine of Party"

As the annexation issue remained on the back burner of American political life in the late 1830s, its status and future prospects were being influenced by the way that the American political nation had evolved over the past decade. The intensely charged Texas matter had appeared just as the United States was settling into a system dominated by two national political parties. The Democrats and Whigs emerged in the 1820s and early 1830s, bitterly fighting from then on for control of the government at local, state, and national levels. The parties developed out of post-1815 disagreements about the future direction of the United States and how that future was to be realized, and out of the need to organize a highly fragmented political scene into a more coherent system able to shape and direct the battles under way. Whigs and Democrats differed strongly from each other over a whole range of policy proposals to foster the American economy and to shape and enhance its society. By the early 1840s, the two parties had etched into public consciousness quite different policy agendas and distinct arguments promoting their own claims and challenging the unacceptable plans of their opponents.[30]

Their differences were always expressed in extremely vituperative language. America's political vocabulary was filled with expressions of the many threats, outrages, and most fearsome demons, always about to strike, that constituted the national situation. Election campaigns reverberated with denunciations, expressions of those fears, and the most dramatically articulated warnings of impending doom. Enemies of republican liberty were everywhere and had to be opposed. Each party made it clear how much was at stake in political warfare, how much the fate of the nation would be decided in the next election, and, most of all, how much its partisan opponents posed serious dangers to the well-being of the United States, given their base intentions and active promotion of "ruinous measures."[31]

Such vigorous presentations of what was at stake in the political world and the realities that undergirded them had the effect intended. The parties bit deeply into the American soil. People listened—and responded. Political leaders and the voters who supported them became deeply committed to their particular party with intensity, conviction, and a great deal of staying power. They followed its lead, worked for its success, voted for its candidates, and repeatedly made it clear how much they were committed to, and how much they believed in, either Whiggery or in Jacksonian Democracy. They considered themselves to be members of mass armies arrayed against one another in perpetual combat for a good cause.[32]

By the late 1830s, such intensely expressed and acted-on partisan commitment and the impulses behind it had become a widely accepted reality in the United States—the norm that largely defined American political culture. As one editor put it, "there never existed so thorough a separation and so exact a delineation and opposition of the two parties, as at present." Americans' strong devotion to what one observer would later call "the shrine of party" everywhere defined, mobilized, organized, focused, and directed the nation's popular politics.[33]

"Democratic Principles are Alike . . . Everywhere"

One of the most important aspects of this emerging party system was that both Whigs and Democrats were well established in, and drew support from, every part of the Union. The parties worked hard to sublimate and overcome differences that lay along local and sectional fault lines. Their focus and behavior crossed sectional lines; their policies and appeals drew people to them regardless of where they lived. Party leaders strongly and repeatedly iterated that northerners, southerners, easterners, and westerners faced the same problems and favored the same solutions: those that were offered by their party. As a result, "Democratic principles are alike," one activist reminded his colleagues, "everywhere. They are the same in New York as in Virginia, in the North as in the South, in the center of the union as at either or every extreme." By the late 1830s, party leaders had largely succeeded in convincing involved Americans of that reality. Both major parties were national in their organization, reach, commitments, and purpose. They acted as such in election campaigns, state legislatures, and Congress and among executive officers at every level of government, and they were perceived as such by their many devoted adherents.[34]

Nevertheless, at the same time that national political parties were taking command of the American scene, they were never unchallenged. There were always some political activists present, leaders and voters alike, who thought otherwise. They had different fears, hopes, and agendas, and they consciously stood, therefore, outside the dominant partisan system, resisting its blandishments and denouncing its reach and power. In particular, from the first, some Americans had found themselves capable of forging sectional identities and commitments, identities that fostered anger against other Americans living elsewhere in the nation, and from time to time led to confrontation with them over specific political policies. As John Quincy Adams's hostile intervention about Texas in 1836 indicated, this sectional consciousness continued to be expressed loudly enough to be noticed and enter into political calculations even as the cross-sectional Whigs and Democrats were rooting themselves in the political soil with so much effect.[35]

There was good reason for this, sectional agitators believed. Slavery was deeply embedded in the national experience and at the center of these sectional rumblings. It was a reality that some Americans tried to ignore, others accepted, and still others confronted and combatted. Among southerners there were always spokesmen ready to defend slavery with passion and determination, because they believed that it was critical to their society and its economic and social well-being. Their arguments were widely accepted in their section even by those many southerners who themselves did not own slaves, though not always with the same rhetorical passion.[36]

This frame of mind was more than a matter of interest, attitude, and expression, however. Some political leaders sought to take advantage of sectional polarization. Their political vocabulary differed in major ways from the partisan rhetoric usually stressed on the political landscape. They held sectional concerns to be the center of affairs in the United States. They argued primarily in sectional terms, stressed their fear and loathing of the values, institutions, and intentions of the people living in other sections of the Union, and sought to reorganize American politics along sectional lines, repeatedly raising dark suspicions about the other section, its excessive power, and its malignant designs against the people and institutions of another area of the Union. In the South, these committed and intransigent sectionalists warned incessantly of the danger that existed in a hostile Union to their way of life and stressed their belief that northerners could not be trusted to go along with them, accept slavery's necessity, and leave the South alone.[37]

Southern politicians were well aware how divided the people of their section usually were over questions of public policy. Most of them accepted this split as normal and not dangerous to their section's basic values and institutions. Others, however, believed that at bedrock southerners' fundamental interests were the same and that there was great danger to those interests in their present situation. Seeing few nuances in the anti-slavery voices among northerners, and not distinguishing between moderate critics of slavery and abolitionists, they argued that northern political leaders would always have to succumb to the pressures of the anti-slavery fanatics living among them. "Vote for a northern President from a free State," one editor warned, "and when the test comes, he will support the abolitionists."[38]

Repeatedly stressing that theme, would-be sectional leaders such as South Carolina's John C. Calhoun warned that unless the people of the slave states united politically in their own defense they had much to lose in the face of an onslaught that would inevitably come from the hostile members of other sections. Magnifying the number of abolitionists, as well as their immediate political importance and potential danger, he and his followers had little use for the national political parties with their transectional claims and conceits that deceived southerners and led them to ignore the dangers they faced. To be sure, Calhoun had been nominally a Democrat for a time and had cooperated with Martin Van Buren on behalf of the party and its policies in the late 1830s and at the outset of the 1840s, but this had been a brief interlude at best. Most of the time, the Calhounites would gladly see the Whigs and Democrats shattered and driven from the scene in favor of a southern-rights coalition drawing on members of both parties to unite and defend their section against the hostile intentions of its predatory enemies.[39]

Southerners were not alone in expressing hostility to the other section. Resistance to southern institutions, to what some saw as the section's excessive power within the Union, and to its aggressive behavior, in Congress and elsewhere, directed against Northern interests had occasionally flared up since the early days of the republic. As we have seen, when John Quincy Adams challenged southerners in the House of Representatives in the mid-1830s and opposed what he believed was their unacceptable push for Texas, he had not stood alone. Outside of Congress, the abolitionists, led by Garrison, Weld, Lundy, Birney, and the rest, were taking an increasing public role in this and other sectional confrontations. Like Adams, they were determined to prevent any further additions of slave territory to the nation and joined "Old Man Eloquent" in offering passionate anti-slavery protests against annexation when its possibility began to be discussed after the Texas Revolution.[40]

At the same time, northern Whigs, while rarely abolitionists, incorporated in their spectrum of ideas and values a range of anti-slavery attitudes, including a fierce opposition to adding further slave territory to the Union. Only a relative few of them, Adams being one of the prime examples, were aggressive in their opposition, given their commitment to holding their party together behind the main issues dividing them from their Democratic adversaries. Nevertheless, their sectional attitudes were frequently close to the surface and a potential source of angry confrontation if stimulated.[41]

THE SECTIONAL SENSITIVITIES expressed on both sides of the Mason-Dixon line had earlier flared up in a most powerful fashion over the admission of Missouri as a slave state in 1819. After a long and acrimonious battle filled with great sectional outbursts against the other side, Congress was able to settle the matter by a compromise, admitting Missouri as a slave state and dividing the rest of the Louisiana Purchase between a free-labor area north of the line—36° 30' north latitude—and another area south of that line in which slavery would be allowed if the people living there desired to have it.[42]

Sectional calm returned to the political arena, although there continued to be occasional outbreaks of sectional sensitivity in subsequent years, as evidenced by John Quincy Adams's assault on Texas in 1836. In the late thirties, these sharp feelings intensified once again as anti-slavery agitation was clearly on the increase in parts of the North, a fact that stimulated, in its turn, tremendous anger among southerners and harsh confrontations and occasional scuffles in Congress between representatives from the different sections. The battle over the "gag rule," for example, a pro-slavery-instigated congressional rule against receiving abolitionist petitions, inflamed the House of Representatives at the opening of each of its sessions in the late 1830s and early 1840s.[43]

The restrictive rule passed (with some critical northern support for it) each time, and the gag was imposed. But this did not stop continued anti-slavery agitation against the South's core institution by petitions, speeches, pamphlets, and newspaper editorials, which intensified, in turn, the southern reaction against the apparently undaunted abolitionist crusade. Overt sectional anger was clearly part of the intellectual framework of American politics as Martin Van Buren settled into the presidency to confront, among other matters, the continued push to annex Texas.[44]

THE BITTER ERUPTIONS between North and South seared the political landscape for a time, and among some participants more permanently. Despite the ferocity of the rhetoric offered, however, and the clear willingness of some activists in both the North and the South to look for a fight with one another, in general these sectional tensions did not as yet shape a wide range of political conflict. While such sectional polarization was important to some, those who put sectional issues ahead of all other matters, that is, those who wished either to advance or retard slavery in the United States, kept meeting serious difficulties. Whatever the intensity of the sectionalist uproar at certain moments, and the reactions evoked by it among politically aware northerners and southerners, the leadership of the two major parties found ways to contain the tensions through evasion and compromise and, most particularly, by their constant harping on what they argued were the more important issues that Americans faced, that is, the traditional ones that the parties had long fought over. As the editor of a leading Ohio Democratic newspaper familiarly put it, in good Jacksonian style, although he and his colleagues might oppose slavery, "we do not waste our energies upon a single sectional evil . . . and let the shylocks of the money power forge the galling chains of a monster bank upon us. Neither do we waste our sympathies upon the slaves when a tariff taxation is bowing our necks to earth at home. We act with a party who fights for liberty upon its broadest basis."[45]

Whig and Democratic leaders below Mason and Dixon's line followed a similar course as they went about their political activities, believing that they, too, had other interests to focus on and that they could control the rhetorical outbursts of "a few reckless men in the South who sought to agitate along sectional lines." They would manage this by shaping their political agendas, as their northern colleagues were doing, to emphasize the range of other policy issues that they considered to be more important to their section's, and the nation's, present and future well-being.[46]

They were right in their belief. Sectional animosities remained a lesser theme among most of those involved in American politics at the end of the 1830s. Most politically involved Americans, while recognizing the differences that existed and the tensions arising from them, did not react positively to, or adopt, the Calhoun-Adams assessment of what was at stake in American politics. They did not take up the sectionalist cause, whatever their personal attitude about slavery or the challenge emanating from the behavior of people in the other section. Most members of the two political parties remained uninterested in "venting sectional grievances."[47] Why should they not? The national political architecture of partisan conflict and management continued to work well for them, and they preferred it in their approach, rhetoric, and behavior on the political landscape to the sectionalist approach to current issues.

As a result, while the elements advancing sectional confrontation were always present on the political scene, and while sectional flare-ups occurred more often than national party leaders wished, the sectional rumblings were only spasmodically intense enough to take over the nation's political agenda. They never cohered into a sustained confrontation between the North and the South that was of sufficient power to overcome the other political impulses present. Thus the angry sectional agitators found themselves to be far in advance of other political leaders and the general public in both sections, and thus very out of step with them, in seeing these matters as the most critical ones facing the nation. As a northern editor summed up, terms such as "Northern and Southern . . . are rarely or never correct, and are only calculated to create unkind sectional feelings which otherwise would not exist."[48]

This was perhaps an optimistic assessment of the way that matters stood as the 1840s got under way, but clearly, while sectional tensions were palpable in American society, national political leaders had learned how to deal with sectional eruptions. More was needed to bring the many Americans who remained unconvinced of their centrality to fall in behind the sectionalists in their vision of a nation hostilely divided by critical issues, institutions, and ways of thinking that defined the different parts of the Union and separated them from one another. We "have seen no evidence of recreancy in our Northern friends, to the faith in which we battled under a Northern leader in 1840," the editor of the *Mobile* [*Ala.*] *Register* editorialized in 1842, "and see only omens of disaster in the attempts to foment divisions within ourselves, resting on sectional grounds."[49]

"Texas Will Be Annexed"/"The Union is Sufficiently Extended"

An issue such as Texas was bound to get caught up in these existing political currents in some direct fashion. And it did. Despite the intensity of the sectional discourse on the matter, raised, as we have seen, by a number of speakers, led by Congressman Adams in the mid-1830s, the annexation proposal was viewed, at the outset, largely through the lens of the prevailing partisan political situation. Although territorial expansion had not been at the center of their concerns in the 1830s, both parties had had something to say about adding more land to the American republic. Each had, not surprisingly, adopted a position congenial to itself, a position that contrasted with that offered by its opponents. It was the Democrats who subscribed to the old Jeffersonian dream of building a landed empire across the continent, an endeavor in whose ultimate achievement Texas would be an important first step.[50]

"Texas will be annexed," an Ohio Democratic congressman celebrated, "and not only Texas, but every inch of land on this continent. Our republic is to be an ocean bound republic." Only good—for all Americans wherever they lived—would come from that expansive achievement. "To me," the Pennsylvania Democratic leader George M. Dallas told a group of supporters,

> the incorporation of Texas into the Federal Union seems not only the opening of a natural and exhaustless resource for the fabrics of the eastern and middle states, the agricultural products of the southern and western, and the activity of our extensive eastern seaboard, but it assumes the aspect of a just and necessary consequence upon the genius and maxims of our confederated system. I regard our present ability to fulfill the high duties of our political

existence, in welcoming successively every community freshly formed upon the North American continent, within the circle of the national compact, as a legitimate and lineal offspring of Gen. Jackson's valor.[51]

In sharp contrast to their opponents, the Whigs articulated intense resistance to any further territorial acquisitions. Their spokesmen constantly repeated their familiar litany, that "the union is sufficently extended and cumbrous without purchasing or accepting any more territory," to make very clear their determined opposition to what they saw as overreaching and destabilizing acquisitions of additional land outside of the nation's borders that brought with them not prosperity and national greatness, as Democratic bluster claimed, but, rather, many difficulties for the nation. The Whigs, one student of their mind set has written, were always primarily interested "in the qualitative development of American society both economically and morally, not its mere quantitative extension."[52]

Nothing was clearer among the Democrats' political antagonists as the Texas debate got under way. To the Whigs, "bloated empires, scattered settlements, and alien people attenuated the bonds of union." As their great leader, the Kentucky slaveholder Henry Clay, told his closest political confidant, "it is much more important that we should unite, harmonize, and improve what we have than attempt to acquire more." Territorial extension, Massachusetts's Whig leader, Daniel Webster, added, "often produces weakness rather than strength. We have a Republic.... Instead of aiming to enlarge its boundaries, let us seek, rather, to strengthen its Union." Nothing could be further from the Democratic Party's long-standing and determined perspective on territorial acquisition as these words were uttered.[53]

THE LINES BETWEEN the nation's two main partisan combatants were, therefore, quite sharply drawn on territorial expansion, perhaps as much as they were on the other policy matters that divided Whigs from Democrats at the end of the 1830s. This was so whatever the hesitations of the leaders of the pro-expansion party, Presidents Jackson and Van Buren, about moving forward on Texas's request for incorporation into the Union in 1836 and 1837. The Whigs were against further expansionist adventures; the Democrats were eager to engage in them, and their leaders had indicated that they were

President John Tyler's first secretary of state, Daniel Webster resisted the annexation of Texas. LIBRARY OF CONGRESS.

only awaiting the proper time, when the diplomatic and domestic complications associated with annexation were resolved, to move ahead to fulfill their expansive dreams in the Southwest.[54] Of course, when Texas's moment would actually be was not apparent, nor was it being intensely searched for by most of the political establishment as Van Buren left office to be replaced by the first Whig president, William Henry Harrison.

Matters, however, never stood still. They were always subject to some unforeseen action that stimulated new impulses and altered the normal trajectory of the nation's concerns and behavior. The partisan imperative was all-powerful; the nation's political leaders remained determined to push Texas, for the present, to the sidelines of American politics. Then President John Tyler unexpectedly took up what appeared to be a moribund political matter and succeeded in moving it to the center of the nation's attention.

2

"AND TYLER TOO"

John Tyler of Virginia, the first vice president to succeed to the presidency upon the death of the incumbent, and then first to be married (to his second wife) while president, had a lot on his mind. He was an anomalous political figure in the early 1840s, an anti-party outsider at a moment when the pressures of intense partisanship had reached unprecedented heights in the public world in which he lived and worked. Faced with a difficult and unsympathetic political landscape, he did not pull back but fought, rather, to maintain his position in spite of the very long odds against him. This determination led him to press for the annexation of Texas. The issue had limped along for more than seven years without result when he took it up. It no longer did so. Given the president's personal doggedness and the exalted position that he held, he was able to frame and advance a new attempt to acquire the republic in ways that added a great deal of controversy to the nation's existing political brew.[1]

"His Accidency"

Tyler was nominally a member of the Whig Party, but one of a particular kind. The Whigs had originated in the 1830s as an anti–Andrew Jackson coalition made up of a range of disparate elements, including a large core of strong nationalists led by Henry Clay, as well as many who celebrated states' rights against what they claimed was Jackson's excessive and destabilizing use of presidential power—that is, what they called his "executive usurpation." The states'-rights element remained an important component of the party's subsequent electoral strategy, which appealed to all who had been calling themselves Whigs to stay together against the Democrats, regardless of any policy differences that there might be among them. That plea, undergirding their campaign slogan, "Tippecanoe and Tyler too," had brought them victory in 1840.[2]

But then things fell apart. After an angry decade in opposition to the Jacksonian Democrats' misbehavior, and fresh from their sweeping electoral triumph, the Clay-led congressional Whigs were determined to establish their party as one with a clear nationalist ideological center. When Congress met in special session in early 1841, the Whig leaders eagerly pushed forward their favored policies reflecting this determination, including proposals for a protective tariff, a national bank, federal financing of internal improvements, and other schemes centering the federal government in the economic arena to an important degree in scope and ways far different from the ideas of their Democratic opponents.[3]

President William Henry Harrison, the Whig standard-bearer in 1840, would probably have gone along with his party's legislative program. He was committed to the party's stance against excessive executive power and made it clear that, unlike Jackson, he would use the president's veto power sparingly, if at all. But he died after only a month in office. His successor, Vice President Tyler, true to his personal belief system, was, once he became president, unwilling to support all of the ambitious nationalist legislative program passed by the Whig Congress. Tyler had deep roots intellectually in the Virginia political tradition, going back to Thomas Jefferson, of suspicion of central power and resistance to its expansion. He and his fellow states'-rights colleagues were deeply hostile to most of the plans of the party mainstream with whom they were yoked and were determined to resist what Clay and his associates were attempting to do. Tyler accepted the tariff bill but stingingly vetoed, and then vetoed again, several versions of the banking legislation sent to his desk, despite the pleas and pressures from the leaders of the party who had made him vice president.[4]

As a result, an ideological chasm opened, and then war broke out, between the nominal party allies gathered at either end of Pennsylvania Avenue. Neither side backed down. Each assailed its opponents with a great deal of fervor. The bitter battle royal culminated

John Tyler, the Accidental President and aggressive expansionist. LIBRARY OF CONGRESS.

when his putative congressional allies formally read Tyler out of the Whig Party, followed by the resignation, in late 1841, of all but one member of his cabinet. (Secretary of State Daniel Webster, who was deeply involved in negotiations with Great Britain over the long-standing boundary problems in the Northeast, remained in office for the time being in order to finish his current task.)[5]

Tyler was left with a small coterie of loyal allies, disparagingly referred to as his "corporal's guard." However unrealistic it may have seemed, given the limited number of his supporters, the new president very much wanted to be reelected in 1844. He understood that he needed a policy initiative that would bring him the additional backing required for him to win a second term. His instrument for creating the necessary momentum in his favor was to accomplish the annexation of Texas to the United States, the popularity of which, he believed, would break the stranglehold that the major parties had on the electorate.[6]

Given his political isolation, Tyler acted from weakness when he took up the Texas issue. "His Accidency," as his enemies disdainfully called him, remained a much hated and ostracized president among the nation's political elites even as he brought Texas back into the public arena. Although he made overtures to the pro-annexation Democrats, and some of them responded favorably, the bulk of that party was as hostile to him as were the Whigs. But neither his weakness nor the widespread negative attitudes toward him prevented the development of his expansionist initiative into a major matter demanding everyone's attention.[7]

Tyler had been a committed expansionist for some time, and his interest was not confined to Texas. (One historian refers to his "enthusiasm for empire and national glory.") The administration also pursued America's claims to the Oregon country in the Pacific Northwest, but Texas took priority, given its importance to American interests and the dangers present if it were not immediately taken up. From 1842 onward, therefore—particularly after Webster, who strongly opposed annexation, resigned from the State Department—the president engaged in secret diplomacy with the Texas government to craft a treaty of annexation. The efforts were led by the new secretary of state, Abel P. Upshur, another Virginia states'-rights advocate at odds with both major parties. A friend of John C. Calhoun, Upshur also exhibited great sensitivity to southern rights, the important role of slavery in the region's economic and social system, and what he saw as the dangers posed to the South by the section's many enemies.[8]

The president, as a Virginia slaveholder, was also dedicated to slavery's health and well-being—and continued survival in the face of the dangers confronting it—but he approached the Texas issue outside of that framework, at least in his public expressions. He believed that there was sufficient support for acquiring Texas among Democrats from all parts of the country, and from some southern Whigs as well, two groups usually quite hostile to him and that commitment, despite their initial rebuffs to the president would bring them into a cross-sectional, cross-party, annexationist coalition that would be to his political advantage. He and Upshur, therefore, proceeded on two pathways. The sectionally sensitive Upshur saw Texas primarily as a way of protecting (and extending) southern slavery in the face of the abolitionist onslaught against it. On the other hand, from the moment that the move to acquire Texas was revived, its proponents in Tyler's circle, as well as those among the

Abel Upshur was President Tyler's right-hand man and a southern rights advocate.
THE NAVAL HISTORICAL CENTER.

expansionist congressional Democrats, and those working on its behalf in the country as a whole, approached it differently. They made great efforts to offer annexation as a major benefit to the entire nation, not as the plan of a particularist cabal interested only in benefiting its own region of the country.[9]

Annexation, Tyler constantly reiterated when he discussed the subject, "was neither local nor sectional, but made its appeal to the interests of the whole Union, and of every state in the Union." Other supporters were quick to follow the president's lead. Acquiring Texas, one citizens' meeting resolved, "would promote the interest of the whole Union and there is no good reason why it should not be immediately done." The republic, after all, offered many attractions to all Americans that should be recognized and appreciated, attractions that were constantly underscored throughout the public debate.[10]

DESPITE THE SECRECY that initially surrounded the treaty negotiations, Texas annexation itself had never quite disappeared from public view. Politicians on both sides of the issue continued to raise it from time to time in 1842 and 1843, expressing all sorts of urgency, warnings, threats, and lamentations about it. Pro-administration newspapers ran articles in favor of annexation before Tyler came out in public on the issue. Thomas W. Gilmer, a Virginia congressman close to the president, wrote a public letter, as early as January 1843, strongly advocating immediate annexation. His effort attracted much notice. Some Democratic state legislatures passed resolutions calling on their representatives in Congress "to urge zealously and perseveringly" for "immediate and indissoluble" annexation. After all, "their people are our people," and nothing should keep the Texas-Americans from being part of the Union as they desired to be.[11]

Behind the scenes, the Tylerites lobbied energetically among important leaders. Mississippi Democrat Senator Robert Walker, the ardent expansionist, was in touch with former president Jackson seeking his endorsement of the annexation efforts. "I think the annexation of Texas depends *on you,*" he told the former president, who still carried great weight with his party associates. The president's men also wooed, with unusual vigor, another important Democrat friendly to expansion, Congressman Charles J. Ingersoll of Pennsylvania, who chaired the House Foreign Affairs Committee.[12]

Senator Walker also made an important foray into the public arena seeking to forestall any potential for sectional confrontation and to mobilize support throughout the Union for a Texas treaty. The Mississippi senator combined in himself the main impulses at play among the pro-expansionists: He was ideologically committed to the Jeffersonian ideal of American continental growth; he had invested in Texas land; and he supported a healthy slave economy. In addition, he was an able, shrewd, experienced, and well-regarded politician.[13]

In early 1844, he put all of these commitments and talents to use when he published a long letter on behalf of bringing Texas into the Union, which ran first in the main administration newspaper in Washington, the *Madisonian.* It was subsequently issued as a pamphlet. One historian has labeled the document, *Letter of Mr. Walker of Mississippi, Relative to the Reannexation of Texas . . . ,* "a masterpiece in which he set forth and reconciled all of the arguments for annexation." He artfully, or disingenously, argued, as the

Democratic Senator Robert John Walker worked closely with President Tyler. LIBRARY OF CONGRESS.

Tylerites were claiming, that there was something in the annexation of Texas for everyone—fertile land for the expansion of agriculture, ports and harbors for American trade, the elimination of the always present British threat to American interests—and, on the slavery issue, he offered those hesitant northerners who, while not abolitionists, were sensitive to slavery's expansion the notion that Texas's admission into the Union would disperse and dilute the institution. Its acquisition would cause, he suggested, many planters to move there with their slaves away from their current homes in the older border slave states whose land was wearing out and becoming uneconomic as a place to utilize slave labor. Ultimately, this diffusion of the slave population southward into Texas would continue until much of what was now slave territory in the border states would no longer be so.[14]

Walker's argument was infused throughout with the widespread racism common to his time among white Americans, a racism that welcomed as much physical separation of the white and black populations in the nation as possible. Such ideas were, he knew, an important element of the expansionist construction of reality, one that was applicable here. The United States faced on its southwestern border a debased population, the argument went, made up of an amalgam of Spaniards, Indians, and blacks. Their presence posed a threat to the white republic's values and strength as a nation. The annexation of Texas would, however, create a further barrier against the possibility of racial debasement as white Americans flooded into and filled the area while the degraded population there was pushed out of the new southwestern lands into Mexico. If Texas was not annexed, on the other hand, the soil exhaustion already under way in the border states would lead to the inevitable emancipation of the black population in those places, with the latter then flooding into the North, a most undesirable outcome for the people living there.[15]

Walker's arguments were widely circulated and became the "textbook" for pro-annexation representatives and senators, particularly in the North, who repeatedly used them among their constituents in support of bringing Texas into the Union, even if slavery existed there at the moment. It was, they believed, an excellent, formidable, and therefore persuasive case for annexation, presenting a reality the pro-annexationists believed in, and one they wanted to remain at the center of everyone's consideration. As Andrew Jackson wrote to his old friend Thomas Hart Benton, "Texas is all important to the North, as it is to the south, and the union would[,] by this annexation and our laws extended over Oregon[,] be established on the rock of ages." The annexation of Texas was, as Tyler and Walker claimed, most definitely a national good.[16]

ON THE OTHER SIDE, the implacable John Quincy Adams was heard from several times, first in an address to his constituents in 1842, and then in a circular letter he, along with several other northern Whigs, issued in early 1843. In both, Adams warned that much was going on concerning Texas that had to be resisted. Slaveowners, he argued, continued to be aggressive and demanding in their behavior. They continued to hold, as they always had, more than their share of power in the Union. (He was referring to the three-fifths clause of the Constitution, which increased the number of southern congressional representatives.) They claimed the right to stifle criticism of their society (through the congressional gag rule against abolitionist petitions), and now they were pushing for additional slave territory in the United States.[17]

Given this mindset and what was now before Congress, Adams and his like-minded anti-slavery associates continued to spy, in the activities of the Tylerites, a conspiracy against northern interests and a southern overreach on its own behalf, that is, "the undue ascendency of the slaveholding power" in the affairs of the nation. There was, consequently, the urgent need to arouse northerners against Tyler and his fellow conspirators as they engaged in these nefarious deeds. Adams and his colleagues were ready to do so and to begin the battle to regain control of public affairs.[18]

Despite these occasional eruptions among those hostile to the president, however, as well as the busy toing and froing among various politicians in the Tyler camp and elsewhere, and the many rumors circulating in Washington and among political activists in many parts of the country, the Texas issue remained relatively undeveloped as a public issue. It was not fully awakened in the political arena until the Tyler treaty went to the Senate in April 1844. Once it arrived there, the Tylerite arguments for annexing the republic were fully laid out by the administration's spokesmen—but with an unexpected, and most fateful, new twist added to them.[19]

"The British Are Coming"

Relations between the United States and Mexico had continued to deteriorate in the early 1840s. The tensions between the two nations involved both long-standing disputes and Mexico's belief that American interest in Texas would provoke even further difficulties between them in the future. Despite a number of diplomatic efforts, the two countries often found themselves on the edge of serious confrontation. At one point, in the fall of 1842, American naval officers occupied the Mexican port of Monterey, in California, in the mistaken notion that the two nations had gone to war. Although that awkward misstep was peacefully settled, the obvious tensions it reflected remained.[20]

Into this stepped the always dangerous (in American eyes) British Empire. In the early forties, existing difficulties in the relations between the United States and Great Britain remained important and significantly framed the Texas issue. There were rumblings between the two nations, as always, over their competing commercial interests, the control of the Oregon Territory, which was jointly occupied by the United States and Britain, and the boundary disputes along the Canadian border; there were long-standing disagreements about fishing rights in the North Atlantic, as well. Americans saw themselves under perpetual, unrelenting threat from a predatory foe determined to bring down their New World republic. As Charles Ingersoll, the Pennsylvania Democrat who chaired the House Foreign Relations Committee, put it in 1844:

> A formidable transatlantic and maritime power, whose territorial possessions by land and water hem us in on every side, from the Gulf of Mexico to the mouth of the Aristook, south, west, north, and east, interposes, threatens our institutions, grasps our territories; endangers our commerce; counteracts our whole system. Can the tribunal of Christendom, to which we owe our amenability, condemn our restoration of Texas under such circumstances?[21]

From the moment that he took office in 1841, Secretary of State Webster had worked hard to calm much of this hostile feeling and resolve outstanding differences. Negotiations went forward on a number of fronts concerning the location of the northeast boundary between the United States and British Canada, as well as about the joint claim of both countries to Oregon. Webster made some progress in his efforts, but many issues remained in dispute as he left office. And, under President Tyler, whatever Webster's diplomatic caution, the United States did not hesitate to identify Great Britain as a danger to the nation and to announce itself as always prepared to flex its muscles against America's oldest enemy.[22]

The Tylerites were particularly concerned about Britain's involvement in Mexican and Texan affairs, an involvement that would immediately threaten American national interests. To begin with, Britain was already too much of a presence south of our border for the administration's, and other annexationists', taste. Mexico's economic and political weaknesses had drawn the attention of European nations, especially the always imperialistically aggressive British, whose interest, in turn, was certain to provoke concern north of the Mexican-American border. The British Empire had never made a secret of its intention to contain the United States and prevent it from expanding its influence beyond its present territorial limits. Here, in Mexico and Texas, was one more chance for them to do so. As one pro-annexation senator summed up, England "is using every effort of skillful diplomacy to acquire an influence in Texas, to be used notoriously to our prejudice." Indeed, there were the dismaying signs that Texas's leadership, frustrated by American hesitation about annexation, seemed willing to go along with Great Britain's plans in their country.[23]

Tyler's concern about the dangers in the Mexican situation was a propaganda bonanza as well as a reality. The president and his colleagues believed that they could use the growing British threat as an effective weapon in uniting many Americans behind their plans to acquire Texas. Britain had to be stopped, their argument went. Otherwise the United States would be thwarted in its expansionist destiny and dangerously threatened by the presence of Britain on the nation's southwestern flank. If the United States did not act promptly, the Texas leaders might agree to go along with the British efforts to pull the republic into their imperial orbit. "We can never admit of European interference in the affairs of this continent," one editor summed up. The annexation of Texas offered border protection to the United States; its acquisition would subvert the very real British designs to establish an impenetrable barrier to America's further westward development.[24]

The British threat had been recognized well beyond the Tyler group and was similarly coupled there with the same determination that British control of Texas must be prevented at all costs. Democratic legislators such as Representative Ingersoll and Senator Woodbury of New Hampshire repeated the mantra that "Great Britain must not control Texas; if such is the alternative, the Untied States must insist on immediate annexation. It is the last struggle for American independence, to be conducted peaceably if we may, but forcibly if we must." The issues were clear: "The dominion of the whole American continent will be seen to be at stake. Shall it rest in America, or in a small island on the coast of Europe? In us and our posterity, or in our oppressor and rival?" In short, "Texas must immediately become American or [it] will soon be British."[25] The Democratic annexationists were, therefore, ready to support the Tyler administration's efforts to acquire Texas whatever their party's ongoing hostility toward "His Accidency" and his administration.

"The Texas Bombshell": A Letter to Richard Pakenham

An explosion aboard the American warship USS *Princeton* late in February 1844 unexpectedly and profoundly affected the Texas issue. President Tyler and his associates believed that they had set the stage well. Whatever particularist (sectional) impulses were present among them had been kept well under wraps as they moved toward an understanding with Texas and planned for the Senate's approval of what they had accomplished. The *Princeton* explosion killed several visiting dignitaries including Secretary of State Upshur, a guest on the ship. In a surprise move, Tyler appointed John C. Calhoun to succeed Upshur. The result would be an unexpected political earthquake: an unprecedented sectional uproar over annexation.[26]

The Texas matter was far advanced when Calhoun entered the State Department. Upshur and the republic's representatives in Washington had already worked out the main lines of an agreement between the two countries. The new secretary of state, a longtime proponent of adding Texas to the United States, swiftly completed the task. The negotiators signed the treaty of annexation incorporating Texas as a territory of the United States early in April 1844. President Tyler submitted it to the Senate for its ratification some days later, on the twenty-second.[27]

But now what? Like Tyler, Calhoun remained outside the pale of the nation's normal political processes as organized by the Whigs and Democrats. And, during the last few years, Calhoun's long-standing states'-rights concerns had been augmented by a much more pointed and intense southern-rights perspective. To him, the South was in even more danger than it had been for some time as its enemies grew in strength within the northern states and the latter grew in population and, therefore, in political strength within the Union. As he saw it, too many policy initiatives had been going against the South at the federal level. This was, unfortunately, likely to continue unless action was taken. Southerners had to assert their rights boldly to protect themselves from the malign power of their enemies. There was no other choice.[28]

Calhoun's intense sectional sensitivity—or extremism, as many viewed it—had won him few additional friends among southern Democrats and Whigs. His intellectual commitments, his public

John C. Calhoun was the public voice of southern interests in, and determination about, Texas. LIBRARY OF CONGRESS.

demeanor, and his use of language in the political arena continued to be at odds with the established political ways of a majority of Americans, including most southerners. But his point of view reinforced his ties to a number of other southern politicians who were similarly aggressively uneasy about the increased assaults on slavery emanating from the North. The Calhoun bloc seemed to have great strength in certain areas, and he continued to be perceived as an important figure in American life even as the reach and influence of the national parties continued to expand. (Among other things, he, too, had contemplated a run at the presidency in 1844, but had withdrawn his name from consideration at the end of 1843 in the face of the unrelenting opposition to him from the established party leaders and the indifference toward him from the overwhelmingly partisan electorate.)[29]

In submitting the treaty to the Senate, the secretary of state, in order to buttress the case for ratification, also forwarded a number of official documents, including correspondence between the principals in bringing the treaty to fruition. Among the material that Calhoun submitted was a recent letter that he had written to the British minister in Washington, Richard Pakenham. The letter followed the main lines of the Tylerite argument for Texas but added to it, and gave it a twist that upset everyone's applecart and changed the existing national, partisan political calculus of the issue.[30]

To Calhoun, and those who followed his lead in the slave states, Texas annexation was overwhelmingly a southern question, one that was vital to their interests. The secretary of state argued directly and potently to the British minister, and to the senators, who also received the letter, that the issue before the nation was the protection of southern slavery, threatened as it was by Britain's persistent intrigues and growing influence in Texas. The treaty, he wrote, had been entered into "in order to preserve a domestic institution." The current British government, like those before it, was hostile to the United States. But, in addition, it was also militantly anti-slavery and committed to the worldwide abolition of the institution. If Texas became a satellite of Britain, therefore, slavery in the neighboring southern states would be immediately threatened by aggressive abolitionist activity promoted by the government in London. As one North Carolina Democrat argued, not untypically of this frame of mind, if the United States did not annex Texas, England would establish itself there, foment Indian attacks on nearby American settlements, then "incite our slaves to rebellion," and ultimately launch an invasion of the United States from its Canadian provinces.[31]

The situation was clear. Slavery had to be protected from such dangers—not only because of its vital economic importance in those places where it now existed, but also because it was a desirable institution in a larger sense, socially important as well as "essential to the peace, safety, and prosperity of states in the union in which it exists." In short, as one of Calhoun's allies summed up, on overcoming the British opposition to the American acquisition of Texas "hinges the very existence of our southern institutions."[32]

WHAT LAY BEHIND CALHOUN'S STRATEGY of directly, unambiguously, and full-throatedly celebrating slavery and promoting sectional advantage in regard to annexation? It certainly ran counter to the way in which the Texas debate had so far been framed by the mainstream promoters of acquiring the republic. As Andrew Jackson wrote, it was "folly to introduce" a matter "that did not belong to the subject."[33] Of course, the ground had already been laid for such introduction within the Tyler administration. The fear of malignant British designs received added force because of a long-standing and growing apprehension among some of the Tyler group that Calhoun was right: that, in addition to everything else that they were up to to thwart the interests of the United States, the British government was determined to engage in a crusade to abolish slavery in Texas, and then elsewhere on the North American continent as well.

Several southern supporters of the president, men particularly close to him in his political isolation, had been meddling in Texas matters for some time and by their actions and words helped shape the way annexation was perceived as the full story began to unfold with Calhoun's letter to Pakenham. These supporters included Duff Green, the Calhounite newspaper editor, employed by Tyler as an agent in London sniffing out what the perfidious British were up to, and Representative Gilmer of Virginia, killed in the *Princeton* explosion, who had often been Tyler's spokesman in the House of Representatives and who had been ardently pushing publicly for the reopening of the Texas matter from the first. Thomas Hart Benton later wrote that he had "discerned the finger of Mr. Calhoun" in Gilmer's 1843 pro-annexation letter, long before the South Carolinian had brought his views forward so definitively. Certainly Green's ominous reports from London and Gilmer's constant prodding about the British danger echoed Calhounite fears about the clear threat to slavery that was emanating from the British government.[34]

Edward Everett, the American minister to England, several times reported back to the State Department that he doubted whether the British government had any abolitionist designs in Texas. Tyler and his close associates distrusted the New Englander Everett, however, and chose to believe the anxious reports of the southern agents they had dispatched to London.[35] Unlike Calhoun, the Tyler group largely kept their fears to themselves, sharing them only with those southerners they were trying to bring behind the treaty. Such reticence was not John C. Calhoun's way. He rarely minced words about his values, where he stood, and his determination to protect slavery, South Carolina, and the South with dogged perseverance, vigor, and relatively little nuance or moderation about the position of his section's enemies. He wanted to talk about slavery, its rights, its needs, and its insecurities because of the looming threats that it faced.

This was a propitious moment to do so, as he saw it. Calhoun and those who thought as he did apparently believed that their time had come—that forging southern political unity was more possible than it had been for some time. First, both political parties were struggling with severe internal strains that, the South Carolinian believed, weakened their influence and opened up opportunities for a different political arrangement. Such was, Calhoun always argued, necessary. Otherwise the South would be at the mercy of its enemies, who would take advantage of the section's internal political divisions. The recent growing opposition to renewing the gag rule against anti-slavery petitions in the House of Representatives offered unambigous evidence of the danger, suggesting that northern congressmen were becoming more sensitive to, and frightened by, the growing anti-slavery sentiment among their constituents.[36]

Calhoun wanted to mobilize southerners to face the danger confronting them. The southern people, A. P. Upshur once said to him, were "far too lethargic upon the vital question [of slavery]. They ought to be roused and made of one mind." The tumult already surrounding the Texas issue provided Calhoun's best opportunity to do so. His Pakenham letter played to this notion. He had joined the abolitionists and such anti-slavery Whigs as John Quincy Adams in bringing slavery to the center of a political situation that others had tied to other impulses. He clearly, deliberately, and optimistically fanned the flames of sectional tensions and cogently established to the sectionalists, north and south, what was at stake in the Texas debate.[37]

THE SECRETARY OF STATE'S LETTER to Pakenham was sent to the British minister on April 18 and given to the Senate the following week. Calhoun's intentions may have been to unite the South behind its perceived danger. What he got was not unity but an uproar. The Pakenham letter accomplished a great deal in texturing the Texas debate and focusing it in a particular way. The presence of certain individuals, such as Upshur, Gilmer, and Calhoun, around the Texas project had already provoked suspicion among some northerners. Calhoun's demarche proved to them what was up and, not surprisingly, provoked a reaction. His contentious language may have been directed at the British, but it confronted Americans as well. His protection-of-slavery argument was not new. It had been heard before. But it had not been, heretofore, pushed into the central consciousness of most annexationists. Now it had been.[38]

Such direct assertion of slavery's interest driving government policy for its own good, as Calhoun propounded in 1844, went beyond the established standards of political discourse. It deliberately challenged the prevailing partisan dynamics of the American political world. His bold move threw some, but not all, of those involved into turmoil. Calhoun's actions could be neither ignored nor readily dismissed. He had given the sectional reasoning an official standing that was both a shock to the majority of political activists involved in the issue of Texas and a major difficulty for them.[39]

His blatant action awakened anger and resistance not only among the acknowledged enemies of slavery but also among some of those who generally tolerated its existence and refused to make an issue of it. Many Democrats who supported annexation continued to do so. They were determined to have Texas. All else—Mexican-American relations, slavery's expansion—however troublesome, was irrelevant. As one of them, Indiana congressman Robert Dale Owen, said, Calhoun had offered "a bad reason for doing a good thing." But several others, led by Missouri's Senator Benton, Calhoun's bitter enemy, and including a number of old Jacksonian leaders, were furious at how Calhoun had tried to set the terms of the debate although he had to know that doing so in this manner would create an intense flare-up among northern Whigs, abolitionists, and, most critically, some Democrats as well. They had never trusted him, and they looked askance at him now. As the veteran editor Francis P. Blair later wrote to Andrew Jackson: "I sincerely believe that Calhoun and his old Junto of conspirators are more than ever anxious to separate the South from the north. They want Texas only as a bone of contention." If the object was to acquire the republic, Calhoun's "strange diplomatic dispatch" was not the way to present the case.[40]

Some historians have argued that anti-slavery sentiment was growing stronger in the North and that even usually indifferent Democratic areas were affected by that increasing opposition to the existence of slave labor in the United States. In this view, the section's representatives were feeling the pressure and had to react by taking stands against the South that they had not done earlier, especially on such matters as the gag rule and, now, the annexation of an area containing slavery. As Silas Wright wrote, "the Texas treaty is made upon a record which is sure to destroy any man from a free state who will go for it."[41]

Of course, the possibility also exists of other matters playing a significant role in all of these crosscurrents. Few northern congressmen liked the gag rule. Many of them were tired of supporting a mandate repressing one of the nation's oldest rights, that of petition. They had accepted the need to support it as the cost of accomplishing the other legislative purposes they were committed to, but their growing resistance to it had been manifest for some time.

Democrats also viewed matters through a lens of national purpose. Their resistance to sectarian obsessions such as Calhoun's was running at full throttle. The arguments that he offered were, in their view, "collateral, irrelevant to the issue, and calculated to affect the question injuriously." They wanted to beat back decisively the secretary of state's attempt to force the issue in his own particular way. One of the appalled Democrats, Senator Benjamin Tappan of Ohio, leaked to the press the supposedly secret documents on the treaty that Calhoun had sent to the Senate. They quickly appeared in anti-slavery New York newspapers and then in others throughout the North.[42]

The sectionalist arguments were clear and sharp. The question that both Calhoun and and his supporters, on one side, and John Quincy Adams and other anti-slavery advocates, on the other, had raised was whether or not the United States should add additional slave territory to the nation and, if it did not, by what right it should refuse to do so. Southerners were quick to argue that they had the constitutional right to bring additional slave territory into the United States, and some of them argued that point with a hair-trigger sensitivity. Northern sectionalists were equally sharp and unyielding. As a result, those who wished to take a national road in order to accomplish annexation were faced with an intense set of fears and suspicions that now filled the atmosphere—and threatened to poison it decisively. To many who favored expansion, the actions clearly came across as a preemptive strike by the highly inflamed southern contrarians against the particular grave threats that they believed their section faced. They were determined to have their way on the Texas issue as a strategic move to accomplish larger, sectionalizing purposes. Calhoun had let the cat out of the bag—and had hurt, thereby, the annexation cause.[43]

The Treaty Is Defeated

With Tyler and Calhoun's demarche, and the public awareness of it, the debate over expansion erupted with great intensity and divisiveness and, not surprisingly, a great deal of sectional feeling and rhetoric. It unsettled the smoothly running structure of national political competition. From the first, Texas had provoked partisan confrontation as well as sectionalist demands for and against annexation, but Calhoun had raised matters to a new level in his letter. His unwelcome footprints were now all over the business at hand. While many politicians did not want to make an issue about slavery, some of them believed that Tyler's whole enterprise, especially the provocation of Calhoun's blatant prosletyzing, and the frame of mind behind it, could not be borne. With a roar, John Quincy Adams reentered the fray once more, joined again by anti-slavery Whigs and abolitionists. Together they made a great deal of noise about what had been revealed about the Texas project: the auspices under which it was being considered, the purposes for which it was being pushed, and the danger that the annexation matter posed to the peace and good order of the country. When the treaty went to the Senate, Adams, never at a loss to find an overheated phrase to make a point, wrote in his diary that "with it went the freedom of the human race." Other opponents of the treaty were no less ready to use similar language.[44]

Predictably, of course, the overdrawn words of the treaty's northern sectionalist opponents did not smooth any of the quite ruffled feathers of their antagonists. Southerners were quick to add their own brand of overheated rhetoric to the mix so that angry words flew back and forth on the floor of the Senate, in newspaper editorials, and in pamphlets issued by proponents and opponents of the treaty, all of it with the usual quota of threats, lamentations, and the kind of fiery language designed to put the other side down once and for all.[45]

THIS BITTER SECTIONAL ROARING was not the end of the matter. The partisans recovered their balance and worked hard to shape the debate in a different way. Calhoun and the northern opponents of slavery lived by a sectional imperative. They were now reminded that other political activists did not. A pro-annexation vanguard held together to try to focus and push forward the issue beyond the sectional tumult raised by the Pakenham letter. Most of those who did so were Democrats, from both North and South. They realized that much was at stake and that there were many reasons why some of their party colleagues would now oppose Tyler's treaty, the president himself, and Calhoun's argument for it. But the bulk of them sought to find a way through the mess toward accomplishing annexation—which was, to them, the main point.[46]

Northern Whigs could be counted upon to oppose the further expansion of slavery—as well as further territorial expansion of any kind. In the highly charged partisan atmosphere of the time, if the outsider Tylerites pushed something, others would resist. Tensions remained particularly high between the president and his former Whig allies, given what had passed between them, but anti-annexation sentiment among the Whigs had, as noted earlier, much deeper roots of belief, interest, and calculation than simply their hatred of John Tyler. Their party had opposed Texas annexation from the outset. The national Whig leader, Henry Clay, wanted the treaty rejected. He was not alone among his party colleagues in his wish. When Tyler reintroduced the issue, Whig state legislatures in the North began to pass anti-annexation resolutions that they sent to Congress as expression of their constituents' will. Vermont Whigs, for example, protested, in familiar terms, against annexation "as unconstitutional and as dangerous to the stability of the Union itself." Many of the resolutions condemned slavery's expansion as well. State party nominating conventions went on record in similar fashion as they met in early 1844.[47]

At the same time, despite the strong pull that party loyalty usually exerted over them, some southern Whigs broke away from their colleagues on the Texas issue. A number of them indicated that they accepted the argument that annexation was an important measure that benefited their section and that, therefore, they would support it when it came to a vote in Congress. Others initially favored voting for it for pragmatic political reasons. They feared that the Democrats' strong advocacy of annexation in the South would be effective enough to make inroads among a number of otherwise loyal Whig voters, causing their party grief at the polls in future elections. They believed they could forestall that outcome by going for Texas now.[48]

Most of the southern Whigs went along with their party's anti-annexation position, however, although they did not intend to emphasize the issue in upcoming election campaigns. Clay told the New York Whig leader, Thurlow Weed, that, in his opinion, the Texas question "will do me no prejudice in the South" in his current battle for the presidency. Sentiment favoring annexation was not as widespread and as powerful there, he argued, as some of his colleagues believed. The bulk of his party supporters in the slave states were inclined to agree, or certainly wanted to agree, with their leader's assessment. They fell in behind Clay and against annexation.[49]

The Democratic situation was more complicated. Anti-slavery advocates and other political enemies of the party had long charged that the party's northern members slavishly followed its southern wing, always ready to submit to the latter's bidding when they were in office. Southerners had dominated the administrations of Andrew Jackson and Martin Van Buren. Both presidents were dependent on southern support at the polls and in Congress and reacted accordingly when dealing with high-ranking appointments to office and with both domestic and foreign issues that affected the South. Remember that as early as 1836, at the time of the Texas Revolution, the ever vigilant John Quincy Adams had argued that what was happening in the Mexican province was not a spontaneous uprising of aggrieved settlers but, rather, part of plot by the slave power, along with its Democratic allies, to increase its section's already substantial dominance of the Union.[50]

If the northern Democrats appeared to some to be as submissive as suggested, there were always limits to any such commitment. Some, generally those who were close to former president Van Buren, had, as we have seen, battled Calhoun for years over his sectionalist paranoia, his hostility to political parties, and his hatred of the Democratic leader. His current demarche over Texas was, to them, the continuation of his dangerous and unacceptable way of behaving in the political arena. Whatever Texas's attraction, Calhoun's argument had complicated the case for annexation by rubbing the slavery issue in the faces of northern Democrats. They wanted no part of an action rooted in the South Carolinian's particular preoccupations and would not, therefore, accept the treaty.[51]

THOSE NORTHERN DEMOCRATS hostile to Calhoun and his framing of the Texas issue were not the sole voice of their party above the Mason-Dixon line. When considering annexation, many other northern and western members of the party refused to think in sectional terms even now. It was not that many of them liked slavery. They did not. But they argued that it was a local matter, not their business, whatever their personal views about it were. It was constitutional, a fact of life in the southern states, and would continue there as long as southerners wished it to. There was no issue to be made about it. Most particularly, they never insisted that no more slave territory would ever become part of the United States. Rather, they took a pragmatic view, and, in their terms, an ideological one, when they considered the annexation of a territory that contained slavery, and they did not think of themselves as submitting to southern dictation when they did so. Determined to maintain their important ties to the southern wing of their party against their common Whig enemies, they reiterated their argument that slavery could be expected to move into additional parts of the North American continent as the country expanded westward, almost certainly into the areas south of the Missouri Compromise line of 30° 30' north latitude. They held to the notion that the earlier compromise line was a fair means of settling the issue so that the more important matters before them (such as continued territorial acquisition) could proceed unhindered. They accepted the Texas treaty even with the Pakenham letter offered as its justification.[52]

WHILE NOT ALL WHIGS AND DEMOCRATS subscribed to their party's position on expansion, the center of gravity of each party's belief system on the matter was distinct and well defined and followed traditional partisan pathways, regardless of the sectional tensions present. As Francis P. Blair, the longtime editor of the Democrats' national newspaper, the Washington *Globe,* who was himself no friend of the treaty, warned Martin Van Buren, the "craze of *acquisitiveness* was very strongly developed in our people especially [among] the Democrats."[53]

Blair was right about his party colleagues—at least most of them. When the Tyler treaty came to a vote in the Senate in early June 1844, it lost rather decisively, with only sixteen senators for passage and thirty-five opposed to it. Party lines largely held on the vote as both northern and southern Whigs maintained their opposition to annexation—which meant, since they controlled the Senate, that the treaty had no chance of being ratified. (All but one Whig voted no, including fourteen from the South.) On the other side, fifteen of the twenty-three Democrats voted for the treaty, including half of the northeastern Democrats, who joined their party's southern and western blocs in favoring Texas annexation.[54]

Nevertheless, the fruits of Calhoun's Pakenham strategy were evident. Jacksonian unity had been strained. Seven northern Democratic senators joined the Whig majority to vote against the submitted treaty. Most of them were not averse to annexation under appropriate conditions but refused to support it under the terms that Calhoun had laid out in the Pakenham letter. They did so despite their long-standing policy of not confronting their southern Democratic allies over the different sectional perspectives present on the scene. Led by Thomas Hart Benton and Silas Wright of New York, the latter Van Buren's closest lieutenant, they took one more opportunity, in their votes against the Texas treaty as presented to the Senate, to slash at the mischief-making Calhoun and his dangerous sectionalist demands on behalf, instead, of Van Buren and the partisan way in American politics.[55]

John Tyler was a most unhappy man in mid-1844. The first phase of his effort on behalf of Texas had ended in shambles. Whatever else might be possible in regard to bringing the republic into the Union, the president's annexation treaty itself was dead. The delighted Whigs believed that beyond this was a larger triumph, that "this mischievous project" had suffered not only a severe blow but, they hoped, a permanent one. Whether or not it was premature to make that judgment, clearly Calhoun's strike on behalf of the importance—actually, predominance—of sectional concerns in the Texas matter had affected the political landscape to a degree sufficient to derail the annexationist impulse—at least in the critical arena of the Senate.[56]

The Whig hopes were premature. Tyler and his colleagues did not give up. On June 10, the president sent a message to the House of

Representatives suggesting that Congress could approach the matter in other ways than through the concluding, and then ratifying, of a formal treaty. He recommended instead that the two houses pass a joint resolution admitting Texas as a state of the Union. However unprecedented that tactic might seem, "the great question," he argued, getting right to the point as the pro-annexationists saw it, "is not as to the manner in which it shall be done, but whether it shall be accomplished or not."[57] Obviously, the president continued to believe that there was a legislative majority in favor of annexation if members would listen to their constituents and, at the same time, put aside the sectional issues that had arisen in the process of pushing the treaty forward.

Could they do so? Under the best of circumstances, achieving annexation clearly faced difficulties, given the strong partisan disagreements on the issue. Whig strength in the Senate, for example, posed a formidable obstacle to the hopes of the annexationists. Beyond that, to complicate matters further, the sectional genie had been let out of the bottle during the Texas debate. Could it be recaptured and contained by the powerful nonsectional partisan influences present? How much damage from Calhoun's pro-slavery obsession would linger among those who were needed in support of Texas? Could such sectional tensions as had appeared be contained sufficiently to bring Texas into the Union on its many nonsectional merits?

Much would depend on how the issue played out in the aftermath of the defeat of the treaty. Certainly, whatever the sentiment for annexation in many quarters, the unconvinced anti-Calhoun northern Democratic senators who had voted against it and the South Carolinian's obnoxious (to them), threatening, particularist version of its virtues had to be brought back in support of the acquisition of Texas. Specifically, they had to be satisfied enough by the policy's alleged many pluses for the Union, and the arguments offered on their behalf, for them to come on board the annexation bandwagon. Alternatively, the political landscape had to shift in ways that would make annexation possible despite the problems that had derailed it in the first half of 1844. Both were to happen, beginning even as the Senate's debates and final decision on the treaty were occurring, and continuing in the months that followed its defeat.

3

"WE CANNOT CARRY VIRGINIA FOR YOU"

Political Earthquake, 1844

American politics had not stood still as Congress wrestled with Tyler's Texas initiative. The political landscape was rarely placid in the middle of the nineteenth century, and it certainly was far from peaceful in the spring of 1844. In fact, it was a particularly tense time even by the highly combative standard that had been established over the previous twenty years. Political leaders and their followers had a great deal to fight about. The angry drama of the battle over the treaty of annexation had significantly roiled the waters in Washington as well as in much of the country at large. At the same time, the run-up to the imminent election to replace John Tyler, with all of the widespread confrontation, provocative bluster, and divisive rhetoric usually associated with such contests, added to the noise and rancor as it assumed a critical role in the unfolding course of national affairs.[1]

The presidential campaign was well under way even as the battle over annexation gained steam in Washington in late spring. While the Texas treaty was before the Senate, the national party conventions were meeting to name their candidates and announce their policy aspirations. The run for the presidency, the range of decisions to be made about it by each party's leaders, and the sense that it would be, almost certainly, a very close battle was therefore never far from anyone's mind as spring gave way to summer.[2]

Both Whigs and Democrats approached the upcoming contest with high hopes and some frustration. The Martin Van Buren–led Democrats felt very keenly their defeat in 1840 and the lost policy opportunities associated with the New Yorker's failure to be reelected. He and they were determined to regain their natural place in command of the nation's government. At the same time, Henry Clay's Whigs might have won four years before, but they believed that they had been cheated of the policy rewards of their victory by Tyler's unexpected succession to the presidency and his implacable opposition to many of their cherished policy initiatives. Both parties looked to 1844 to redress their frustrations and advance their particular cause. Neither was in the mood to compromise on the matters that separated them from one another, or see any virtue in the other's views about public affairs. This election would be, as such always were in the partisan confrontations of the age, a real and a rhetorical war to define the nature of the Union and to articulate the policy measures necessary to promote its prosperity and its people's freedom.[3]

Most observers started out believing that the upcoming contest would follow familiar pathways. The recognized leaders of the two main parties, Clay and Van Buren, would be the candidates, facing one another in a battle that would focus primarily on the traditional issue agendas that each had long espoused: what should be the reach of central government power, and what were the proper policies necessary to restore and expand the American economy. Neither party expected, at the outset, to have much to say about territorial expansion, particularly about Texas.[4]

Van Buren and Clay were old antagonists. They had been dueling against each other for twenty years. Each had helped to define his party's stance on the issues, and each's colleagues had chosen him several times to run for president. Clay had never won the prize, losing in both 1824 and 1832. Van Buren's victory in 1836 had been followed by his defeat four years later. Now, each was in the field again; each was hungry to win and gain the position he believed he had earned. They were personally friendly with one another despite their sharp political differences and persistent rivalry, but their friendship did not weaken their determination to beat the other to the top of the political ladder.[5]

Clay and Van Buren were not alone as they prepared for the battle. Both John C. Calhoun and John Tyler had announced their intention to run for the presidency as independent candidates, free of the inhibiting party shackles that they both despised, and with Texas annexation as a major part of their appeal to the voters. They were

Whig leader Henry Clay publicly opposed annexation but feared the consequences of his stance. LIBRARY OF CONGRESS.

confident that the country was ready for them and the policies that each was committed to.

Although they worried the leaders of the two major parties for a time, their day in the sun was short-lived. Neither's candidacy lasted for very long. The response to Calhoun's offered him little encouragement, and he withdrew from the contest even before the campaign got under way—at the turn of the year 1843–44.[6]

The rallying cry for "Tyler and Texas" lasted longer, as the president's corporal's guard assiduously promoted his cause. They especially began to court pro-annexation Democrats in the hope of expanding his support base. As a result of their energetic activities on his behalf, and his own stubborn determination, Tyler hung on for some time. His supporters held a nominating convention on his behalf as late as May 1844, coterminous with the Democratic National Convention, but, as with Calhoun, these efforts failed to generate much enthusiasm among political activists beyond Tyler's original small band of supporters or to cause a rush of popular support to him. The president therefore eventually, if reluctantly, faced political reality, abandoned his plans, and ended his candidacy.[7]

This failure of both outsiders to mount much of a challenge to the two major parties underscored the power and control that the Whigs and Democrats had exerted over the political arena since their full emergence in the late 1830s, a power and control that continued, significantly, to hamstring alternative outcries from developing into significant political crusades. To be sure, an anti-slavery, and anti-Texas, Liberty Party was, for the second time, also in the presidential contest behind the Kentucky abolitionist James Birney (and would campaign until the end), but few observers believed at the outset that it would attract enough popular support to be a significant force in shaping either the nature of the campaign or the final outcome of the election itself. (In 1840, Birney had received just over seven thousand popular votes for president.)[8]

The Ordeal of Martin Van Buren

Clay and Van Buren prepared for their impending battle in the usual way, consulting with trusted colleagues, keeping in touch with key leaders of their party in the states, and planning the direction that their campaign would take. All seemed as it should be. But everyone's expectation as to the nature of the campaign turned out to be only partly accurate. A range of divisive matters over domestic policy—and then, most critically, about Texas—got in the way with a force that threw off all of their confident expectations.

Some of what occurred was the normal jostling within the parties over specific candidates and particular legislative priorities, jostling that the leaders of each coalition expected to occur in the pre-convention season. There was a sharpened intensity to it, however, given the effect on everyone's outlooks of Whig and Democratic disappointments over the past four years. To be sure, it was also expected that most of these strains would be tamped down when the parties organized themselves for the upcoming election. Loyalty behind the candidates and policies selected at party conventions was always demanded and usually achieved. Even the pro-Calhoun, and anti-party, Charleston *Mercury* recognized, in 1843, when Calhoun and his followers were still allied with the Democrats, that "if there is any division in the Democratic Party, it will be before the convention, not after."[9] It was such commitment to the party as a whole that gave the Whigs and Democrats the strength that each of them exhibited in the 1840s. Still both parties went through a process of smoothing out internal differences and finding bases for agreement so as to maximize their ability to bring their supporters together to work in a common cause.[10]

The Whigs had always had their share of differences over specific priorities, favored candidates, and, now, how best to recoup what they had lost in the Tyler debacle, but their pathway to the campaign was relatively smooth. Henry Clay was their favorite and would be named without difficulty when the party convened in its national convention on May 1. Clay received all of the delegates' votes for president on the only nominating ballot taken. It took three roll calls for the convention to name Theodore Frelinghuysen of New Jersey as the vice-presidential candidate. The party did not issue an official platform but, rather, published a short statement of its principles. This mentioned the Whig commitment to "a well-regulated currency" and "a tariff to defray the necessary expenses of the government, and discriminating with specific reference to protection of the domestic labor of the country." Official platform or not, the party remained committed to its well-established approach to the national economy—while, at the same time, its convention's brief statement of principles did not mention Texas annexation or territorial expansion at all.[11]

Optimism among the Whigs was quite high as they entered the campaign behind their greatest leader. After several years of downturn in their fortunes, they were now ready to build on what they believed were all of the good omens they spied on the political landscape and take firm control of both the presidency and Congress. Their newspapers and private correspondence were filled with their confident expectations. As one of them exulted, the Whigs "will succeed by an overwhelming margin in the coming election."[12] Some of what they said was cant, designed for public consumption to hearten the faithful and get them out working for their party. But much of it also reflected the strong positive feelings of the party's leadership when they discussed the upcoming campaign with one another.

In contrast, their opponents did not seem to be on as solid ground as the Whigs were—nor, it turned out, as confident. In early 1844, the Democracy was not only a party that had been badly defeated four years before, but a troubled one as well—in the words of one historian, "leaderless and mutinous" since its loss in 1840.[13] In the run-up toward the election, the still formidable bloc that looked to Martin Van Buren as the party's leader found themselves powerfully challenged within the party that they had led for so long. Some of that challenge constituted a leadership succession crisis. The Jacksonian generation was aging and beginning to pass from the scene. Arguing over who would succeed it in leading the party—and the nation—was roiling the waters with furious intensity. The old verities of succession, from Jackson to Van Buren to, perhaps, Thomas Hart Benton, were no longer universally accepted once Van Buren had gone down to defeat in his reelection effort four years before. Younger party activists were pushing their elders very hard for more access to offices and some real power for themselves. They did so in increasingly confrontational terms: "Let the old dynasty be restored," one rebellious Democrat wrote, "and the superannuated and broken down politicians will have full swing & we modernizers must step into the rear rank of the political cohorts." He and others who thought as he did were not prepared to accept that. They believed that their time at the head of the Democratic column had arrived.[14]

PART OF THIS LEADERSHIP CRISIS stemmed from another fact: The Democrats faced the upcoming election divided over the electoral viability of their presumed candidate. Although Van Buren was still largely acclaimed as the party's leader, at least publicly, and expected to win the nomination at Baltimore when the Democrats convened, many had considered him to be a severely weakened presidential candidate long before the Texas issue appeared on the scene. His electoral margins at the national level, even in his presidential victory in 1836, had never been prepossessing. His loss to Harrison four years later had made his vulnerability a major concern to party leaders. Although the Democrats had done well in state and congressional elections in 1842 and 1843, due, most likely, to the Whigs' serious disarray, they had not done as well as they wanted to in a number of key states, in Andrew Jackson's Tennessee, for example. And, whatever positive outcomes they had enjoyed since 1840, the memory of Van Buren's electoral weaknesses lingered. The sense of being in danger when the American people next voted was never far from the surface among many always nervous party leaders.[15]

Could Van Buren win the upcoming contest? Many Democrats

Martin Van Buren was the leader of the Democratic Party until he was overthrown by James Polk. Van Buren saw annexation as a dangerous policy. LIBRARY OF CONGRESS.

thought not: "I do not see how he is to be elected if nominated" was the conclusion of one of many such exchanges among party activists as the convention neared. Leaders in the competitive large states were particularly worried about the ex-president being at the top of their party's ticket. Among others, Pennsylvania Democrats were reported to be in "an uproar" against his candidacy, while in Tennessee "many had grown weary of following the New Yorker down the road to defeat."[16]

Most Democrats who spoke out on the issue, including editors usually loyal to the leadership in their newspapers as well as party supporters in private correspondence, had previously gone along with the apparent inevitability (and justice) of Van Buren's renomination. But as they exchanged with one another evidence of his—and their—possible electoral weakness, some leaders hoped that a more attractive candidate would emerge to replace him. "Saving the Democratic Party from the rout that awaits [it] under Mr. Van Buren" became a rallying cry among a range of party activists in the few months remaining before the national convention was scheduled to meet in Baltimore.[17]

The differences among the Democrats were never confined only to personalities, particular candidates, and the problems associated with a generational transition. There was always a policy dimension to the party's factionalism. It was rooted in increasingly serious differences over the party's traditional policy agenda, and it gave Van Buren much trouble as the convention approached. Conflicting views about the usual policy issues—tariffs, banking and currency, and the government financing of internal improvements—had not only continued to be the basic substance of political conflict *between* the parties but also now played a significant role in the warfare *among* Democratic factions in the run-up to the party's nomination decision. In the late 1830s, some Democrats sought new directions for, and reconfigured definitions of, its purposes and policy commitments.[18]

For a time the tariff issue became the center of contentious discussion in party circles. Democrats had usually supported relatively low rates on imports in comparison to Whig preferences, but they had divided, and continued to divide, over where to locate those rates, although a significant majority favored placing them at the lower end of the scale. Other Democrats, however, had supported the Whig-sponsored tariff of 1842, which had raised duties for the first time in a decade. Their defection had provoked a great deal of anger in party circles, as well as suspicion of Van Buren, since several of his closest associates had voted for that tariff. The Van Burenites' "treason" on the issue was widely held against him among free-trade southerners and Democrats holding similar views elsewhere.[19]

At the same time, a number of Democrats demanded more willingness by party leaders, in the face of the economic collapse of the late thirties, to revise traditional Democratic financial policy initiatives. They wanted, in particular, the party to support the chartering of more state and private banks and to back the issuance of paper money, both designed to stimulate trade in the face of the weakened economy. They added to that demands for government funding of internal improvements construction as another means of boosting the depressed economy by putting unemployed people to work on these projects and, at the same time, by lowering the cost of transporting goods. In contrast, Van Buren and his supporters strongly disagreed. They continued, instead, to hold fast to the hard-money, anti-banking, and anti-federal-power ideas that, they argued—with great vigor—defined their party. They saw no reason to shift their long-standing beliefs about these core matters into new channels and every reason to maintain their commitments to those ideas and policies that had long distinguished the Democrats from their opponents.[20]

Finally, there was much talk of a "Young Democracy" bloc within the party, a group distinguished by its members' stalwart commitment to territorial expansion and the fullest development of America's continental mission to reach far beyond the nation's current borders. These Democrats were particularly strong among veteran western party members such as Lewis Cass of Michigan and William Allen of Ohio, as well as the young Stephen A. Douglas, just beginning to make his mark in Illinois politics, but they had many adherents elsewhere as well. There was an increasing sense of urgency among them, given British machinations on the nation's borders, and a sense of an opportunity too long delayed, both in Texas and in the long-coveted Oregon country. They were eager to get on with the nation's territorial "manifest destiny" and impatient of further hesitation among their party's leading lights and the arguments the latter repeatedly expressed against the nation's further landed expansion at the current time.[21]

Assaults against Van Buren from friends of John C. Calhoun had been a constant of the New Yorker's national career since he had replaced the South Carolinian as Jackson's political heir in the early 1830s. Calhoun's associates in his home state and in other parts of the South still refused to accept the legitimacy, or the finality, of that succession. Now, with an election looming, their assaults were renewed with particular vigor. They were aimed at stirring up as much anger against Van Buren and his allies before the Democratic convention as they could, both among southerners and in areas of the North where Calhoun had some political support due to his traditional, no-holds-barred, states'-rights outlook, which some northern Democrats shared. In the South, the Calhounites focused on Congress's defeat of the gag rule against anti-slavery petitions and passage of the tariff bill in 1842, always underlining the fact that some of Van Buren's associates had voted in the anti-southern position on both issues. Calhoun himself argued, further, that the former president's hostility to the Pakenham letter "clearly proved that Van Buren was courting the abolitionists." The conclusion that followed from the New Yorker's outrageous heresy was clear: Southerners "cannot trust [him] and ought not to contribute to his success."[22]

Some of these assaults were aimed originally at securing for

Calhoun his rightful nomination as president, which had been previously denied to him by the manipulative artfulness of Van Buren, the "Sly Fox," during Jackson's presidency and since. But some of these efforts reflected larger themes, particularly the fears of some southern leaders close to Calhoun, fears that echoed his notions of the forces threatening all southerners, which had been unleashed and were growing stronger. "The combination in Christendom against the slaveholding interest," the Virginia Calhounite Robert M. T. Hunter wrote in late 1843, "the course of English diplomacy abroad, the state of Northern feeling at home, and the present necessity for maintaining the balance of power between the free and slaveholding states constitute a crisis which gives an importance to this question and also to the election of a Southern president." In such circumstances, Van Buren would not do. Nor would Clay, a southerner, but one who was opposed to the annexation of Texas and who was in thrall to the anti-slavery elements that controlled his party. What, then, was the South to do?[23]

These differences, and the attitudes emanating from them, added much to the internal friction surrounding ex-president Van Buren's candidacy. At the same time, his position was also weakened by the political situation in his home state, with its many desperately needed electoral votes. The New York Democrats echoed the party's condition elsewhere, being particularly badly split between the ex-president's supporters and other party activists over banking policy and the financing of canal construction in the state. Here again, these policy and personal differences between the traditional Jacksonians around Van Buren, the "radicals," or, increasingly, the "Barnburners," and a more entrepreneurial bloc of "conservatives," or "Hunkers," disgusted with Van Buren's policy rigidity even in the face of new conditions, appeared to be intractable. Senator Wright referred to the Hunkers, in fact, as "the untrue portion" of the party. As the comment reveals, the New York Democrats seemed unwilling, by the early forties, to repair the dangerous split in their ranks, some of them even threatening to run separate tickets in upcoming local and statewide elections, with all of the confusion and difficulties that would follow for the national party seeking to reclaim its place in Washington.[24]

The sum total of these internal party confrontations, in New York State and elsewhere, suggested deep trouble for the Democracy, particularly given that there were as yet few signs of a possible reconciliation among the warring factions even as activities connected with the presidential race began to get into high gear. "The breach between the V's and the anti-V's has become impassible," a Tennessee congressman close to the highly interested former congressman James K. Polk wrote to the latter from Washington just before the party's national convention was scheduled to convene.[25]

SUCH DISAGREEMENTS, and the constant airing of their difficulties by the different Democratic factions as had become commonplace at the beginning of 1844, were not unusual in American politics. Party members often bickered among themselves and blustered about their nonnegotiable demands, but they usually found ways to resolve, or at least paper over, their differences in time for the election campaign. There seemed to be a different quality at work here, however. The divisive focus on Van Buren was particularly noteworthy given the widespread acceptance of him heretofore, enthusiastically or otherwise, by loyal Democrats, and it gave the internal battles a great deal of steam as the convention's delegates began to assemble.

Still, Van Buren remained the party leader. After a brief period of withdrawal from public activities after the 1840 election, he and his friends had worked hard to maintain his place at the top of the coalition that he had done so much to build. Their efforts had been largely successful despite the frequent grousing against him. He continued to have a great deal of support among party activists and, thanks to the actions taken in his favor by state party meetings throughout the country, had amassed enough convention delegates pledged to vote for him to give him a majority of those who would be voting to name the presidential candidate.[26]

Testaments to the ex-president's strength appeared in newspaper editorials and in private correspondence. "The mass of the Democratic party in this state," a Missouri Democrat told Lewis Cass, who had his own hopes that year, "follow their old leader [Benton] in support of Mr. Van Buren." Van Buren was, an Ohio Democrat wrote, "our strongest man." "It is plain," a party editor argued, "that the nomination of Mr. Van Buren, above all others, will rally the force of the party." Reading these testimonials, Van Buren and his associates could be confident that they remained in command of the Democratic Party and that, whatever unhappy strains were evident among party members, and despite the opposition that had developed to his candidacy in the years since 1840, neither would be a barrier to his renomination and then successful run for reelection.[27]

What upset their calculations and provoked a party revolution was that all of the hesitations about Van Buren and the resistance to his renomination in 1844 could be effectively woven together and dramatically focused by what Silas Wright referred to as "this Texas mania." The contentious issue proved strong enough, in conjunction with the other elements already in play, to tip the balance against the ex-president and lead to his replacement by a more electorally and ideologically attractive candidate.[28]

Candidates for national office often received letters from party members seeking a statement about some policy matter or other. The responses to such letters were used as the basis for newspaper editorials in the party press to enlighten, stimulate, and reassure the faithful and were quoted by local speakers in electoral rallies on behalf of the candidate. Van Buren had received a number of interrogatories seeking his views on Texas annexation, which, the writers claimed, were not widely known. The candidate decided to respond to one of them, written by William Hammet, a hithero obscure Mississippi congressman and an unpledged delegate to the Democratic National Convention.[29]

In a long-winded, complex, and typically cautious argument, filled with dependent clauses and many rhetorical uncertainties, Van Buren did not foreclose the annexation of Texas, but he found many good reasons to hesitate at this juncture. Whatever virtues there might be in acquiring Texas, he argued, it could not happen right away. The diplomatic fallout from it would further disrupt our already strained relations with Mexico and would cause problems for America's place and reputation in the world. Many observers would see annexation as an unacceptable and unworthy act of aggression against the Mexicans. Given that, "should not everyone," he wrote,

> who sincerely loves his country—who venerates its time-honored and glorious institutions—who dwells with pride and delight on associations connected with our rise, progress and present condition—on the steady step with which we advanced to our present eminence, in despite of the hostility, and in contempt of the bitter revilings of the enemies of freedom in all parts of the globe—

> consider, and that deeply, whether we would not, by the immediate annexation of Texas, place a weapon in the hands of those who now look upon us and our institutions with distrustful and envious eyes that would do us more real lasting injury as a nation, than the acquisition of such a territory, valuable as it undoubtedly is, could possibly repair?[30]

Annexation should occur only, he concluded, when its accomplishment would be necessary to forestall an action by others that threatened the United States, or would be a real benefit to the nation and not have disruptive consequences on American relations with Mexico or its national honor, or, finally, after the American people had shown their clear support for such annexation by their votes for pro-annexation candidates for office, "be the consequences what they may." Then he, as the chief executive, would undertake to effect annexation.[31]

"More Than a Crime"

The Hammet letter was fatal to Van Buren. It increased opposition to his renomination and crystallized the strong sense already present among party members that he could not win. When it appeared in the Washington *Globe* at the end of April, it provoked outraged cries from annexationists and from Van Buren's many party enemies. Even if they parsed the letter with care and nuance, and recognized that Van Buren was not shutting off annexation entirely, the flavor and direction of his rhetoric seemed clear. What so many read as Van Buren's timidity and resistance amid the mass of his cautionary verbiage was far from acceptable to the rising spirits of many loyalists in the post-Jackson Democratic Party, even some of those who had up to now favored Van Buren's nomination. He had demonstrated that he was a man of the past, no longer with them as Jacksonian Democracy evolved beyond the hesitancies about expansion of the previous decade. He was not giving them what they wanted most: *immediate* annexation. Instead, restive Democrats saw in his letter not a reasoned argument that would bring Texas into the Union in due course but, rather, a too negative resistance to what was required—taking the necessary steps to annex the republic without further hesitation. Texas had been around long enough. It was time to move on the issue. Van Buren apparently did not agree.

As a result, there was a fierce reaction against the party's leading candidate from within the party, a reaction on a far wider basis than anything that had threatened him up to this point.[32]

Even some of Van Buren's strongest supporters were shaken. In Virginia, for example, there was great anguish among loyal Democrats. No one had been closer to the New Yorker than Thomas Ritchie, longtime editor of the Richmond *Enquirer*, and Democratic leader in that state. He and Van Buren had been closely linked in the building of the Democratic Party in the 1820s and had always been together since. Ritchie had worked to forestall growing sentiment for Calhoun among Virginia's Democrats in the early forties and had at least partly succeeded in getting party leaders there to fall in, and stay, behind the ex-president. But Ritchie was also aware of the powerful pull of Texas annexation on his state's Democrats. As he wrote before Tyler withdrew from the contest, "if we have no Texas candidate but Capt. John Tyler *he will carry off a few thousand* [votes] from Mr. V. B. which *per se* would be sufficient to defeat Mr. V. B. in Virginia."[33]

Now Tyler's chances and hopes were not prospering, but the problem of Virginia's situation as the presidential election approached had grown worse for the Democrats. They had just had an unexpected setback in the state's April legislative elections, a fact that shook Ritchie and his associates deeply. The party was clearly in perilous condition in the state. Van Buren's letter to Hammet was the last straw to his once loyal friends in this situation of great danger to all that the Democrats stood for and wanted to achieve. "I am compelled to come to the conclusion," Ritchie now wrote to his longtime friend and ally, "that we cannot carry Virginia for you."[34]

What made it worse to Ritchie, and other outraged party members, was the apparent similarity of Van Buren's views and hesitations to those of the party's arch antagonist, Henry Clay. The latter also published a letter about annexation, which appeared in the Whig press at almost the same moment that Van Buren's letter to Hammet became public. He was against it, which was no surprise. More to the point, the simultaneous appearance of the letters was certainly suspicious and smelled of collusion. That would not do. The configuration of elements seemed, to many, too much for the party to bear in its quest to return to national power. Whether collusion had actually occurred or not, Van Buren had, one later wrote about the affair, "committed, as Talleyrand said, 'more than a crime. It was a Blunder.'"[35]

Texas annexation ensured the destruction of Van Buren as a viable Democratic presidential candidate. There were differences between Clay's position on Texas and that of the ex-President, but those differences were lost in Van Buren's verbiage and his seeming denial of what annexationists now demanded—and expected quickly. Given the load that he already carried—the perception of him as a weak candidate, and the sharp disagreements with him over the party's policy commitments—his opponents and the faint of heart among state and local party leaders were now able to put it all together, powerfully challenge his nomination, and move aggressively to put their party fully behind the annexation movement. Amos Kendall, the longtime Democratic political strategist, summed it up well to his old leader, Andrew Jackson. "Extensive distrust in reference to his political strength," he wrote, "had been created before the Texas question arose, and his course on that furnished an opportunity to give him a finishing blow." Jackson agreed. If more in sorrow than otherwise, he, too, no longer believed that Van Buren was an appropriate or viable Democratic candidate in this year of expansionist opportunity—and necessity.[36]

VAN BUREN AND HIS CLOSEST COLLEAGUES had believed that the letter to Hammet would strengthen the ex-president in his quest for renomination, or at least contain the issue for the moment; otherwise why write it? They recognized the reality of the uproar against him when the letter appeared but did not believe it would last nor be devastating to their purpose. As one of the shrewdest among them wrote, "feeling will, by and by, settle down to a better state."[37]

But this was a highly politicized moment of crisis for party members, not a time for ponderously written, reflective complexities and presentations too easily read in ways harmful to the writer. Van Buren's motives and the way that he approached the Texas issue in his letter reflected many things: his innate caution about new issues generally and about Texas in particular, his calculations about the electoral situation, and an overconfidence about his ability to command the party. But, as Andrew Jackson sorrowfully summed up in reaction to Van Buren's words, "you might as well, it appears to me, attempt to turn the current of the Mississippi as to turn the democracy from the annexation of Texas to the United States."[38]

Texas had added a great deal of force to the Democratic policy

In this 1844 cartoon, Van Buren is ridiculed for his attempt to defer annexation, which has cost him the support of his party colleagues and his chance for renomination. LIBRARY OF CONGRESS.

differences and to the wariness felt in many quarters of the party concerning Van Buren's strength as a presidential candidate. The stage was set for an uproar at the least, further divisions at the worst. The annexation issue had Democrats roaring at one another and widening and deepening a chasm among unhappy party members just as they were about to meet and make momentous decisions about their course in the looming election.

"Young Hickory" and "the Reannexation of Texas . . ."

The Democrats convened in national convention in the Odd Fellows' Hall in Baltimore on May 27, 1844. Earlier party conventions had gone rather smoothly, each presidential nominee being quickly named on the first ballot, the only one necessary in a ceremony of consensual harmony. Not this time. From the first moments of the meeting, Van Buren's opponents seized their opportunities and outgeneraled the veteran political managers leading the New Yorker's forces. He was tripped up by shrewd (and devious) tactical manuevering and because the Texas issue was effectively used against him. The decisive moment occurred right at the opening when leaders of the anti–Van Buren bloc adroitly seized control of the meeting while the delegates were milling around in the still disorganized proceedings. They shouted through the selection of their own chairman and, more significantly, pushed through by voice vote their particular set of rules to govern the proceedings.[39]

The sudden strike by Van Buren's opponents at the opening of the convention sealed his fate, although it took several days for the end to come. Specifically, the annexationist bloc moved the adoption, as a convention rule, of a two-thirds majority requirement for a candidate to receive the party's nomination. This supermajority notion was not new. It had been established in previous Democratic meetings going back to 1832, ironically then instituted in order to underscore the widespread party support for Van Buren's nomination as vice president on Jackson's ticket. On the other hand, it had not been used four years before when Van Buren had been renominated for the office that he already held.[40]

The Van Burenites vigorously protested but were beaten in a roll-call vote in which a number of delegates who were formally pledged to Van Buren's nomination voted against his interests on the two-thirds manueuver. The mood of delegates from all parts of the country was clear enough. Expansion was on their minds, and they wished to find a suitable candidate who would get behind it with appropriate commitment and the necessary energy. Although Van Buren received 146 votes on the first nominating ballot, a majority of the 266 accredited delegates, and led on the next three roll calls, it did him no good. He was losing votes when each new tally was made, and it was clear that he would never attract the support of the two-thirds of the delegates necessary for him to win. All of this took place amid much bitterness that constantly spilled over in speeches on the floor, for and against Van Buren. The situation inside the hall was ominous. The party seemed to be on the verge of destroying its electoral chances because of the differences on Texas.[41]

As Van Buren's delegate totals sagged, those for Michigan's Lewis Cass increased, reaching 123 on the seventh ballot. The sixty-one-year-old Cass was a loyal Jacksonian and longtime officeholder who was quite popular among Democrats in the western states. Despite his popularity and strong committment to expansion, however, he was not going to get the votes necessary to be nominated. The members of the Van Buren bloc were dead set against him, believing that he had been in the forefront of those working to bring down their leader. They were strong enough to block Cass's nomination, or anyone else's, if they stayed together as the convention continued to vote. They seemed determined to do so. The situation thus remained ominous as the meeting staggered along. The crisis ended only when, after holding on to their hopes as long as they could, and in order to avert a catastrophe for the party, the Van Burenites reluctantly gave way and ultimately accepted the nomination of James K. Polk of Tennessee, considered to be, in the eyes of many of the New Yorkers, a tried and true Jacksonian in his outlook and policy commitments. He was also politically close to the ex-president: He had come into the convention holding the inside track for the vice presidential nomination on a Van Buren ticket.[42]

In addition, Polk was, of course, a dedicated expansionist, strongly in favor of bringing Texas into the Union. He was nominated on the ninth ballot to run on a platform of traditional Democratic policy proposals and enumeration of past glories, as well as a plank calling for "the reannexation of Texas and the reoccupation of

Oregon" (adding the other longed-for prize to the expansionists' want list) at, the plank concluded, "*the earliest practicable moment*" [italics added]. The last was a wonderfully ambiguous phrase that lacked the sense of urgency and immediatism that had been so prominent among the exigent expansionists in the run-up to the convention. In a sop to the defeated, the plank was drafted by one of the leaders of the New York Van Buren group, either Silas Wright or Benjamin F. Butler.[43]

Nevertheless, whoever actually wrote the plank, territorial expansion had now become a central tenet of the Democratic Party's creed more directly than ever before, both rhetorically and in its leadership's clear intentions about it. It was something that many party members fervently believed in and, they were convinced, that the American people wanted. Finally, it was most certainly, as they had always seen it and claimed in their rhetoric about the issue, in the national interest to bring Texas into the Union.

THE DEMOCRATIC PARTY had passed through a severe trial in which the old leadership had been brought down in favor of post-Jackson leaders imbued with both traditional party values *and* the great desire for the immediate achievement of the nation's manifest destiny to spread to the southwest and to the Pacific coast. At one level, Van Buren's defeat, although unexpected, could be seen as a normal political overturn of the kind that was to become familiar in both parties in future years and had happened to Henry Clay at the Whig convention in the previous election. But such an upset was new to the Democrats who had grown accustomed to the seamless transitions of the party's top leadership characteristic of their history since their emergence as an organized party in the 1830s. What now would follow the trauma that they had just been through?

The question was partly answered when the new leaders of the Democracy moved to nominate Van Buren's closest political friend and most loyal lieutenant, Senator Silas Wright, as their candidate for the vice presidency. Wright was as much against immediate annexation as was his chief, and he was extremely bitter about what had happened to Van Buren. (He had been at the center of events and had been quick to spot conspiracies against his leader early on. He was characterized as "furious" because of what had occurred in the convention.) Because of his ingrained loyalty to his party leader and friend, and his state of mind as a result of what had happened to him, he turned down the nomination and rejected all overtures to reconsider—a very bad omen for a party that had just had such a divisive, wrenching experience. (The convention finally turned to George M. Dallas of Pennsylvania, a relative of the expansionist leader Robert J. Walker, and named him to the second spot on the ticket.)[44]

As the convention proceeded, whatever qualms, and worse, there may have been, the party leaders worked overtime to heal the inflicted wounds. They were successful. In fact, the Democrats emerged from their convention in good shape, relatively united and ready to do battle. Those fretful Democrats who had been so concerned about their party's weaknesses and fragmentation before the convention widely acclaimed Polk's nomination. They saw in him a "Young Hickory," who would recapture the Democrats' most glorious moments and lead them to even greater heights. The nomination energized the party activists, who then went eagerly to work on behalf of their ticket.[45]

Most critically of all, Van Buren, whatever his private feelings, and true to form, did not sulk in his tent but called on his followers to put their talents and their energies to work to elect Polk and Dallas. Side by side with the internal tensions that had brought him down were the impulses keeping party members such as the ex-president and his followers loyal to the institution and the causes it espoused despite their differences. Van Buren and his lieutenants were not happy about what had happened at Baltimore, but in the spirit of party loyalty they accepted the decision of the convention and went along, if not entirely warmly. Their task was made easier—or more bearable—because of the candidate who had replaced their leader. "If we could not have Mr. Van Buren," John A. Dix wrote, "certainly they could not do well as to give us Mr. Polk. . . . He had the goodwill of the entire Van Buren faction." Silas Wright agreed. "I will support cheerfully Mr. Polk for the Presidency," he wrote at the end of the convention, "and hope in my head he may be elected."[46]

Some anti-slavery New York Democrats tried to have it both ways, issuing a circular letter saying that they, too, would support Polk while, at the same time, "rejecting the resolution respecting Texas."[47] But that was not Van Buren's way, or that of most Democrats. The convention had chosen its candidates and they were duty bound, as loyal Democrats, to support them. The duly chosen nominees had to be elected whatever differences existed over Polk's approach to Texas.

That consensual, unifying ideal, of course, was not always fully adhered to, but in Van Buren's case, after Polk's nomination, it was. Whatever the depth of his personal disappointments, he remained, and acted as, the loyal Democrat that he was. He also made it clear to his supporters that they were expected to do the same, and they did. Silas Wright even went beyond his commitment to the remaining-faithful-to-the-cause rhetoric. His reluctant willingness to leave his Senate seat and run for governor of New York was, party strategists believed, a boon to Polk. As they saw it, the popular Wright's active presence would significantly strengthen the national ticket's chances in the largest state in the Union. Elsewhere, as well, Van Burenites fell into line. They joined Democrats "of every shade of opinion" who now "blended in a bold and ardent stand." The shrine of party still held sway among them.[48]

"Who Is James K. Polk?"

The parties quickly squared off behind their candidates. They had many things to talk about. The campaign was soon awash in heated discussion of the variety of issues that divided the parties from one another. Most of them were familiar matters that had cross-sectional support (or opposition). Both parties encountered bumps along the way in their efforts; each's expectations and confidence went up and down as the days passed; both made adjustments in their approaches and arguments as they went along; but both largely kept their eyes on the main lines of the issues separating them, what they believed, and what troubled them about their opponents.

The Whigs began with their traditional concern for leadership qualities. They were delighted with Polk's nomination. In their eyes, he was an unknown politician of little discernible appeal, talent, or strength. They were confident that he would never be able to stand up to the likes of Henry Clay. He had served in Congress and had been Speaker of the House in the first half of the 1830s, but he had never proven himself as a national leader—that is, in modern terms, a mover and shaker. In their statement of principles and in the campaign, Whigs made much of Clay's superior experience on the national stage and his recognized qualities as a gifted leader. In comparison to his stature, "who," their editors and speakers derisively asked, "is James K. Polk?"[49]

Beyond individuals, and as expected, the parties continued to fight on the old ramparts established in the Jacksonian administration and further developed since. Each's editors and speakers vigorously and repeatedly pushed their party's usual perspectives on public policy and the public good. As Michael Holt has written, the Whigs wanted "to etch the sharpest possible line" between themselves and the Democrats on traditional economic issues since that was, they believed, the surest way to mobilize the maximum Whig vote, as they had successfully done in 1840. Democratic strategists concurred from their own corner, believing that such drawing of the sharpest lines between the parties on such matters redounded to their advantage.[50]

THE DEMOCRATIC CAMPAIGN, to be sure, added a fillip to this stress on traditionalism. Party leaders combined the theme of restoration in government affairs and the traditional policy approaches of the party with the expansionist enthusiasm that had clearly grown in their ranks beyond what Van Buren had once hoped were its containable boundaries. Whatever hesitations some Democrats had on the matter, they were drowned out by the positive noise of the pro-annexationists in command. The latter believed not only in immediately acquiring Texas but also in its efficacy as an issue for them. They thoroughly aired their position in all sections of the country. They were convinced that there were votes to be gained on Texas beyond the party core in many areas of pro-annexation enthusiasm, especially among southern Whigs. One of their pamphlets, *The South in Danger* (written by the very busy Robert J. Walker), addressed Clay's followers in the slave states, calling on them to do their duty by voting against Clay and his everlastingly hostile to the South—and to annexation—northern Whig allies.[51]

As the parties developed their campaign themes and assessed their strategies, there were always difficulties to be overcome. Each party's concerns about the closeness of the race were underscored when spokesmen for both presidential candidates occasionally fudged their party's usual policy commitments for electoral purposes. (This was not done as often as later political folklore claimed, since the other side was always quick to jump on and expose any such deviations from party orthodoxy. Such jumping on and exposure of any such duplicity certainly occurred here.) Nevertheless, special local and sectional situations prompted some attempts at deception or ambiguity. Polk's supporters in Pennsylvania, for example, proclaimed their candidate's backing for a higher tariff than Democrats generally espoused or than "Young Hickory" had ever previously publicly favored.[52]

With the Whigs it was Texas. At the outset of the campaign both parties worked hard to remind voters of where they stood on the annexation issue in those areas of the nation where they believed that it had particular prominence and importance. On most policy matters, as noted, they presented their views always within the prevailing partisan framework. Expansion, too, was approached in this way. Democrats emphasized that all their arguments about bringing Texas into the Union reflected their normal political directions, discourse, and visions. Whatever the sectional elements that appeared in the campaign concerning the annexation of slaveholding territory, they tried very hard to domesticate them and proceed to mobilize the Democratic electorate as they always had.[53]

The Whigs also worked hard to approach matters in normal partisan terms. Most of them continued to echo their long-standing position that the addition of Texas was unnecessary to America's needs and a potentially dangerous error. But whatever the partisan quality to the general debate over expansion, North-South differences came into play among Whigs as well in reaction to the sectional heat raised by Calhoun's linking of annexation with the security of slavery. Northern Whigs were particularly harsh about "the reckless folly" of acquiring Texas. Many of them expressed strong anti-slavery sentiments when they discussed the issue. They focused a great deal of attention on the sectional machinations of Tyler and Calhoun and, now, the rash pro-slavery expansionism of Polk and the post–Van Buren Democrats.[54]

In contrast, some southern Whigs continued to view the issue as a difficult one for them. They were not sure that they could oppose annexation very strongly given the sectionalist impulses unleashed from the beginning by some of their adversaries and now further developed by Calhoun in his Pakenham letter. These Whigs continued to believe, as they had from the first, that the sectionalist argument for annexation as a way to protect slavery was attracting potential voters who otherwise would be expected to support Clay. Their determination not to be caught on the wrong side of the issue of promoting their section's security, and seeing their party's cause hurt as a result, remained a powerful inducement as they pondered what course they should take.[55]

Another election year pro-annexation cartoon. This one suggests that only abolitionists and other extremists oppose the acquisition of Texas. LIBRARY OF CONGRESS.

Others among the southern wing, in contrast, went along with their party's general position, reiterating their opposition to further territorial expansion and the diplomatic consequences that would ensue, including war with Mexico. A Whig mass meeting in Louisiana resolved, for example, that, "however desirable the extension of territory by the annexation of Texas might be, the Whigs of Louisiana are unanimously opposed to the measure unless compatible with the honor of the country and the stability of the Union." They made it clear that they accepted Clay's opinion at the outset of the campaign that the Texas issue was "a miserable political humbug," and took up, instead, the usual Whig agenda as their main rallying point.[56]

But, to underline the backing and filling that occurred in this closest of elections, a concerned Clay ultimately straddled on Texas in the South. In two letters to Alabama newspaper editors, he amended his previous all-out opposition to annexation and suggested that if certain conditions were met he would agree to acquiring the republic when he became president. He had "no objection" to annexation if it could be accomplished "without dishonor—without war, with the common consent of the Union, and upon just and fair terms."[57]

Clay's Alabama letters did not really change very much in policy terms. His position remained ambiguous. While now accepting eventual annexation, his statements still contained clear differences over timing and conditions from those of the much more ardent pro-annexationists leading the Democrats. More important, the conditions that he set were not likely to be achieved anytime soon—if ever. Once again, however, nuances were lost in the heat of the campaign, and different groups reacted to their perceptions of the direction and apparent substance of Clay's current stance. In short, some voters now believed that Clay supported annexation.[58]

Did the letters change a great deal about the election? Whatever backtracking Clay attempted on the issue in them was almost certainly futile. Reflecting the tensions between the partisan and sectional states of mind, many northern Whigs were appalled by the letters due to Clay's apparent shift of position. It was an action that made New York's William H. Seward "gloomy" and certainly angered most of his like-minded colleagues. Still, Seward was not alone among them in continuing to support his party's national ticket. The longtime anti-slavery congressman Joshua Giddings of Ohio also supported Clay as the campaign got under way. If he, Seward, and other anti-slavery northern Whigs were deeply angry about Clay's shift, they never lost sight of the fact that the Democrats were the real enemy and that Henry Clay was greatly preferable to Polk.[59]

Democrats made much of the Whig candidate's waffling and apparent electorally driven shift, reminding those voters who might be taken in of the Whigs' traditional anti-expansionism. They argued that if Clay was moving away from that, it was a highly suspicious move and undoubtedly duplicitous, an example of the Whig leader's lack of principle and his desperate search for votes. As one party editor summed up, "he turns so rapidly that vertigo and dizziness prevail."[60] Democrats had never been impressed by Clay's integrity or any of his other claims to superior merit as a statesman, and his behavior during this election campaign confirmed their deep skepticism—a skepticism that they continued to make much of in their campaigning right up to election day.

After the intense campaign of the fall, the country went to the polls in early November and then settled down to await the announcement of the results that would be forwarded from local polling stations to county seats, and then to state capitals, to be tallied, checked, and, finally, announced. Voting places were crowded throughout the country. Almost 80 percent of those eligible turned out to record their choice. When all of the returns were finally counted, Polk won an extraordinarily close election with a little under 50 percent of the popular vote, beating Clay by about thirty-eight thousand of the 2.7 million cast. He would enjoy a Democratic-controlled Congress in support of his administration as well. The Liberty Party gathered just over sixty thousand votes in the North, enough, some have suggested, to tip New York State, and the election, to Polk. (This assumes that the Liberty voters would have supported Clay at the polls in the absence of their party on the ballot as an alternative.)[61]

"Young Hickory" was to be president of the United States. The Democrats had successfully come through the turmoil caused by their internal difficulties and won the election behind an old-style party leader who was also, like his mentor, Andrew Jackson, an exuberant expansionist, eager to bring Texas and Oregon and, it turned out, other areas as well into the American Union. As the jubilant Democratic loyalists saw it, the political landscape had returned to its normal colors after four years of the uproar caused by their partisan enemies. The party's leaders and their many supporters, along with the policy preferences that they all held, were now firmly in command of the nation's governing apparatus and could proceed to enact the many legislative policies and accomplish the necessary executive actions that were mandated in their national platform and their other statements of purpose issued during the campaign—including all that they had had to say about territorial expansion.[62]

In the absence of public opinion polls, it is not immediately apparent what impact the Texas issue had on popular voting in 1844. Some historians suggest that pro-Texas sentiment increased the Democratic vote in the South and that Clay's Alabama letters may have cost him support among northern Whigs who went to the Liberty Party instead. Certainly, those party leaders who wished to believe in the power of the Texas issue, taking the pulse of the voters in election rallies, convinced themselves that annexation was popular among enough people to have made a difference. But the election turned out to be about many things: the elements comprising the ongoing battle between Whigs and Democrats with their competing visions of appropriate policies, as well as the impact on some voters of the Texas issue as framed by Calhoun. When all of it is tallied, most of the popular voting largely followed the electorate's already established commitments to one party or the other, while the positions taken about Texas and Oregon probably did not change as many minds on election day as the heat of the campaign rhetoric, and the hopes and worries of party leaders, suggested would happen.[63]

That was certainly the opinion of a number of contemporary observers. The Maine Democratic leader, John Fairfield, told Polk that Texas had been touched on only briefly in his state's elections; the tariff and bank issues had "been the principal topics on both sides."[64] (Democratic support increased in other northern states as well, despite the hostility to annexation in a number of areas.) In many states, the pattern of the vote in 1844 generally echoed results in earlier elections, allowing for new voters. In Virginia, for example, Polk's percentage of the vote in all parts of the state in 1844 was about the same as Democratic totals in the same places in the off-year 1843 congressional elections. Elsewhere, voters in other parts of the Union similarly echoed their own past behavior when they went to the polls that fall.[65]

One important matter shaping the vote in the North, where many Whigs had articulated an anti-slavery-extension position, had little to do either with Texas or with the traditional economic issues dividing the parties. Ethnoreligious tensions were particularly high in a number of northern states that fall, and some local nativist, anti-immigrant parties had appeared on the scene railing against what they perceived to be the dangers from a flood of undigestible immigrants entering the United States. The Democrats had long attracted support from newly arrived immigrants from Ireland and parts of the Continent. The Whigs repelled them, and in 1844, party leaders in New York and Pennsylvania allied themselves with the nativists, expecting important electoral gains from their alliance. (Frelinghuysen's nomination as vice president was part of that strategy.) But, as Michael Holt has effectively shown, what the Whig strategy produced instead was a surge of immigrants to the polls to support the Democrats because of matters concerned with their own security and the prejudices exhibited by the Whigs against them.[66]

As noted, this had nothing directly to do with Texas except to help the Democrats win a number of northern states by close margins—and the national election. The election primarily revolved, however, around the usual mixture of different elements—existing loyalties and policy commitments, the perceived horrors that would follow if the other side got in, the particular attraction of some matter or other—with no one issue, except perhaps previous party allegiance, determining the eventual outcome. The point was that the drama of that year could be internalized as one more example of a bothersome sectional uproar that was subsequently tamed by the dominant processes of American politics. The election of 1844 was neither a nationwide referendum on Texas nor a clear example of the sectionalizing of the political arena. What it was, above all else, was a Democratic victory.[67]

4

"TEXAS WILL BE ANNEXED"

THE FIRST FRUITS OF JAMES K. Polk's victory was, not unexpectedly, the annexation of Texas. The fervent annexationists of the previous spring were still in office and, like many others, chose to read the presidential election as a statement of the voters' positive attitude about the issue. (Considering the fifty-fifty division of the vote, that seems something of a stretch.) They therefore proceeded to accomplish what they wanted to do all along. The annexationists' leader, John Tyler, urged on by Secretary of State Calhoun, made one more intervention on the issue, again significantly roiling the political waters as he did so.[1] Polk would not take office until early March, four months after his victory. The newly elected Twenty-ninth Congress would not convene in its first session until December 1845, thirteen months after the national election (unless called earlier to Washington by the president). However, the existing Congress, the Twenty-eighth, whose upper house had refused to ratify the annexation treaty the previous spring, would meet one last time in a short so-called lame-duck session one month after Polk's victory. When it did, early in December 1844, it found the Texas annexation issue once more awaiting it.

The Triumph of Annexation and the Annexationists

President Tyler presented his final annual message to the assembled members of Congress on December 3. The recent presidential contest confirmed, he happily told his listeners, that "a controlling majority of the people [in their votes for Polk] and a large majority of the States [through legislative resolutions] have declared in favor of immediate annexation." It was time, therefore, for Congress to act decisively on the matter. He called on them to do so by passing a joint resolution admitting the republic to the Union, an action that would need only a majority in each house rather than the two-thirds vote of the Senate called for in order to ratify a treaty.[2]

Tyler was not alone in pressing for action as soon as possible in the aftermath of the election. Despite the fact that Polk's close victory had not been a clear-cut referendum on Texas—even given Tyler's assertion that it was, and the impact that the issue had had on some voters—once the contest was over, pro-annexationists joined Tyler in speaking and acting as if it had been, loudly, insistently, repeatedly. Democratic editors intensified their support for annexation, as did their spokesmen in Congress and elsewhere, both citing the November outcome to make their case. "Texas will be annexed," an Ohio Democratic congressman exulted in January, "and not only Texas," he went on, "but every inch of land on this continent. Our republic is to be an ocean-bound republic." The exuberant message had sunk home. Even the anti-expansionist New York *Evening Post* admitted, "That there is a large majority who would be glad to see Texas, in some way or other, united to this country, there can be no doubt."[3]

In response to these pressures and the acknowledged widespread desire for annexation, both houses of Congress were quickly inundated by a range of bills to accomplish Texas's entry; seven appeared in the Senate, another ten in the House.[4] The ensuing debates over them revealed the same lines of contention as earlier, with a clear pro-annexation majority in the House of Representatives and the Senate more uncertain. Some northern Democrats in both houses continued to be restless about how the party had worked out its problems in 1844 as well as to be uncertain—and distressed—about annexation. (One measure of the persistent anger expressed in some quarters was the repeal of the gag rule against anti-slavery petitions in the House at the opening of this session, a repeal made possible by increased northern Democratic support for the move.)[5]

Still, the majority for bringing Texas into the Union was there, whatever the resistance, if it could be brought together. It came down, in the congressional deliberations, to finding the most agreeable means of effecting annexation, rather than deciding whether it should be done or not. Much time was taken up, therefore, in seeking a consensual means of achieving the agreed-on purpose. The large bloc of pro-annexation congressmen among the Democrats were told that they should pursue "a circumspect and conciliatory course." They should not spend time haggling over the details of how, exactly, Texas would be brought into the Union. Nor should those northern Democrats who remained hesitant, or not fully convinced, continue to battle against the clear tide of pro-annexation feeling. In seeking some means of soothing differences on the issue, "conciliation" among them was also now to be the order of the day.[6]

The appeals to consensus among the Democrats worked. It took time and much effort to achieve it, but even the Van Buren group were reported as seeking, from the first, "a fair and liberal compromise." In the aftermath of Polk's victory, most of their leaders were not prepared to make an issue over slavery's expansion, which some of them had jibbed about repeatedly in earlier debates. In fact, despite all of the efforts made to get them to back off, some continued to do so even now, but their holdout was clearly a distinctly minority view in the prevailing climate of accomplishing annexation that distinguished and defined their party's position.[7]

The final stages of the deliberations revealed, therefore, all of the arts of partisan politics that had been evolving over the past two decades: the pushing forward of a compromise bill that would attract enough votes by forsaking some clarity on issues of internal dispute among the Democrats for a certain ambiguity on details instead, as well as much pressure from party supporters and the constant intervention of party leaders, including a certain amount from James K. Polk, not yet president but very active behind the scenes.[8]

Stephen A. Douglas in the House and Thomas Hart Benton in the Senate tried to ease the continuing sting of Calhoun's Pakenham maneuver. Douglas, for example, introduced an amendment limiting the area of Texas open to slavery to that below the line 36° 30', the old Missouri Compromise boundary between free and possible slave territory. To be sure, there was very little of Texas north of that line, even given the province's leaders' extravagant territorial claims. Nevertheless, the amendment indicated a sense, even among ardent expansionists such as Douglas, that it was desirable to meliorate whatever sectional hostility remained among some of the Van Buren Democrats so that the main object, Texas entering the Union, would, at last, be attained.[9]

In the Senate, Calhoun's South Carolina colleague, George McDuffie, offered a bill that simply repeated the terms of the defeated treaty. That was unacceptable to the same senators who had voted against the treaty in the first place. The resistant Democrats around Van Buren then sought to take the initiative. Speaking for many of that group, Senator Benton demanded further negotiations with Texas over the republic's boundaries and a new treaty to resolve other issues, including Texas's debt problems. He wanted to admit only the settled eastern portion of the republic as a slave state and to organize the rest of the republic's land area into a new Southwest Territory (with slavery permitted only in half of that territory). Subsequently, in the spirit of compromise, he removed most of his bill's restrictive, and or controversial, elements. His bare-bones substitute admitted Texas as a state as soon as the details could be worked out in further negotiations between the United States and the republic.[10]

As the debates unfolded, most Whigs continued their opposition as before, and in quite familiar terms. On the House floor, Congressman Caleb Smith of Indiana, a state where a great deal of pro-annexation sentiment had been repeatedly expressed and widely reported, unabashedly made the familiar clear once again, that he and other Whigs "who oppose the annexation of Texas, are satisfied with the Union as it is. . . . Our territory is already sufficiently extensive to promote the welfare of all."[11]

The Whigs also focused on the means chosen to accomplish annexation, arguing that the joint-resolution pathway was unconstitutional. In addition, they brought up the often troubling question of Texas's debts, a question that they had used against agreeing to annexation in the earlier debates, even as the various bill writers tried to finesse that issue (usually by making Texas responsible for paying off its obligations). As the debate dragged on, Democrats accused Whigs of deliberately procrastinating in order to wear everyone down and hopefully defeat the bill. That behavior had to be ended. It was time, the editor of the Washington *Globe* wrote, to bring "this unprofitable discussion" to a close.[12]

A young congressman and senator, Douglas was an ardent supporter of western expansion. LIBRARY OF CONGRESS.

THE SECTIONAL RUMBLINGS stoked by Calhoun and the subsequent backlash against him were still present as Congress considered a new approach to annexation, but the fallout from them remained unclear. The different responses of many northern and some southern Whigs to the annexation of Texas remained as they had been. Northern members of the party were sharply against it, with editors of party newspapers and speakers to party audiences in various parts of the North continuing the same anti-southern assaults that they had voiced since the issue had emerged under Calhoun's aegis earlier in the year. Unfortunately, their party colleagues were, an exasperated southern Whig wrote, "wickedly narrowing it down to a simple question of pro & anti slavery."[13]

In these final hours, many of the southern Whigs continued to be against annexation as well, if not for the reason given by their anti-slavery northern colleagues. They repeated, once more, the argument that they had offered during the campaign: that annexation would not be a benefit to the country, as the overly exuberant expansionists claimed, but, rather, would cause a great many destabilizing

Thomas Hart Benton was a veteran Jacksonian leader who saw Calhoun's policies as threatening the Union.
LIBRARY OF CONGRESS.

internal problems that would be difficult for the nation to resolve. The annexation of Texas remained, to this bedeviled group, what it had always been: not a good idea, no matter what the Democrats claimed for it.[14]

At the same time, as long foreshadowed in the ongoing debates within the party, other southern Whigs once more broke with their party colleagues, both north and south. Annexation would, they again argued, in fact, benefit the South, and their constituents, being convinced of that, evinced much support for Texas annexation. These representatives could not, therefore, they familiarly repeated, afford to continue their opposition. It would seriously hurt them and their party electorally, not only in the immediate term but almost certainly later as well, as their opposition to an unusually popular policy continued to be used against them by their Democratic antagonists.[15]

There were also sectional fault lines among the Democrats. As the debate got under way, Representative Jacob Brinkerhoff of Ohio characterized the efforts to acquire Texas by his colleagues as "your

Southern, your sectional, your intensely selfish scheme of annexation." New York party members seemed to be especially divided. One of them, George Rathbun, a congressman from upstate, warned his colleagues that their constituents opposed the further extension of slavery and that they should, therefore, oppose annexation. But another New York congressman, Chesselden Ellis, answered his colleagues in traditional Democratic (northern or southern) terms: "Texas, sir, must be ours. Its acquisition is identified with the great interests of the country. That my vote will represent the opinions and feelings of the democracy of my district, I have the best reason to know. That I will accord with the general sentiment of the democracy of New York and of the Union, I have as little reason to doubt."[16]

Behind the colloquy among these northern Democrats were their ongoing efforts to overcome their differences and find the much more important "common ground" that they were sure existed on the issue—or on any issue that they might initially have disagreements about. As Martin Van Buren wrote, in concluding his part in dealing with the issue, "in respect to the Texas matter, I have had my say, and am disposed to abide [by] the opinion of my countrymen."[17]

That attitude was clearly in the air as Congress worked its way through the matter. In the House, Milton Brown, a Whig congressman from Tennessee, following that line, and seeking to get the issue out of the way once and for all, broke ranks with most of his party colleagues to introduce the resolution that ultimately passed that body. His bill called for the admission of the whole area of Texas as a state (with slavery if the Texans wanted it) and the provision that additional states could thereafter be carved out of the area if Texans agreed to it. Significantly, the Democratic caucus voted to support Brown's resolution over any of those offered by members of their own party. It gave them what they wanted and might draw some Whig support, end the debate once and for all, and get Texas into the Union. Finally, Douglas's 36° 30' clause was accepted by Brown and became part of the joint resolution passed in the House.[18]

"His Honor Is Sufficient Security"

When the House and Senate voted on the issue in early 1845, the lineup was clear. Whatever the sectional themes that had been expressed, party unity was high, if never perfect, as the roll was called. In the House, eight Whigs (all from the South) and 112 Democrats, from all over the Union, voted for Brown's resolution. Seventy-two Whigs (including seventeen from the South) and twenty-six Democrats (about one-third of those who came from the northern states) voted against the bill. Among the latter, it was observed that "the distinct friends of Mr. Wright [that is, the Van Burenites] stood out to the last." Despite this continued hesitation by some congressmen in Van Buren's circle about the sectionalist impulses present, Democratic unity averaged 80 percent of its members. The Whigs, in their turn, averaged 90 percent unity. Southern Whigs, to be sure, divided, two-thirds of them opposing the bill and one-third supporting it. Nevertheless, to repeat, partisan lines, always sneeringly referred to by the other side as reflecting "party drill" (i.e., pressure from the leadership, not independence of mind), predominated in the House's voting behavior whatever the sectional cracks that had surfaced throughout the legislative process.[19]

In the Senate, the two approaches offered—Brown's version calling for immediate admission of Texas, and Benton's plan calling for ultimate admission but only after further negotiations—were united, at Robert J. Walker's suggestion, as different sections of one bill, with Congress giving the president of the United States the authority to choose which of the two pathways to entry he wished to offer to the Texans. The 27–25 vote passing the combined proposal, with three Whig senators voting for the resolution, was very close, if conclusive enough.[20]

Fortunately for the pro-annexationists, Benton and his fellow friends of Van Buren went along with the two-headed compromise. They apparently believed that they had an understanding that the incoming President Polk, not the outgoing, despised Tyler, would carry out the terms of the joint resolution and that the new president would opt for the Benton version and negotiate a new treaty with Texas. Silas Wright was assured that Polk would do so: "His assurance was given to others as well as myself," New York's Senator Dix reported, "and his honor is sufficient security." Benton also told his colleagues that the expansionist leader, Senator Walker, known to be close politically to both Tyler and Polk, had said to many senators that Tyler would leave the final stages of the matter to the incoming president. "Thus quieted in their apprehensions," Benton later wrote, "five senators voted for the act of admission who would not otherwise have done so."[21]

But the expected procedure did not happen. Tyler did not sit by and wait for Polk's accession to office. Instead, he moved quickly (on Secretary of State Calhoun's advice) after signing the bill to offer Brown's version of annexation to Texas, sending a courier with the offer to the republic's capital. When he entered office a few days later, Polk had the opportunity to recall the envoy that Tyler had dispatched but decided not to do so. Nor was he willing to change the terms that were being offered in favor of Benton's still-more-negotiations approach. He briefly halted the courier to think about it but then allowed him to proceed. Polk denied, then and later, having made any promises to act differently once in office and argued that if he had followed the Benton route the delay would have meant "that Texas would probably have been lost to the Union." Whatever the truth of a claim of bad faith, the new president, who had been kept informed of the situation in Congress, also seemed determined to end any further hesitation and to settle the issue once and for all and thus preclude both further divisive debate and the danger his plans would face if internal party disagreements continued to fester among those who should now be united.[22]

WHAT WAS THE SIGNIFICANCE of all of this political activity in the parties' back rooms, on the convention floor, on the campaign hustings, in the legislative arena, and, finally, in the White House, in 1844 and early 1845? The political revolution of 1844 at the summit of American politics was, first of all, about the leadership of the Democratic Party. Second, it focused intense concern on territorial expansion as a significant issue in national politics. Third, the immediate annexationists, led by Tyler, Calhoun, and now Polk, had won. Texas annexation was finally an accomplished fact after the long and acrimonious fight unleashed by the outgoing president and his secretary of state.

Was there more to it than that? At first glance, the political world had settled down to its normal routines and operations as James K. Polk entered office with the Texas controversy behind all of them. Some politicians on both sides of the issue, and their followers, were licking wounds incurred during the battle. Still, there was every chance, as Polk hoped, that those wounds would quickly heal and not erupt into anything more now that the issue had been brought to a conclusion. There was nothing more to fight about.

THE SITUATION REMAINED more problematic than Polk's hopes for it, however. The pro-annexation majority was delighted as the president's courier sped on his way to the Texas capital, but there was less to be delighted about than they knew. The congressional resolution of the long-smoldering issue was seen by some contemporaries, and by later historians, as both an end and a beginning. First, it signaled an end to the divisive controversy that had held the political stage for too long, one fueled by the range of political, economic, sectional, and diplomatic impulses that defined and shaped the American scene. At the same time, some suggest that it proved to be a beginning, an important first step toward the weakening of the national political structure so carefully constructed to avoid and harness the consequences of internal fragmentation in the United States. The elements of angry and persistent sectional tension were present (as they had always been). Ammunition for its further growth had been fired off during the Texas battle and given it an impetus into national politics that seemed quite ominous to some observers and decisive in shaping what was to follow afterward.

Perhaps. The question, in its aftermath, was whether these strains would affect things beyond the election of Polk and the successful completion of the annexation of Texas, as well as beyond the political leadership level where so much of the battle had so far occurred. The quite real sectional tensions present were only one aspect of the political calculus that had led to the final result. The threat sectionalism posed had not yet become a full-scale war. That there were differences between the North and the South was acknowledged by many. Yet none of the potential weakening process inherent in persistent North-South conflict had cohered, as Polk took the oath of office, into a clear-cut force strong enough to affect controversial matters in new, and dangerous, ways. The partisan qualities that primarily defined American political life had once again largely contained the sectional tensions that had appeared, no matter how aggressively some political activists pushed them onto popular consciousness.

In sum, more was needed to bring together and focus all that had occurred, and was still present on the scene, that divided northerners from southerners and to make it into the kind of critical moment that would have consequences that reached beyond its own starting point. To repeat, that had not yet happened, as it had not happened in earlier moments of sectional confrontation, despite the uproar of the last year and all of the dire warnings and frightened forebodings that had been expressed. This turned out, however, not to be the last word in the drama of Texas annexation. The sense of closure felt by many participants when the joint resolution passed and the president acted to finalize the process once and for all turned out to be premature. Texas was in the Union. More was still to come. Ironically, President Polk was to be the agent of further unleashing of the forces that would imprint Texas on the national consciousness well beyond the immediate question of annexation.

5

"PROLIFIC OF EVIL AND PREGNANT WITH BLOODY FRUIT"

On July 4, 1845, a Texas constitutional convention convened by the republic's president, Ansel Jones, met to consider an ordinance accepting the United States' annexation proposal. There had continued to be disagreements among Texans about the American offer and political manuevering to defeat it. These difficulties were now overcome, and the ordinance passed overwhelmingly. In October the last steps were taken. The people of Texas voted to ratify the convention's action. The news of their official acceptance, in the form originally proposed by Milton Brown, reached Washington just in time for President Polk to announce it to the members of the new, Democratically controlled Twenty-ninth Congress when they convened in its first session in early December.[1]

A number of Whig newspaper editors and other party spokesmen had continued their protests against the admission of Texas in the months since Congress had passed the joint resolution. Prominent party leaders in Massachusetts led by Charles Francis Adams (John Quincy's son), Henry Wilson, and Charles Sumner, joining with members of the Liberty Party in their state, formed a Massachusetts State Texas Committee to engage in a last-ditch effort to mobilize further opposition. Their primary weapon was an editorial and petition campaign that they vigorously pushed among their neighbors. Party leaders from other states also kept up the fight as best they could, in debate and by their representatives in Washington offering motions against the admission of Texas when Congress reconvened.[2]

The anger—and anguish—of those opposed to annexation continued to be intense and obviously heartfelt, but it remained ineffective. The Whigs themselves were divided. While some engaged in what one Democratic editor called a "useless, stale, flat and unprofitable debate," many others among them had given up the battle. "I cannot think it good policy to waste our efforts on the impossible" was the response of one Massachusetts Whig leader to the efforts by his colleagues to mount continued opposition. As the historian Justin Smith has summed up the situation, "the day for such efforts had evidently passed." It was time, the *Democratic Review* concluded, "for opposition to the annexation of Texas to cease."[3]

The majority position on the long-contested matter was clear, and annexation proponents were in a position in the new Congress to bring the matter to a close. In short order, as the year 1845 came to an end, and despite the continued rumblings against doing so, each house passed, and the president then signed, a bill formally admitting Texas into the Union as its twenty-eighth state. The draining and seemingly interminable annexation process was at last completed.[4]

This was the close of a chapter, not the end of the matter, however. Texas was now part of the Union. Whether to annex it or not was no longer an issue. But the potent political uproar it had induced was not quickly forgotten. Once again, as in the Texas debate itself, the political machinations among different individuals and groups in the months and years that followed the final steps completing annexation, and the missteps and misunderstandings that accompanied them, had an immense impact on the substance and direction of American politics. The messy fallout from the battle to make Texas part of the United States became a critical factor shaping the way that events subsequently unfolded and, most critically, how they were interpreted, and reacted to, on the political landscape.

Polk Triumphant

The impact of the Texas affair on future events had already begun to develop long before the final steps completing annexation had been taken. James K. Polk and his wife, Sara, arrived in Washington in early 1845 to lead a new political beginning. They and their fellow Democrats had every reason to enjoy a sense of well-being and triumph. The party had come together effectively in the 1844 election and regained control of the national government despite initial sharp disagreements about candidates and policy measures. During the campaign the Democrats had highlighted "Young Hickory's" commitment to traditional Jacksonian policies and the continuity that he represented, from the days of Andrew Jackson and Martin Van Buren to the present, even as the party had now entered a new era. Moreover, when President-elect Polk left his home in Tennessee early in the year for his inauguration, he remained determined to maintain that good feeling and the unity that he and the Democracy now enjoyed.[5]

The sense of where they were was clear to the Democratic leadership. Despite lingering tensions among the old and new party leaders, and evidence of some continuing sectional anger as well—a colleague warned Polk that he would "have a delicate game to play between the North and the South" in the party—all seemed healthier than it had been in some time as the Jacksonians once more took over the reins of government and the shaping of the nation's future. "We see nothing to distract" the Democrats arriving for the opening of Congress, one party newspaper said with some smugness, "and feel quite sure that the utmost good feeling will prevail." Martin Van Buren certainly seemed content as Polk took office. "I am well satisfied that the P[resident] elect goes to Washington with the most upright intentions" was his comment as the year began.[6]

Polk agreed that all the positive vibrations running through Democratic ranks reflected his own position, and he intended to bolster the positives by using his victory to live up to the party's often stated campaign promises—the ambitious program articulated in the national platform and during the campaign. He intended to restore the Jacksonian–Van Buren perspective in government operations by pushing through a range of traditional Democratic economic policies while resisting unacceptable attempts to enlarge the national government's domestic responsibilities. He also made quite clear his intention to move beyond the now obsolete hesitancies exhibited by Jackson and Van Buren in the past with a vigorous program of territorial expansion.[7]

The president-elect arrived in Washington in mid-February and took the oath of office on March 4. He was only forty-nine years old, the youngest president to that time. Despite his comparative youth,

President James Polk was a strong annexationist who brought Texas into the Union despite opposition. LIBRARY OF CONGRESS.

he had had an extensive political career, beginning with service in the Tennessee legislature when he was in his late twenties. He was familiar with Washington, having served in the House of Representatives from 1825 to 1839 (the last four years as its Speaker), leaving to become governor of his home state for two years. Losing his reelection bid in 1841, and then another race for that office in 1843, he had remained politically active awaiting (and working to effect) an expected call back to the national scene. (He had hoped to be selected as Van Buren's vice-presidential running mate in 1840 but had lost out to Kentucky's Richard M. Johnson.)[8]

Polk's closest associates during the last years before his election as president had been state politicians in Tennessee and members of the congressional delegation from his home state, led by the veteran and politically astute Cave Johnson. Johnson had been an important behind-the-scenes figure at Baltimore and was very much in evidence in early 1845 as Polk began to organize his administration. One particular role that he played was to keep in touch with the Van

Buren Democrats in Washington, first while the new President was still in Tennessee and then when he came east.[9]

The Whigs had sneered at the new president's lack of national experience and standing as a statesman. That criticism had been effectively overcome during the presidential campaign, but the opposition's negative attitudes toward Polk remained a central facet of the political scene as he entered office. Even as his administration settled in, partisan political divisions remained as sharp as ever, and political complexities as difficult as they had always been. The Whigs, despite their minority status in Congress, had no intention of being quiet about any of Polk's initiatives—and they were not. As a result, the new administration was characterized by an intense period of quite traditional, unremittingly contentious two-party confrontation dividing Democrats from Whigs over the familiar issues of their era, in particular the old standbys: banking, tariffs, and whether or not there should be federal financing of internal improvements: rivers-and-harbors development and road building.[10]

The president brought all of these issues forward once again in his inaugural address when he reiterated, as he had promised, the commitments written into the Democratic platform and pressed for the enactment of the party's version of the policies needed—consciously echoing, as he did so, the approaches of Jackson and Van Buren before him. Ours, he reminded Congress, "was intended to be a plain and frugal government." We, he continued, "need no national banks." He was "opposed to a tariff for protection merely." As to expansion and foreign policy, the president "confidently believed that our system may be safely extended to the utmost bounds of our territorial limits." Finally, "our title to the country of Oregon is 'clear and unquestionable.'"[11]

As Polk intended, the inaugural address proved to be only the first step in a well-designed agenda for action, not just a hopeful wish list of promises. Polk proved to be a strong and determined president. He and his congressional allies would succeed in passing their domestic agenda through the House and Senate during the first two years of his administration despite the continuing Whig protests and their constant efforts to derail the Democratic program. A low tariff and the independent treasury became the law of the land in 1846. The president also vetoed a bill in that year to expand the federal government's financing of internal improvements construction, although some Democrats from the upper Midwest, reacting to constituency demands, supported the bill and the need for federal assistance at certain moments, even for local transportation projects that had no credible claims to having a national focus.[12]

The president's expansionist goals, too, were achieved after, not unexpectedly, being largely fought out in partisan terms. Polk's avid commitment to America's continental destiny not only led to the formal completion of Texas annexation but, by 1846, also included the adding of much of the Oregon Territory to the United States as the president first blustered a great deal about, and then settled by treaty, the boundary dispute over the area with Great Britain. He continued the cycle of acquisition when, after provoking and winning a war with Mexico, the United States added, from its defeated enemy, large portions of the Pacific coast south of Oregon, and an impressive chunk of the territory west of Texas as well.[13]

Democrats were generally as enthusiastic about the administration's expansionist accomplishments as they were about its domestic initiatives. Whig opposition, as noted, remained strong and persisted even as it failed to achieve its anti-Polk objectives either in the domestic realm or by stopping the war with Mexico or preventing thereafter the seizure of more territory from the defeated Mexicans. Whig congressmen, in full roar, fought hard to undercut the president and his supporters and humiliate them if they could. They did not like anything that Polk was up to, any of the policies that the rejuvenated Democrats were now pushing through Congress. "We look in vain," one of their campaign pamphlets argued in 1846, "for any act of public or private good" in the administration's policies. "This twenty-ninth Congress," a Whig member lamented, "will have earned for itself the reputation of having done less good, and inflicted more evil upon the country, than any Congress which has convened under the Constitution." But, so far as blocking those policies, they looked in vain as well. Whatever their passion and determination, the Whigs did not have the votes.[14]

The Van Buren Factor

Polk and the Democrats were riding high as they savored their triumphs. Matters, however, were never going only one way. What also happened moved beyond the persistent differences between Democrats and Whigs to involve the edgy Van Buren group among the northern Democracy in a harsh confrontation with the administration and its supporters. From the beginning of his run for the presidency, candidate Polk had repeatedly expressed much gratitude to Van Buren. The New Yorker's "magnanimous" and "powerful support" at the outset and during the months that followed was "characteristic of the man," Polk told his close colleagues. It "places me under lasting obligation to him." Shortly after the election, the new president wrote to thank his predecessor. There was no one, he told the ex-president, to whom the Democracy "are more indebted for their success."[15]

Van Buren and his allies agreed—not because they thought that they had done something unusual but, rather, because they had successfully fought their way out of the trap that Calhoun and Tyler had set for them, as well as bypassing the dead end that the Democratic convention had forced them into. They remained a significant component of the party's elite despite the attacks on them, loyal to it and pressing hard to further its fortunes. New York's Democratic voters had been a key element in Polk's victory, the outcome there being energized and, in fact, caused, as they claimed, by the efforts of the ex-president and his deeply committed longtime colleagues.[16]

At the same time, everything was not entirely friendship and good relations, whatever the surface indications of goodwill. Not surprisingly, the various Democratic blocs reacted with different degrees of warmth to the new president. Many of the Democrats from outside New York State who had supported Van Buren at Baltimore joined the hardcore Polk loyalists, and readily fell in behind the new leader of the party during the campaign and as he prepared to enter office. In addition to them, however, were those particularly close to Van Buren, loyal to his standing among the Democracy, and committed to pushing his claims on the new administration. The core of this Van Buren bloc was, of course, the New York Democrats who had been with the ex-president for many years, had gone down the line with him at the Baltimore convention, and still looked to him for their lead in party affairs.[17]

Their loyalty to Van Buren did not make them hostile to President Polk as his term began, despite the claims of some observers, both friends and enemies, that they were. Polk's close ally

Congressman Aaron Brown of Tennessee warned the new president that "*our whole* difficulty is with the N. York Democrats. They show a strong leaning against us."[18] Brown's comment was prescient about future events but not accurate as to the situation at the beginning of the Polk administration. The Van Burenites had not, to be sure, lost their heart to Polk as had so many other Democrats. But, in early 1845, having demonstrated their commitment, including their willingness to go along with the annexation of Texas whatever their reservations, and their effectiveness in winning New York for Polk, not only were their feelings of friendship toward the president comparatively strong, but their expectations as to their future relations with him remained optimistic as well. They believed that things would continue as normal: that the president would follow the usual, if unwritten, rules of the party in his dealings with them, including finding important places for some of them within his administration. Those who saw themselves as the inheritors of the glorious days of Andrew Jackson and the upholders of his political way anticipated that they would continue to be recognized as part of the ruling elite of the movement as they had been since the beginning.[19]

The new president was not unaware that behind the professions of loyalty there was much disappointment and frustration among his New York allies, as well as many potential tensions that could emerge because of them. As he began to construct his government, he was reminded of the sensitivities present and that he should be heedful of "the fatal shock" to the confidence of the Van Burenites as to "the faith and fidelity of their southern brethren" because of what had happened to their leader at the Baltimore convention. Polk was not immune to their feelings. His close friend Cave Johnson reminded him, once again, that "many of the northern Democrats have become very uneasy lest southern influence should prevail over northern with you." They feared that "you are inclined to favor the southern democrats at the expense of the northern." The Van Burenites wanted a concrete sign from the president of his loyalty to them.[20]

Polk began well. He took the opportunity to face down the skeptical and suspicious in his dealings with Van Buren over the winter of 1844–45. He acted impeccably toward the party's former leader then, writing to him asking advice about cabinet appointments. Van

Buren had responded warmly in return, offering suggestions about the cabinet's makeup and appointments to other offices. Relations appeared redolent of their long association as Jacksonian leaders and men accustomed to mutually accommodating to each other's needs and position. Everyone's positive expections remained very high as a result. The president had come through.[21]

Things began to change when Polk announced his first appointments. The Van Burenites found their hopes shattered. The president did not do as they hoped he would. Polk found nothing wrong with the Van Buren bloc's notion that they expected to be part of his administration, but he stumbled in critical ways in his dealings with them so that he seemed, as they saw it, to be ignoring their suggestions, challenging their importance, and demeaning their position as part of the Democracy. Their reactions were to be expected. What the Van Burenites saw first as the president's indifference and then as his hostility to his party colleagues could not help but create a situation in which the cooperative relationships among the leading Democrats began to unravel, with the Texas crisis, the root of it all, taking on a critical meaning within the Van Buren group that would lead to important consequences for them, their party, and, ultimately, the nation as well.[22]

"New York Is . . . Betrayed"

Polk had some difficulty in constructing his cabinet and identifying the right people for other major posts in his administration. Who was to get what office occupied much of his time, first in Nashville and then after he arrived in Washington. As always, there were many prominent party claimants for the main offices to be filled. He had received much advice, pro and con, about particular candidates. As he listened to the various suggestions, demands, and entreaties of would-be officeholders and their congressional supporters, he reminded his advisors and other allies that he wanted, most of all, to establish an effective cabinet that balanced, as much as possible, the various blocs, ideological, sectional, and otherwise, within the Democratic Party.[23]

Recognizing his obligation, Polk quite appropriately, in the Van Buren wing's eyes, offered the Treasury Department early on to Silas Wright—although Van Buren and his allies had at first expected, and preferred, to have one of their number head the more prestigious State Department. That office went instead to the expansionist Pennsylvania senator James Buchanan. Wright, having just been elected governor of New York, felt obligated to stay in Albany and serve out his term. He therefore turned down the president's offer. Polk then made a commitment to the ex-president and his friends that he would appoint, in Wright's place, whomever they suggested for the position.[24]

But even the offer of the treasury disappeared as all sorts of complexities and confusions boiled to the surface within the Polk circle, and the incoming president changed his mind several times. Van Buren first recommended the talented and experienced Benjamin F. Butler, his close friend, as the best choice for the post. Butler, Van Buren's former law partner, had served in several posts including the cabinet, as attorney general under Jackson and Van Buren. Polk, in the meantime, caught up in what one historian calls "the chess game" of cabinet building, and juggling his lists constantly as he heard from various party blocs, selected, instead of Butler, the ubiquitous Robert J. Walker, the Mississippian who had played such a leading role in forging both Texas annexation and then "Young Hickory's" nomination. At the same time, he was considered a reliable free trader by his southern peers in the party, which the Van Burenites, including Butler, were not. Having decided on Walker, Polk then told Van Buren that he would appoint a nominee of his to the somewhat lesser, but still respectable, cabinet post of secretary of war.[25]

Van Buren and his colleagues did not think that the War Department was a good enough appointment, given who they were and what they had earned in Polk's cause during the campaign. After much soul-searching among themselves, however, they once more deferred to their party's new leader. Van Buren suggested Butler for the offered post, even though the latter, at first, did not want to serve in that position. The ex-president also listed other, lesser-known New Yorkers as appropriate candidates if Butler refused to accept Polk's offer. In the meantime, Van Buren worked hard to make Butler change his mind. By the time that he persuaded the latter to agree to go to the War Department and had his acceptance forwarded to Washington, Polk had grown impatient—and skittish—about the delay in constructing his cabinet. Ignoring Van

Buren's other suggestions, he named William L. Marcy, another major New York politician and a former governor of the state, to the post.[26]

This was a crucial error. A range of Democrats had vigorously pushed Marcy's appointment, but when Polk named him it meant that New York's seat in the cabinet would be held by a man who Van Buren and his friends considered to be their enemy. Marcy was a leading member of the conservative Hunker group in the Empire State who had worked so hard to bring down the ex-president and his supporters and who continued to cause great difficulty for the fractious Democratic Party there even as state elections loomed on the horizon. If anything, the divisions between the warring blocs were growing even wider and deeper than they had been. "I am satisfied," one observer wrote, "that we cannot patch matters up in this state, and that the project of harmonizing must be henceforth in great measure discarded." And the president, despite his later disclaimers, had been informed about the angry divisions in the New York party.[27]

A loyal supporter of Polk's policies, William Marcy was an enemy of Van Buren. LIBRARY OF CONGRESS.

Marcy's appointment, therefore, could hardly be considered a friendly action on Polk's part. Whatever the president's denial of evil intent or of any hostility toward them, his action outraged the Van Buren group. At the very least, Polk had acted in a way contrary to their expectations and understanding of what they had the right to receive from him. They had been loyal to the party ticket and to Polk. The president, however, had not been loyal to them. Quite the opposite, in fact. He had fallen, as they saw it, under the influence of those party groups who were the most deeply antagonistic to Van Buren. His actions indicated that Cass, Buchanan, and Walker, the leaders of the anti–Van Buren phalanx in 1844, had the new president's ear and they did not.[28]

Finally, Polk, capping the changes he was making in the party's leadership, and despite the advice of Andrew Jackson that he not do so, replaced the loyal Jacksonian and longtime Van Buren supporter Francis P. Blair as editor of the Democrats' national newspaper, the Washington *Globe.* Blair had been as lukewarm as the ex-president about Texas annexation and publicly hostile to the project before the national convention dictated otherwise. Polk established, in Blair and the *Globe*'s place, a new publication, the Washington *Union,* to be edited by, of all people, Thomas Ritchie, the Virginia Democratic leader, once Van Buren's close ally, who had so stunningly defected from him over Texas to join the anti–Van Buren bandwagon at Baltimore.[29]

This was the key moment in the unfolding drama. Van Buren's everlasting patience in political dealings, even with antagonists, had reached its limit. He and his associates made no bones of their bitter disappointment, loudly and pointedly, to the president. "New York is, I fear, betrayed" by Polk's "unwarrantable course on the formulation of the cabinet" was the angry characterization of one of them in response to the blows that he saw raining down on their group. The new president's appointments policy was "marked" with "hostility, aggressive hostility. . . . towards New York" (meaning the Van Buren bloc). They did not deserve this.[30]

The Democrats who were close to Polk, northern and southern, did not agree with the accusations against the president and his advisors and were dismissive of the outrage expressed by the Van Burenites. They also maintained a secure majority of support among the party faithful even as tempers rose and hostility increased. The staunchness of most Democrats behind the president was unsurprising given the power of party loyalty, their acceptance of party discipline as a norm to be followed, and their strong belief in the efficacy of party organization and behavior in furthering their ideological purposes. In the view of these Democratic stalwarts, Polk, the party's leader, had been open, as he repeatedly and vigorously asserted, to all of the Democratic blocs. He had dealt as fairly with each of them as he could regardless of their stance during the nomination battle in 1844 or where they came from. If some did not believe in his good intentions, that was not his fault.[31]

Whatever the expectations were, the old and new leaders of the Democratic Party were probably destined to tangle, despite their personal inclinations and professions of friendship as Polk took the oath of office. A great deal was at stake, and a great many feelings, while hidden, were close to the surface. But there is no convincing evidence that Polk wanted to alienate the Van Buren group at the outset of his administration. His choices for each appointment made sense to him. He had intended, he wrote, "to know no divisions of the democratic party" and, therefore, when it came to patronage, "to do equal and exact justice to every portion of the Republican [i.e., Democratic] Party."[32] He believed himself, at least as he expressed it in his correspondence, to be acting as a national Democrat and furthering his goals for the party and for the country.

Some historians have demurred from Polk's claims about himself. They suggest that he was much more a partisan of southern values and interests than recognized either originally by contemporaries such as the Van Burenites or since by scholars who label him a national Democrat in the Jacksonian tradition. His actions in his appointments, and in other decisions as well, reflect, therefore, not the careful balancing of party interests that he claimed to be seeking. Rather, they reflect a sectional loyalty (encompassing Democrats from outside the region who were loyal to southern interests) that was more important to him than has usually been acknowledged.[33]

It is more likely, however, that Polk had stumbled badly not out of malice or because of his pro-slavery bent (which was certainly part of his makeup as a slaveholder) but, rather, because of his relative inexperience, his impatience, and his failure to appreciate the full ramifications of making these decisions on heavily contested ground or to foresee the impact that his choice would have on the Van Buren group, as well as other party members viewing the same set of circumstances. In fact, as the Van Burenite anger grew, members of the Calhoun bloc were, ironically, complaining, in their turn, that "instead of an independent man, we have elected a Pres[iden]t bound hand and foot to the Van's." All of Polk's appointments so far, Duff Green wrote to Calhoun, have been given to "partisans of Van Buren."[34]

With both sides yapping against him, Polk may have believed that he had acted equally between the contestants. Beyond that, the situation was more complicated for the President than Van Buren and his associates or the Calhounites allowed. Polk had acted clumsily and not in the friendliest manner toward Van Buren, beset, as the new president believed himself to be, by a party characterized by a high degree of leadership turmoil alongside its general unity on policy matters. He wanted to work with the Van Burenites (and the Calhoun sympathizers as well) if they would accept his leadership. He told one of Van Buren's closest allies that he "would on no account do anything" that might give the ex-president "displeasure." He had tried, if more halfheartedly than he might have, to meet the demands of the New Yorkers. Van Buren and his colleagues had been offered their share of offices under the new administration. The ex-president also had warm friends, such as Secretary of the Navy George Bancroft, in the new cabinet. Other officials, such as Cave Johnson, appointed to be postmaster general, were quite friendly as well.[35]

That had not been enough, as the dismayed Van Buren group saw matters. The issue was the level of appointments that the president should have offered to them so as to recognize their continued centrality to the Democracy. Unfortunately, the cost of satisfying the bloc was, Polk apparently came to believe, too high to pay, too upsetting to the arrangements he wanted to make. In his eyes, Van Buren and his allies demanded too much, their sensitivities and feelings of disappointment went too far, and they were too quick to try to flex muscles that they no longer had. As the president later wrote, "I will do, as I have done, Mr. Martin Van Buren's friends full justice in the bestowal of public patronage, but I cannot proscribe all others of the Democratic party in order to gain their good will . . . I will adhere strictly to my principles without identifying myself with any faction or clique of the Democratic party."[36]

The president, therefore, refused to change what he had done in naming his cabinet and expressed little sympathy for the Van Burenites' complaints and sense of injustice. He did offer the ex-president and his colleagues other important positions in his administration in order to repair the damage. He suggested that Van Buren himself go to London as minister to the Court of St. James's—a position that he originally offered to Calhoun and then to two other prominent South Carolinians. Some of Polk's offers were accepted. Van Buren refused to go to England, but Butler became United States attorney in New York City, for instance, and other New Yorkers close to Van Buren were named to lesser positions in the administration.[37]

Whatever the calculations or commitments that impelled Polk to act as he did, or his efforts to reach out to them, the Van Burenites remained appalled and hostile. They continued to consider the offices offered to them to be grossly inadequate—even insulting—considering their status as Democrats and refused to be placated by the president's post-cabinet offers. Polk may not have wanted to give displeasure to the ex-president, but, as the latter and his friends believed, he apparently found it necessary to do so when the chips were down during the appointment process for the highest positions within his government. And, in one last blow to the Van Burenites' concept of what was proper and what was not, he had then, they argued, quite unacceptably split the patronage that he offered to New Yorkers between the contending blocs in the Empire State. The whole experience of the first few months of the Polk administration had been capped by even more of the hostility toward them that he had demonstrated from the outset of his term in office.[38]

As those feelings took hold among them and their frustrations grew, Van Buren and his friends began to move beyond simply reacting strongly against what was happening, as they had been doing, and, most significantly, began to construct an understanding of the reasons for their fate under Polk's leadership. It was, when fully formulated, an understanding that challenged the president's integrity and cast him and his closest colleagues in a very base light indeed. They argued that what the president was doing was a most dangerous assault on a core, necessary element of the American political process, an element that had made the process as effective as it had proved to be.

"Mutual Forbearance"

Both Van Buren and Polk were experienced Democratic leaders who fully subscribed to the critical need for party unity as the key to victory and the subsequent achievement of their policy goals, but that commitment did not dominate their relationship in 1845 and thereafter. The hostility that blew up in the first days of the Polk administration persisted as the president continued to make his own way while the Van Burenites were forced to look on in dismay at the continuing degradation of their position. They came to see what was happening to them in a particular light. Their enemies then suggested, and some historians have since, that their reaction to Polk's actions was due primarily to their loss of power and position within the party—that it was for individual and personal, not more cosmic, i.e., admirable, reasons. Van Buren and his associates wanted revenge because of their dethronement by the Polk administration.[39]

Other historians have argued, in contrast, as noted earlier, that the Van Burenites' confrontation with Polk and his followers, and the turn that it subsequently took as their opposition hardened, should be attributed largely to their growing sensitivity to rising anti-slavery sentiment in their home districts, a sentiment that considered the acquisition of Texas and subsequent actions by Polk in a most unfavorable light. Such sentiment posed an imminent threat to the Van Burenites' ability to hold the offices that they occupied as members of Congress and the state legislatures. They had, therefore, strong ideological and electoral reasons to cut out a distinct position for themselves that was clearly hostile to the Polk administration's apparent southern and conservative tilt.[40]

These factors did play a role in shaping the Van Buren bloc's reaction to their situation. They were scrambling to deal with a number of disturbing matters that had suddenly engulfed them. Certainly, for one, in closely competitive races, anti-slavery voters' defections, or their increased turnout to vote against the Democrats, could be lethal to some of the latter's candidates. Moreover, as they contemplated the shambles of their situation under Polk, it was also not surprising that they thought not simply in terms of revenge only or, as they moved to counter the assault on them, that they sought to hurt the southerners in command of the party for their destructive hubris.

Nevertheless, whatever the impact of such influences on building up their reactions, something else of some importance was also working on the leaders of the Van Buren wing as they assessed their situation in 1845 and 1846. As the New Yorkers saw it, what was happening was not merely internal partisan bickering, common among all political parties; nor were their heavily bruised feelings simply due to patronage disappointments, the clash of personalities between them and other leading Democrats, or the threats posed to them at the polls. Their calculus of the situation included but also went beyond such matters. These men were political activists and reacted to events in broad political, not only electoral, terms. They constantly calculated how specific events affected themselves and their constituents. Here, they focused so much on their party situation because their world continued to be circumscribed by their belief that healthy—that is, dominant—*national* political parties were the key to the successful achievement of the promise and aspirations of the American democratic experience.[41]

Van Buren, the builder of the political party system, had shown them the way. A politician to the depth of his soul, he had led his followers to live their public lives in a particular environment, embedded fully in the great power of the national parties and with a deep understanding of, and commitment to, the way that the Democrats and Whigs engaged in public business. Like their leader, they were party loyalists to the core, primarily focusing on the critical transsectional issue conflicts that they considered to be the crux of national politics. The Van Buren bloc had demonstrated, time after time, the importance to them of the partisan dimension of American politics: national reach, organization, ideology, leadership, commitment, and loyalty.[42]

Socialized as they were by partisan norms and ways of thinking, the Van Burenites therefore reacted in terms of that approach now. To them, the battle in which they were engaged, whatever else people might see in it, was about their party and the necessity to secure its dominant role in America's affairs for as long as possible. This attitude had a specific meaning in the context of the Polk administration's actions. Of particular concern to them, as they formulated their plans, was that the partisan dimension was sustained by the cooperation among all Democrats in setting the party agenda and by the acceptance of the equality of all members of the Democracy in achieving that cooperation. The Van Burenite conception of politics stressed loyalty to the interests of the whole body of Democrats throughout the Union in order to maintain the party's full strength and to enhance its unity, power, and authority, all in order to fulfill its commitments and accomplish its larger goals and policy purposes.

Party members understood that there would always be some differences among them over priorities, personnel, and other details within the array of the general agreements about public affairs that defined Democrats. But such differences could always be overcome, and obviously had to be, for the common partisan good. First and foremost, they got along with one another, and expected to continue to do so as they fought their battles against their common enemies.

At the core of their approach, in other words, was the notion that the Democratic Party thrived by a careful balancing among the different groups that constituted its basic support. Anything that disrupted that balance would hurt the party. As a result, they operated by an unwritten law that recognized each group's claims and rights and that balanced out the various needs of each bloc so that no group was slighted, its priorities ignored, or its proper role unrecognized. Van Buren had once called for "mutual forbearance and reciprocal concession" among the engaged combatants during a government crisis in the early thirties. He and his like-minded followers applied the same principle to the Democratic Party thereafter. The reciprocal support of each other through compromise was the dominant watchword by which party members lived and could hope to attain all that they wished to accomplish in the political realm.[43]

The party's internal politics was filled with such reciprocal agreements and understandings over policies. For one example, as the Van Burenites saw it, the demands for the whole of Oregon and for the successful annexation of Texas were properly yoked together in the party platform, balancing one group's priority with another's within the Democrats' general support of expansion. Such reciprocity produced a sense of balance among them and a willingness to work together on behalf of everyone's needs—their common purpose.[44]

That was the crucial point. There was to be no backing and filling against individual party groups, no chicanery in dealing with each other, no double-crossing of anyone with legitimate claims on the party. Thus, as they pointedly reiterated from first to last, while Martin Van Buren had lost his place as the leader of the Democrats, he and his followers were still entitled, as a recognized and powerful party bloc, to have their interests acknowledged and needs accepted and accommodated at an appropriate level by the other members of the coalition.

The problem with Polk was that his behavior and the forces behind him threatened to disrupt the Democratic Party. This was not so much over specific policy issues—there was much, if not always total, agreement there. The president's record in securing the Democrats' long-standing domestic policy agenda was an exemplary one despite the anger of those Democrats who felt that Polk should not have vetoed the rivers-and-harbors bill.[45] But the Van Buren bloc believed that Polk had, at the same time, undercut the very basic premise of balance and reciprocity. In his appointments policies he had betrayed one part of the coalition in order to serve the interests of another far beyond its due. His actions in constructing his administration violated the core principle of internal accommodation and equality among the different party blocs.

That, in turn, led to the crux of the problem as the Van Burenites viewed matters. To those who had fought together alongside the ex-president in the fires of the Bank War and the nullification controversy a decade earlier, who had stood together on behalf of traditional Democratic policies in the late thirties and early forties, something devastating was happening to their cherished party. By his personnel choices and his behavior toward the Van Buren group, Polk had weakened and endangered the party and what its members were trying to get done. In addition to his obvious southern tilt, he had supported those who were no longer faithful to the ideals and policies of the Jacksonian revolution and who were, as a result, the sworn enemies of the Van Buren bloc. Such men, disloyal as they were to the party's traditional ideals, did not deserve the kind of balanced consideration that true loyalists did. But the new president "has done everything," a leading Van Burenite complained, "to build up the Conservatives, who are the enemies avowed of President Van Buren and Gov. Wright." That would not do.[46]

THERE IS A DISTINCTION TO BE MADE, therefore, as the reasons for particular actions are searched for, between acting out of frustration and revenge and, acting, instead, because of larger ideological concerns and conceptions of politics and how it had to be carried out to reach desired goals. Both elements were present, but the latter seems to have predominated in the minds of Van Buren and his associates because, as they saw it, if the balances were not restored and the party's traditional understandings not recognized, it would no longer be able to function as a grand coalition of the like-minded. It would become instead a dysfunctional mass of squabbling politicians. Its energies would turn inward, and the organization would implode in fragments and chaos.[47]

The Van Burenites' whole world was coming apart, and they reacted strongly. They could do nothing else. Until now, they had followed their basic line: controlling whatever anti-slavery and anti-southern feelings they had in the interest of promoting their national purpose by keeping their unity across sectional lines, emphasizing what held them together, downplaying what divided them. Now, they clearly had to reconsider their approach, given what had been happening to the party and to themselves. Stunned, appalled, and angry, they were determined to defeat the assaults of their erstwhile partners against their interests and against the interests, and the true meaning, of the party founded by Andrew Jackson.

The Van Buren group's language of betrayal and partisan debasement was persistent, repetitive, and intense. Something bad was occurring, and they did not like it one bit. They wanted their party back. They wanted the Democracy clearly and firmly set in its traditional policy mold and with its traditional structure of understandings and accommodations, and they wanted the full recognition of their critical role as part of its leadership. The party was worth saving. More than that, it was necessary to do so. Its current leaders needed to be given a sharp jolt to make them understand that what they were up to was unacceptable to other party members and dangerous to all of their political goals.

BEYOND THE EMOTIVE ANGER expressed by the Van Buren group lurked a critical question: They understood what was happening, but what underlay these assaults on them and the party? Why were they being pushed aside despite the impact it would have on the Democracy? They came to believe that the answer went well beyond Polk and his personal malice and his shortcomings as a party leader, although, to be sure, whatever else was in the mix, they remained appalled at "Young Hickory's" notably maladroit handling of events. Nor did they accept the president's continued innocent explanations of his motives and his intentions toward them. The Van Burenites perceived too many connections among all of the things that had occurred over the past year to believe them to be happenstance, simply the stumbles, disengenuous misunderstandings, or unacceptable inattention of an overworked, preoccupied, very busy leader. In the divisive hothouse atmosphere prevailing in Washington and New York, the pungent odor of conspiracy was much in the air as the Van Burenites sorted out the situation in which they found themselves.[48]

"Western Rights Have Been Trampled On"

The story that they developed began with the way that the president had dealt with his cabinet and other appointments when he entered office, but their understanding was strongly fueled by events that followed the conflict over the senior-level choices that Polk had made. Until 1846, as noted above, despite their simmering anger, the group around Van Buren as well as other northern Democrats supported the president's program as it worked its way through Congress, but then Polk's controversial foreign policy initiatives not only brought new recruits to the anti-administration group but also strongly fed their sense of despair and betrayal. They also definitively clinched the accuracy of the explanation that the dissident Democrats were developing as to what was going on.[49]

Polk's forceful expansionism added a great deal of additional territory to the United States, in keeping with his party's platform and his own remarks in his inaugural address.[50] But how he did it, and what he found necessary to cede in order to accomplish his purpose, only deepened the chasm separating him and his allies from others within the Democratic coalition. A number of western expansionists, the so-called 54° 40' men, became convinced that the president had sold them out on Oregon and, in consequence, joined the already disgruntled Van Buren bloc in opposition to Polk. Like the

Van Burenites, these expansionists saw in Polk's diplomatic actions not only dismissal of their demands but also an interconnection of events, beginning with Texas annexation, that they believed were fouling the Democrats' nest.

It could be argued that Polk and Secretary of State Buchanan handled the Oregon matter with great skill given the comparative military strength of England and the United States. They avoided war and gained a great deal. The most fervent Democratic expansionists did not think so. From the beginning of the debates over reclaiming Oregon, they were suspicious, distrustful of the administration, and ready to vent their anger against other party members who appeared to be less committed to acquiring all of the territory in dispute than they believed they should be. The objects of their suspicions were those close to the president, many of them from the South. It began in Congress as the debate got under way. "I cannot but regret," one of the expansionists wrote, "the position affirmed by the South, in the Senate, on the subject of our rights to Oregon. . . . Is it treachery? Is it bad faith?"[51]

That was bad enough. Then the president deserted them as well. Specifically, the administration at first engaged in a great deal of

James Buchanan, secretary of state under James Polk, favored America's continental expansion. LIBRARY OF CONGRESS.

aggressive blustering about our legitimate claim to the whole of Oregon, all the way to the most extensive boundary sought by the most committed expansionists. Then it entered into a treaty with Great Britain compromising our demands and accepting a reduced territory whose border lay along the forty-ninth parallel, not 54° 40'. This was done at the same time that Polk refused to compromise on the southern border, accepting Texas's inflated assertion as to the extent of its territory. The administration did so even at the cost of a war with Mexico. To back up his claim, the president sent American troops into the farthest reaches of Texas's boundary claim, thereby setting the stage for a clash with the Mexican army. When that clash happened, it became the reason for Polk to ask Congress for a declaration of war to counter Mexico's clear aggression against our troops, which, he argued, had occurred on American soil.[52]

The differences between the two cases were noticed. The president proved willing to go to war to gain potential rewards for slaveholders, that is, to add territory to the Union that many saw as likely to open up new areas for slavery. At the same time, he compromised away the just territorial claims of free-state expansionists in areas where slavery was unlikely to go and could never prosper. "The rule seems to be," a New York congressman remarked, "to grasp in one direction all the territory within our reach, and to abandon that to which we are justly entitled in the other."[53]

The expansionists differed among themselves at a number of points, but they generally agreed that because of the president's deceptive actions over territorial expansion in the Northwest, the Polk administration had, for its own purposes, struck at the basic roots anchoring the party's commitment to work together. In their case, as with the Van Burenites, the same disturbing reality had to be faced. That "western rights have been trampled upon" by a supposedly friendly administration was the conclusion they drew, accompanied by warnings that they had to oppose the president and his supporters in order to thwart his plans and achieve their own desires. In no other manner than in full-scale resistance to the administration on the things that singly mattered to its members would it be possible to overcome the president's clear southern tilt as he pursued his further expansionist efforts. "How long," the editor of the Cleveland *Plain Dealer* asked, "will the Democracy of the North and the Great West submit to the political domineering of this slave oligarchy of the South?" Anyone who now remained loyal to the administration as it engaged in its erroneous actions "should be marked with the curse of Cain."[54]

To be sure, Oregon, like Texas, was never solely a sectional issue. There were southern expansionists who joined their northern colleagues in favor of the 54° 40' boundary line. "Oregon is ours by right," an Arkansas editor declared. "We wish to occupy it; therefore we *will* occupy it." There should be, he concluded, no "craven" negotiations to reduce American claims below 54° 40'.[55] But, once again, nuance about the situation was lost as the issue came to fruition amid a growing resistance within the Democratic Party to the way the Polk administration was operating. The warnings of a number of the president's Tennessee colleagues at the outset of the Polk era about the sensitivities of, and disagreements between, sectional blocs in the Democratic Party were turning out to be compellingly accurate.

Again, as when he constructed his cabinet, Polk was aware of the sensitivities present in the Oregon situation. There may not have been any explicit commitment to a quid pro quo that linked acquiring all of Texas and the reoccupation of all of Oregon, but the unhappy western Democrats who believed that such an understanding existed were not alone in their outlook. Even a number of southern Democrats thought that there had been at least an implicit commitment on the issue. The Georgia party leader, Howell Cobb, lamented that "the course pursued by the Southern democracy about Oregon had had the effect of alienating the good feelings of many of our northern and western democrats and thereby rendering the harmonious and united action of our party more difficult than it would have been had all the South stood square upon that great question as *some of us did.*" Cobb was seconded by John Lumpkin, a Georgia colleague, who wrote to him, "I agree with you that the Southern democracy have not *redeemed their pledge* to their northern allies" in regard to Texas and Oregon [italics added].[56]

There was still more at issue in the foreign policy arena. The onset and course of what his Whig opponents quickly labeled "Mr. Polk's war" confirmed the hesitations that Van Buren and others had had about bringing Texas into the Union before Mexico could be persuaded to agree to its annexation by the United States. Despite successive American victories on the battlefield, the war became a long and controversial episode. The Whigs quickly took the lead in framing the controversy. While claiming that they supported our troops in the field and voting for the supplies the army needed, they proved themselves, unsurprisingly, to be strongly opposed to Polk's initiatives concerning Mexico, using the same kind of extremely denunciatory language that they had put forward to challenge Democratic domestic initiatives. They assailed the president for his willingness to take whatever action he deemed to be necessary in order to acquire the territory that he and other Democrats coveted on the Pacific, including his deliberately provoking a war and then lying about Mexico's responsibility for starting the conflict. As the war progressed and they sensed public disillusionment and smelled electoral blood, the Whigs heightened the temperature and became ever more angry and accusatory. "We regard this war," one of their editors wrote, "as the great political and moral crime of the period." They went on to suggest that Polk's "eager passion for blood and carnage" and his "lawless usurpations" in carrying out his aggressive policies against the Mexicans disgraced himself, his party, and, most of all, the country.[57]

Further, among the Whigs, as well as among many suspicious Democrats, it became clear that one purpose of the war went beyond securing Texas's border claims to encompass the additional seizure of land in the Southwest from America's southern neighbor and, now, enemy. This realization, too, supported the growing notion among them that the administration's purposes were always southward in their orientation. Polk had gone to war (albeit with much support from Democrats everywhere) primarily to benefit one section of the Union. "The Texas outrage" was the beginning. "The interests of slavery demanded the annexation, the Baltimore convention decreed it, and they were obeyed" by Polk and his colleagues. "This war is one of the first fruits of the annexation of Texas," a Massachusetts Whig congressman argued, "and that measure was got up and consummated to extend and perpetuate slavery."[58]

On the Democratic side, many fewer of those engaged accepted that argument against the president. It is important to note, once again, that throughout Polk's administration Democratic loyalty remained almost as strong behind the president on Oregon and on the war with Mexico as it was on his domestic policies. Most Democrats had no reason not to remain committed to their party leader and his policies as the conflict in the Southwest erupted, for instance, and they were quick to assail the Whigs' "rabid . . . rancor of party spirit . . . so far from all just ideas of patriotism when the country is engaged in a war."[59]

But the developing bitter argument over the administration's actions certainly focused attention on the larger directions being taken and the ultimate purposes of Polk and his allies. Within the president's party, despite the extensive support for him both domestically and about the war, two groups of some significance—in character and weight, if not in their total numbers—were deeply incensed about what they saw as his continuing missteps and determined to right the wrongs that they believed they had suffered at his hands.

The growing opposition to Polk from these usually ardent loyal Democrats was palpable. As the political firestorm over the president's policies on the nation's borders grew in intensity, a sense of unease, suspicion, anger, and, most dramatically, occasional paranoia now hardened into a much more focused political impulse among the Van Buren bloc—and increasingly among the most forceful northern and western Democratic expansionists as well. As one historian has summed up, Polk and the southerners in his administration had, in one way or another, alienated every group of northern Democrats "between his inauguration and the beginning of August 1846."[60]

Not quite. Not all of the northern Democrats had become hostile to the president. They had become a divided lot. As a result, these party members from the free states, both Van Burenites and the others present as well, increased the intensity of their bitter public arguments with one another about what was going on. As they did so, they soon enough split into recognizable pro- and anti-Polk factions that found it more and more difficult to cooperate in an easy and regular fashion, as they had in the past and normally would be expected to continue to do under the leadership of a Democratic president. The extent and seriousness of this split varied from state to state. It was particularly marked in Van Buren's New York and in a number of midwestern states that were the home of the most ardent expansionists. The divisions drew sustenance from other issues that the Democrats had been wrestling with as well as from the events now occurring in Washington. In these states, real, divisive concerns and the vehement articulation of them were taking a toll on the unity of the recently victorious party. The Polk administration was turning out to be not a happy moment in the history of the Jacksonian coalition.[61]

"A Long Premeditated Crusade"

What was crucial to all of these Democrats as they viewed the shambles of the administration's initiatives was that it was all of a piece. Each successive event, going back to the original provocation of the strike by the Tyler administration over Texas, was connected to every other. The sum of these connections revealed to the restive Democrats the presence of a larger pattern. It was a pattern that gave Texas even more significance, well beyond anything that it had already achieved. President Polk's behavior since coming to power had put the Texas battle into a most troubling light.

The notion of a slaveholders' conspiracy to control the Union had been around in American politics for some time. It had been largely confined to a few anti-slavery activists usually considered extreme in their views about all aspects of public policy. Texas annexation, the abolitionist Benjamin Lundy argued when the issue first arose in 1836, was "a long premeditated crusade . . . set on foot by slaveholders, land speculators, etc., with the view of reestablishing, extending, and perpetuating the system of slavery and the slave trade." John Quincy Adams had made a similar argument on the floor of the House of Representatives then. Other expressions of the same theme—or accusation—had been heard throughout the decade that followed, whenever Texas was mentioned.[62]

The notion of a dominant slave power was certainly rampant among many northern Whigs, but for the first time the argument was beginning to reach a wider audience. The Van Buren Democrats had always rejected that staple notion as promoted by anti-slavery spokesmen. They had never seen evidence supporting claims that a slave-power conspiracy existed, one that sought to dominate American politics and would allow no one to stand in its way. But now, as they considered matters in 1845–46, the evidence was piling up that there was a great deal more to the long-rejected claim than they had realized.[63]

Although President Polk and his associates dominated the Democratic Party, and shaped its direction, ostensibly in the name of all party members, wherever they resided, the architecture of southern control of the party, the aggressive slave power in command, was in full view for all to see. Southern footprints were present in every action that had been taken in the expansionist enterprise and in too many other actions of the president and his cronies.[64]

Step by step the picture had unfolded. Calhoun and Tyler had given it away with the Pakenham letter framing the Texas matter as a pro-slavery issue. Then came Van Buren's defeat for renomination by the manipulation of the national convention's rules because he had run afoul of southern demands on him and the party. That had been followed by Robert Walker's legislative maneuvering over the joint resolution in order to get the bill through. Finally, Polk, in his Texas decisions, the fiasco of cabinet construction, and his lying about Oregon, had betrayed solemn intraparty agreements in favor of the party's southern extremists and their northern Hunker allies.

Polk's deceptions had begun with his accepting Tyler's final actions on Texas annexation and allowing the process to go forward. In so doing, the new president, whom one historian has called "a skilled political dissimulator," had reneged on his commitment to the Van Buren wing to act otherwise. That misadventure was but the first step. "It was not a barren fraud," Senator Benton later wrote, "but one prolific of evil and pregnant with bloody fruit." Much had then followed to confirm what had been initially perceived. Polk's malevolence and deceit had underscored the southerners' uncompromising hunger for domination in alliance with the president and his northern satraps. There could be no other explanation of the events of the last two years. The southerners' "Democracy & Patriotism appears to go with *Interests, Sectional feeling* & *Southern policys* [*sic*]."[65]

Van Buren and his colleagues were used to, in the words of one historian, "bending before southern pressure," but they now found themselves in an entirely new situation. The southerners had overreached. Demanding that the party pursue only their own special interest, as they were doing, went far beyond the acceptable. They obviously did not want equality and reciprocity among the groups constituting the Democracy but, rather, wanted absolute control of party affairs.[66]

ANTI-SOUTHERN ANGER, and fears of being dominated by one regional group or another, were not new in American politics. Even the Van Buren Democrats had experienced such fears. In their struggle against Calhoun during the 1830s, they had to counter repeatedly the South Carolinian's claim that a northern president—such as Van Buren wished to be—could not be trusted by southerners. Until now, however, a distinction had been made between *perceived* domination, such as the Van Buren group and other Democrats believed to be characteristic of the conspiracy arguments of the anti-slavery leaders, and *actual* domination, which the aggrieved New Yorkers and their allies now believed was revealed in the Polk appointments and the president's subsequent behavior. The former could be dismissed. The latter was extremely dangerous to the Democratic Party and its critical mission.[67]

Van Buren's supporters' uncomfortableness about slavery, and their resistance to the idea of adding more slave territory to the Union, did not lead most of them to take a confrontational stand about either, nor to make the differences into issues dividing the angry northerners from their party brethren from the South. They had continued to tolerate whatever disagreements there were between them and their southern allies, accepting, year after year, that the internal accommodation of different priorities and candidate choices within the party continued to be the most singularly important matter, whatever else might get in the way.[68]

But now the northern Democracy's willingness to suppress anti-southern feelings, in the interest of party unity and its mission, no longer made sense. Such submission as the southerners demanded could not go on. To repeat the long-standing Van Buren mantra, political parties, the key to the working of American politics, could not function effectively if the Polk group's attempt to exclude loyal party members from their rightful place in the leadership continued. The party had to come first, for what it was and for what it meant as a national institution. If uncontrolled sectional rapacity tried to override that fact, then it must be resisted with all of the energy and power available to those under attack. The "bad faith and intrigue" against them made only one course possible. It was time to draw a line against their enemies.[69]

WAS THERE, AS THE GROWING BELIEF CLAIMED, a full-fledged, well-thought-out, organized southern conspiracy to dominate the Democratic Party at the expense of its other constituencies? Had Calhounite notions of the need for aggressive southern control of the political arena come to fruition under the leadership of James K. Polk? Probably not to the degree charged by the frustrated northerners. Southern Democratic politics was more complicated than that, and Polk's behavior more congruent with Democratic aims than the Van Burenites and their expansionist allies admitted. There were still many Van Buren supporters in the slave states, for example. They were not part of any alleged conspiracy against him. At the same time, Polk's realism about comparative power, within the party, on the one hand, and between the United States and the British Empire and the United States and Mexico, on the other, led him to make decisions that had accomplished a great deal that most Democrats supported with great enthusiasm, even as they offended certain party groups and caused them to look for, and find, dark connections and evil purposes in many of the administration's initiatives.[70]

Still, the critical matter was that, whether or not there was an actual southern conspiracy, Polk's actions had suggested the possibility that there was one. That possibility energized opposition to him and his supporters and led his party opponents to construct an explanation of what was going on that had as its centerpiece the reality of a southern assault on them and of an administration willingly in thrall to the party's southern wing. As the historian David Davis has suggested, "once men were disposed to perceive every event as part of a subtle systematic plot, there was no room for accident, blunder, or human frailty." There certainly was not such room among the Van Buren Democrats and their expansionist colleagues in the middle years of the Polk administration.[71]

The dissident Democrats' particular construction of reality turned out to be the central factor in all of the growing tumult among them in the Polk years, with significant consequences for the party and for the nation, consequences that would soon enough be felt. They understood all too well what was happening and who was to blame.

As John Van Buren, the ex-president's son, wrote to New York senator John A. Dix, contemplating the situation in which they found themselves, "How helpless and contemptible the Administration has become. Polk's consolidation of the party by throwing all the honest men overboard has resulted as might have been expected," in division and impending diaster. The "punic faith" and "selfish and treacherous" behavior of the president and his southern allies were going to bring them all down.[72]

6

"NEITHER SLAVERY NOR INVOLUNTARY SERVITUDE"

SAM HOUSTON AND THOMAS JEFFERSON RUSK, the state of Texas's first United States senators, along with Timothy Pilsbury and David Kaufman, their two colleagues newly elected to the House of Representatives, arrived in Washington and took their seats in Congress early in 1846.[1] By then, the fruits of annexation included not only the appearance of these Texans in the nation's capital but an ongoing political controversy as well. The Texans discovered very quickly how angry were some Democrats against the Polk administration, and how determined to do something to challenge the way that the political situation had developed over the past year.

The question for the Democrats hostile to the administration was, what exactly could they do about Polk's perfidy? Contempt for the president, and verbal lashings of him and his colleagues, were insufficient, in the current situation, to restore the Jacksonian Democratic Party to its true path.[2] Stopping the nation's expansionist push was not likely even though resistance to adding more territory continued to come from the Whigs, some of the Democrats, and, now, John C. Calhoun and his followers as well. (Back in the Senate, the South Carolinian introduced a resolution at the end of 1847 against the United States holding on to any of the Mexican territory seized by American troops once the war had ended.)[3] There was little chance of such restraint being accepted as national policy, given the current political environment, but could the Polk-led drive across the continent be circumscribed in some way that would make the Van Burenites' (and others') resistance to the administration not only clear but effective as well?

On the other side of the political spectrum, the Whigs, most particularly the northern anti-slavery bloc among them (those labeled "Conscience" Whigs), were, as always, ready and eager to act in some fashion against a president whom they despised and feared for his partisan initiatives and his aggressiveness in carrying them out. The fact that the Whigs were, at the moment, the minority party in the national government did not lessen their determination to battle the administration, but they faced the same problem as the Democratic dissidents. What, exactly, could they do?[4]

The answer appeared in the summer of 1846 when the persistent rumblings against Polk and his allies, the overreaching southern Democrats, came together in a particular plan of action. Before that moment, anti-slavery extension groups in the North had worked to contain slavery, while Van Buren and other party leaders, north and south, had sought to contain the slavery issue. And, generally, when activists had pushed sectional themes, the fact that they were considered to be extremists, well outside the pale of normal politics, limited their impact. Now those truisms changed.

If Polk and his allies, disregarding "the obligations of party," were going to push others aside solely in their own sectional interest, then there was no longer any reason for the northern Democrats affected by their actions to try to contain sectional and anti-slavery tendencies among themselves and their constituents. "The conviction is forced upon [us] . . . ," one of the anti-Polk dissidents argued, "that the South is incapable of keeping faith with the North, no matter how sacred the obligation, if even a seeming sectional interest or prejudice stands in the way." They therefore had to respond directly, as strongly as they could, against the southern offensive against them.[5]

The Wilmot Proviso

David Wilmot, a Pennsylvania Democrat, had entered the House of Representatives as a first-term congressman as the Polk administration got under way. His general approach to policy matters and his voting record in the House at the outset of his term were quite supportive of the president, but he was also close to the Van Buren bloc, with some political problems and resentments of his own,

David Wilmot was the young Democratic congressman who brought the controversy to a head when he introduced his anti-slavery extension proviso. LIBRARY OF CONGRESS.

enough for him to become the instrument of the Van Burenites' counterattack against the southern-dominated administration. Wilmot and a group of House colleagues—both Democrats, most of them Van Buren supporters, and a number of the anti-slavery northern Whigs—all of them determined to strike a blow against the arrogant southerners controlling affairs, overcame the usual partisan restraints that they lived by. Amid the harsh rumblings of anger on all sides, they met together several times as Congress neared adjournment in early August. Out of their meetings emerged an amendment to the president's request for an appropriation to pay for peace negotiations with Mexico. It was an amendment designed to face up to the group's Polk-led enemies in a direct and clear-cut manner.[6]

Wilmot's unambiguously worded amendment borrowed the language of the Northwest Ordinance of 1787 mandating that "neither slavery nor involuntary servitude shall ever exist" in the Old Northwest, the area north of the Ohio River. The 1846 version banned the introduction of slavery into any of the territories—California and New Mexico, and perhaps more—that the administration expected to acquire from Mexico as a result of the peace treaty that would eventually end the war.[7]

The Proviso encapsulated all of the elements that had come together in the Polk years among those stung by the administration's behavior and policies: genuine anti-slavery sentiment, political calculations, and the rising hatred of the president, his party cronies, and his one-sided sectional orientation. Whatever the many policy and ideological differences between Barnburners, expansionists, and northern Whigs, for the moment they could work together by focusing on the major point before them: the arrant misbehavior of the administration and its southern allies.

In addition, whatever other motives impelled him, Wilmot, in his comments on the House floor when he introduced the resolution, and in later stages of the debate over it as well, echoed the same racist themes that, ironically, Mississippi's Robert J. Walker had expressed two years before in his letter advocating the annexation of Texas. Wilmot articulated his determination to maintain the new territories for the benefit of the white population of the United States and to protect areas where "farmers and laborers" who were "of my own race and color" would settle "without the disgrace which association with slave labor" would bring to them, a "dishonor and degradation" that they refused to accept.[8]

Whether or not this was a maneuver to attract support from those who were otherwise indifferent to slavery's expansion, Wilmot's racist perspective reflected the attitudes of many of his fellow northern Democrats, Van Buren supporters or not. The idea that this was a white man's republic was widespread and frequently expressed in the nation's political discourse. Wherever they went from this point onward, for instance, the Van Burenites generally subscribed to this notion even as they opposed slavery's further extension. Only a relative few of them ever appeared to be motivated by a commitment to egalitarianism reaching beyond the white community, or any other humanitarian impulses directed toward nonwhites.[9]

THE PROVISO PASSED the House of Representatives when first introduced largely on a sectional roll call. It did not come to a vote in the Senate before Congress adjourned, however, amid confusion and cross-purposes among the members. Nevertheless, an important action had been taken. Meant as a shock and a provocation to those in political control, whatever else the amendment may also have been, it was certainly noticed in political circles, welcomed by some and denounced by others. It did not immediately cause as deafening an uproar in the political nation as it might have. As time passed, however, the implications of the Wilmot group's action began to sink in throughout the political landscape. As it did so, this move to restrict slavery in new territories touched a highly sensitive nerve with great force.[10]

In the first place, this was something without precedent for Democrats, allegedly loyal to their party and its principles through thick and thin. They were working in concert with their natural Whig enemies against an administration of their own party. Second, they were making a sectional response to what many of them saw as a partisan conundrum, building upon the great deal of sectional bitterness that had been intensifying among both northern Democrats and Whigs since Calhoun's Pakenham gambit about Texas and all that followed from that provocation in order to regain control of their party. Third, as many of their party peers pointed out, the substance of their attack against the South was outside the boundaries of normal political discourse. None of this was welcome—or acceptable.[11]

The Proviso, therefore, led to an eruption of hostile sectional responses, rhetorical and, more compellingly, behavioral as well. In the first instance, the Barnburners, in a sharply worded published address, largely written by Martin Van Buren, defended their support of the Proviso. They noted that the Mexican territory acquired by the United States was "now free from the *pollution* of slavery." It was a rather harsh way for them to put it, no matter how accurate it may have been, given their record and long toleration of slavery.[12]

In return, southern Democrats assailed their former party allies with similar passion, outraged as they were by what they considered to be an unprovoked, unfair, and unconstitutional attack on themselves and their society. They were especially aggrieved because they continued to believe that whatever overreaching was happening on the political scene was not being done by them but by the Van Buren group and its allies for their own base purposes, not for the good of the party or the nation. The southern "anti-Proviso frenzy," as William Freehling describes it, centered on both the present and future threats to their place in a union dominated by a northern majority that they claimed was intent on unfairly challenging and denigrating their section and denying them their rights in the territories.[13]

Their strong feeling directly led to the expressed determination of some southern Democrats not to support any presidential candidate of their party who supported the Proviso and its denial of southern rights. Furthermore, they demanded Democratic Party commitment to the notion that citizens of the United States had the right to settle, with their property, in any territory acquired by the nation. (This so-called Alabama Platform, quickly adopted by a number of state party conventions in the South, drew a great deal of attention in the run-up to the Democratic National Convention in 1848.)[14]

Many northern Democrats continued to support the president and were no less appalled than were the southerners at the way the Van Burenites were acting. The latter, in fact, kept encountering the reality that most of the northern Democrats were not with them as they expressed their unhappiness with Polk, raised their voices on behalf of the Wilmot Proviso, and exhibited, in their general demeanor, clear hostility to a Democratic administration. They considered the Barnburners to be political renegades. The present spectacle of cross-party cooperation against alleged southern overaggressiveness infuriated them. It was an attempt by "the Democratic—Abolition—Whig branch of the opposition . . . acting in concert for the accomplishment of a common object—hostility to, and a desire to embarrass the present administration." The Proviso, their weapon to accomplish this, was but a "stalking horse for factious and ambitious politicians," an evil "bird of ill omen," designed "to give aid and comfort to the enemy." It was, in short, nothing more than a "firebrand thrown in to distract the friends of the administration." Those behind its introduction were motivated solely "by an inveterate hatred" of the president and his policies.[15]

The administration Democrats (and the Van Burenites, too) still accepted the fact that they had to tolerate slavery as a reality in the United States, something about which they, as a party, could do little, even if some of them were inclined to do something. It was constitutionally protected at the local levels where the power of decision about it lay. We should not, Vice President Dallas argued, "interfere with the peculiar affairs" of the American people. It was up to them to decide how they wanted to live. Democrats, whatever the unhappiness some of them may have felt about the institution of slavery, could go no further than that. Therefore, "we do hope and pray that our Democratic friends in Congress will cease the agitation of the slavery question." Such agitation was "fraught with incalculable evil."[16]

Polk was both dismayed and furious about the challenge to his administration and himself embodied in Wilmot's proviso, particularly by the support for it from Democrats. "Such an agitation" as had erupted due to the introduction of the measure was, he wrote, "not only unwise, but wicked." Thinking primarily in political terms, as he always did, he assailed Wilmot and his allies harshly. Their behavior "divides and distracts the Democratic Party" and materially boosted the Whigs' "prospects for coming to power."[17]

Tension and Uncertainty

The political temperature had certainly been raised along sectional fault lines. Despite the anger present and the crossing of swords at its introduction, however, the Wilmot Proviso did not immediately accomplish one of its main purposes, that of restoring the balances within the Democratic Party. It did have other effects. In the four years after its introduction, angry sectional bickering over the territories became the order of the day in the political arena. It kept arising in the halls of Congress, appearing in partisan newspaper editorials, being included in state legislative resolutions supporting or opposing the Proviso, and being declaimed in campaign speeches throughout the nation. The angry divisions held up congressional organization of territories, both Oregon and the new areas acquired from Mexico in the peace treaty in 1848. No acceptable formula could be found to deal with the place of slavery in these areas. The tumult managed to irritate and frustrate everyone involved, especially the president, who hoped to guide provisoless territorial organization bills through the legislative process. In that sense, the Van Buren group (and the hostile Whigs) had accomplished some part of their purpose, if only part.[18]

Interestingly, despite all that was occurring to draw clear sectional lines, partisan influences and anti-sectional perspectives continued to influence political events as the Polk administration began to wind down. While the lineup of forces opposed to the president included unhappy Democrats, given past experience and the normal processes of politics, the latter were expected to return to their party home after a period of venting their grievances. That expected continuing commitment was especially important to party leaders since Whig hostility to the war and to the president who had, in their view, unjustly and unconstitutionally started it continued to grow more and more widespread, intense, and unyielding. Abraham Lincoln, a first-term congressman from Illinois with a sharp tongue and noted debating style, made a name for himself as a fervent and persistent partisan of the Whig cause against the war. His speeches on the floor of the House challenged the president's claim that Mexico had been the aggressor on American territory. In one of his many efforts Lincoln lashed out at the Democratic president as "a bewildered, confounded, and miserably-perplexed man." Other Whigs joined in with comparable vehemence.[19]

In the face of such assaults and what lay behind them, most of the Van Burenites, even as they assailed those aspects of Polk's actions that threatened the party, remained conscious of their long-standing partisan commitment. Francis P. Blair wrote to the elder Van Buren, for instance, to remind him that, whatever their hesitancies about Polk and those who surrounded him, "we are obliged to support the war & in supporting it must support the Administration." Many of the Van Burenites agreed, if more reluctantly than at earlier times. They did not see themselves as separating from their partisan home. They were, after all, Democrats, with all that that meant, and had little in common with Polk's other adversaries. "Have their long cherished principles less value or fewer charms, than in former years and previous campaigns?" one editor asked. The answer, he and others argued, was no. Party loyalty would remain. It was the key element in their political lives, as it had been for some time past.[20]

Polk's tenure in office had little to fear—despite some degree of anxiety on his part as events unfolded—so long as most Democrats followed that line, ignored the party's internal difficulties as much as they could, and maintained their unity against their Whig opponents when party interests were at stake. Given the sharp political divisions over the president's domestic and war policies, such interests were at stake most of the time.

Veteran Democratic newspaper editor Francis P. Blair was loyal to Martin Van Buren and an opponent of annexation. LIBRARY OF CONGRESS.

Even as the sectional temperature rose on both sides of the Mason-Dixon line, therefore, partisan influences began to have an effect on the Democratic dissidents. Some of the Van Buren bloc, Congressman Preston King for one, wanted to maintain their push against the administration and the extension of slavery. A loyal Barnburner from Silas Wright's home area in northern New York, who was quite close to Wright and other Democratic leaders, he never hesitated in his determination. He introduced an even stricter version of Wilmot's measure in the next Congress, in the absence of the Pennsylvanian from the House floor, and provoked another uproar with his strong advocacy of it, assisted by others of similar outlook.[21]

Other Democratic supporters of ex-president Van Buren, however, began to think about pulling back, given their second thoughts about the extent of their challenge and the charge that they had gone too far. A good many of Van Buren's allies who had joined with him to confront the president now calmed down significantly. Such men as Thomas Hart Benton and some of the 54° 40' men led the way despite their still-smoldering fury about Texas and Oregon. They had wanted to restore the Democratic Party to its regular ways of operating, not rip it apart over the question of slavery in the territories. They believed that they had made their point. The administration and its southern allies, however angry they were because of the Van Burenites' actions, would have to take notice of the latter's demands and expectations, and thus make the necessary moves to restore the Democrats' unity to its accustomed place in party affairs. Or so the party mutineers argued—and wanted to believe.[22]

NORTHERN WHIGS WERE ALSO UNCERTAIN as to how far they intended to push sectional themes. Their opposition to slavery extension remained important; most of them supported the Wilmot Proviso. The revolt of the Van Burenites against the Polk administration had given them an opportunity, they believed, to get much further politically than they had been able to do up until now as Polk had so successfully pushed his policy initiatives. At the same time, a large bloc of them wanted to retain their ties to their southern wing and not engage in any activities that would further exacerbate any of the strains that now existed between them. They had other things they wanted to accomplish, together, if they could. Whigs, one of their northern editors wrote, "have not associated together for the purpose of abolishing slavery." As with the Democrats, their other policy priorities demanded that they stay together, united against their partisan opponents.[23]

One way of doing that, if their differences over the extension of slavery into new territories threatened to split them apart, was, they argued, for the United States not to acquire any more territory as a result of the war. "We want no more territory" became their (not unfamiliar) catchword as the Mexican War moved toward a conclusion. The Democrats denounced them for "sacrificing the rights and honor of the nation" by turning their backs on expansion's many benefits, but to the Whigs, their approach allowed them to focus on the issue that divided them from Democrats—more territory or not—rather than on one that divided the sections from one another.[24]

Free Soil

There was some hope, therefore, that the hostility provoked by the Wilmot Proviso would quiet down despite the fact that someone always reintroduced it and pushed it vigorously whenever Congress tried to deal with organizing the Mexican Cession. But the hopes for normalcy proved short-lived as things began to fall apart once again. The Van Buren Democrats again faced a crisis that led them to challenge the normal processes of American politics by drawing a sectional line. Their persisting and often overpowering conflict with the Hunker faction in New York State—a faction still supported, the Van Burenites believed, by the Polk administration—erupted once more in 1846–47. As it did so it increased, even more than earlier, the outrage that the Barnburnery felt toward their adversaries and their situation. All of their anger, suspicions, and fears culminated in an even more dramatic backlash against their party enemies, who, in their ever consistent view, began with New York's Hunkers but then, most critically, reached beyond them into the White House.[25]

What energized this internal party conflict beyond earlier situations and brought it to a most confrontational and destructive head was Silas Wright's travails in 1846 and 1847. He had not enjoyed being governor of New York, both because of his personal desire to be elsewhere and because he was beset by a range of all but unresolvable political difficulties, including the continued sharp divisions within the state's Democratic Party. Despite it all, always a good party soldier, he reluctantly agreed to run for reelection in 1846 in order to hold the largest state in the Union for his party. This time he lost.[26]

His defeat provoked a renewed uproar from the outraged Van Buren bloc. It had happened, they claimed, because of the base treachery of other Democrats. Their Hunker party enemies, the very ones who had been so well rewarded by Polk, were, they charged, "*the cause*" of "the political assassination of Silas Wright." Unconscionably, the Hunkers preferred the victory of a Whig to that of a member of their own party, if the latter was a Barnburner. They had refused to turn out at the polls to support their party's nominee, Governor Wright, because he was the longtime second-in-command of the Van Buren group. Many of the Hunkers had been "openmouthed in opposition" to him throughout the campaign.[27]

And members of the Polk administration had encouraged the Hunkers in their vile apostasy, or so the Van Burenites chose to believe. Polk had actually warned his advisors that Wright should

Silas Wright was Van Buren's main lieutenant as senator and governor of New York. His death stoked bitter recriminations. LIBRARY OF CONGRESS.

not be undercut, whatever the Barnburner provocations against the administration, and that he intended to give the New Yorker his full support as well as that of his subordinates. How far his associates followed the president's directive remains an open question. Certainly, the Barnburners were unconvinced by the president's claims. John A. Dix remarked in his *Memoirs* that it could not be doubted "that the influence of the Government in Washington was thrown against" Wright.[28]

Once again, as the Van Buren group saw it, they had encountered treachery from Polk's southern-dominated government, whose leaders feared that Wright would become the party's presidential candidate in 1848. (It should be noted that the Democrats did poorly generally in the 1846 congressional and state elections. Wright was not their only lost cause that year.) Nevertheless, the Barnburners believed that, whatever had happened elsewhere, Wright would have won in New York if he had received the full support of party members.[29]

Then Wright died within a year of his defeat. His unexpected and premature passing (he was only fifty-two) devastated his Barnburner allies. Given all that had happened, his death greatly intensified the tension and paranoia that they manifested against the Polk administration. As they mourned him, they were persuaded that members of the that administration, along with their allies in New York (whom one of the Van Buren leaders referred to as "regicides"), were responsible for Wright's passing as they had been for his election loss. They charged that he had never recovered from that defeat, a defeat that should not have happened. Their anger, rational or not, provoked a determination to punish the authors of the tragedy in order to ensure that the treachery that had caused it would never again happen to devastate the Democratic Party.[30]

Polk was quick to dismiss the many charges hurled at him by the distraught Van Burenites. It was time, he argued, that the Barnburners contained their misplaced anger. It was not he but they, with their wild, disruptive, accusations, who were distending the reciprocal relationships within the party and threatening its prospects. He wrote in his diary that Wright was, in fact, his "personal and [political] friend," reiterating that he had warned the Hunkers against working against him, or refusing to vote for him, in his race for governor and had condemned any of them who did so. The president saw himself, as he always did, as acting only in the best interests of the whole party, never only one portion of it as his enemies charged.[31]

All of this was far from the Texas controversy but was, nevertheless, closely connected to it. The different perspectives loudly offered and rebutted about Wright and the Democrats' situation sharpened the sense of sectionally rooted confrontation stretching back to the Pakenham letter and what followed from it. What had started as a Van Burenite attempt to restore their party standing had grown well beyond that. The language of betrayal continued to be widespread, anything but calmly presented, and deeply provoking to all of those involved in these most fractious debates. To the Van Buren group, the "sectional rapacity" of the southerners and their northern allies remained the key issue. They reiterated the point that they had earlier, and always, "exposed themselves to political embarrassment and injury" because of their long-standing commitment to their southern colleagues and support for them over such matters as the gag rule and abolitionist attacks on slavery. In return, they had been double-crossed, ignored, and degraded.[32]

IF THINGS WERE NOT DIFFICULT ENOUGH, the events surrounding Texas annexation returned to bedevil the already hothouse politics of the late 1840s, once more sharpening the sense of betrayal that the Van Buren Democrats and their allies felt about the actions of the president and his colleagues. The dissident Van Burenites went after the president for his alleged deception in 1844 when he had promised, they claimed, that he would follow the Benton formula for annexing Texas, not the one offered by Milton Brown. Senator Benjamin Tappan wrote to the New York *Evening Post* that he had been told then, by a southern senator, that Polk authorized him to say that if the [Texas] resolution passed, "*he would not use the House resolution, but would submit the Senate amendment as the sole proposition to Texas.*" Because of that assurance, Senators Benton and Tappan and three other previously hesitant Democrats voted for the joint resolution.[33]

Polk flatly and angrily denied Tappan's accusation and the evidence produced to support it. He said that he had no memory of the conversation that was now reported to have taken place and that he "certainly never understood myself as pledged to select that mode," that is, Benton's approach to acquiring Texas only after further negotiations. He caustically referred to "the misunderstanding, not to say, total perversion, of me or my meaning, if any such conversation was held."[34]

Polk's principal biographer, Charles Sellers, does not totally believe him, suggesting that "clearly Polk deceived" on this occasion, consciously or not, and that he probably had made some kind of rhetorical suggestion to the Benton group that he shared their views on the matter and would follow their lead. What he actually said may have been more ambiguous than Tappan later suggested, but, whatever the case, the reappearance of this episode of charge and countercharge, attack and denial, at this moment further poisoned the relationships among the top Democrats and pushed them even deeper into the chasm that divided them.[35]

Not unexpectedly, most Democrats continued to remain loyal to the administration. Few northern party members outside of the Van Buren orbit doubted Polk, questioned his actions, or accepted the case being made against him by his party enemies. At the same time, the southerners among them, while also rejecting the indictment of their behavior, and the wild charges against the southern-born president being pressed by members of his own party, insisted that there was a quite different reality now framing American politics from the one that the Van Buren Democrats were espousing. It was they and their institutions who were under assault from anti-slavery zealots now joined by members of their own party. They therefore echoed the claim that the situation in which they found themselves vis-à-vis their party was intolerable. From Washington, the Democratic newspaper editor John L. O'Sullivan described them as being especially "furious about the Proviso. No Proviso man, they say, can get a single Southern vote."[36]

That determination would not be tested in 1848. The culmination of the by now long-running confrontation between Polk and his challengers was the unthinkable. The formation of the Free Soil Party in the summer of 1848 completed the circle of political turmoil begun when Tyler entered into the Texas adventure five years before. The Van Buren bloc had had enough. To recover the ground that they had lost since 1844, and to deal with the continued assaults on them from their party enemies, they acted in a most uncharacteristic and stunning way. In conjunction with their allies in the Wilmot Proviso endeavor among the northern Whigs and other anti-slavery activists, Van Buren and his supporters now became a major component of a third-party alternative to the Democrats and Whigs in the presidential election of 1848.[37]

For the great promoter of party loyalty, Van Buren, to become enmeshed in such an experience was all but unimaginable to most politically conscious Americans. Until then, "no man was more solicitous to preserve the integrity of the Democratic party" than its primary founder and builder. He was New York's, and the nation's, leading partisan. But, in his terms, unfortunately, it was necessary to draw a line. Things had gotten so far out of hand because of the actions of Polk and his followers that defection from them and a direct challenge to their interests were now necessary, however shocking such were to many sensibilities.[38]

How they got to that point underscored, once more, their determination to regain their place in the Democratic Party—or else. In 1847, the New York State Democrats had split apart at their state convention in their continuing battle for control of the party. The Barnburners insisted on including the language of the Wilmot Proviso in the party's state platform. The Hunkers strongly resisted. The latter controlled the convention and won the day on that issue, on their choice of candidates, and on other matters separating the two sides. The result was a walkout by the Barnburners, a call by their leaders to another state convention that they would control, and the selection, by each faction, of separate lists of delegates accredited to the Democratic National Convention scheduled to meet in the following May, once more in Baltimore, the scene of Van Buren's humiliation four years before.[39]

At the latter meeting, the Van Burenites lost again. They demanded that they be recognized as what they considered themselves to be: the true Democrats of their state, and the sole legitimate representatives of New York. Given that, the convention must seat only their delegates. The unhappy delegates from the other states, forced to find some way out of the impasse, offered, at best, a compromise, splitting New York's votes in the convention between the two factions. It was also clear that the convention was going to name the anti–Van Buren Michigan senator Lewis Cass as their candidate on a platform that did not include the Wilmot Proviso language. This was all too much to bear. Not having been treated by the convention "on terms of equality and reciprocity," the Van Buren bloc walked out. The Hunkers, also insulted by not being recognized as the sole legitimate delegates from New York, stayed on but refused to vote in the balloting for the party's presidential nominee.[40]

Believing, still, that they had not left the party but that the party had left them and that something needed to be done about that, the Van Buren group, with many hesitations along the way, concluded, in the aftermath of their walkout at Baltimore, that only an independent political movement would accomplish their purposes. They were determined to "bring the despots & ingrates of the South & their obsequious sattelites [*sic*] of the North to their senses." What is the remedy for correcting erring parties? the Van Buren group's campaign newspaper asked. "That remedy consists in deserting a party," was its no longer surprising answer, "rendering asunder all its ties, and planting ourselves upon those just and true principles upon which all republics must be based. A new party is formed, the republic is saved." They had come far, now astonishingly breaking a long-standing political contract previously seen as of the greatest importance to them, one that had always occupied the predominant place in their political existence.[41]

The dissidents began meeting with others sympathetic to their purposes in a series of gatherings, culminating in a convention at Buffalo, New York, in early August. Despite the many hesitancies that they, too, had, especially about acting in concert with Van Buren Democrats, their longtime enemies, prominent anti-slavery Whigs, shocked by their party's nomination for president of Zachary Taylor, a Mexican War general who was also a slaveholder, ultimately proved willing to come to Buffalo. There the Barnburners, along with these Wilmot Proviso Whigs and those members of the Liberty Party who had long sought to broaden out their movement, organized the Free Soil Party, denounced "the aggressions of the Slave Power," and espoused the Proviso and no more slave territory as its centerpiece. Anti-slavery, anti-Polkism, and anti-expansionism brought together a previously incompatible coalition, each part of it joining for its own reasons. Although they originated as distinct elements, with different purposes impelling them, their purposes had been cross-fertilized and become one as the fallout from Texas and Polkism had spread.[42]

The Van Burenites were the key to the birth of this coalition, and they continued to dominate the Free Soil scene as the members of the party went after the southerners in the campaign that followed. They provided the fire and the political experience, sagacity, and muscle (in terms of numbers), not to mention the presidential candidate, of the new party. How many people made up the Van Buren faction (or each of the others) is difficult to determine. Not all of those who had challenged Polk and his associates since 1845 joined the Free Soil excitement. Some of them associated themselves with the movement for a time and then backed away; some Van Buren loyalists stayed home, sticking with the Democratic Party from the first, and never became Free Soilers. The original Van Buren group, stretching back to the time of the 1844 convention, formed the core of the Democrats who went into Free Soil. They probably made up about half, or a little less, of the total number of New York Democrats, many fewer in other states. Whatever their numbers, they were a most forceful presence in the movement, noticed, thought about, cheered, and cursed throughout the political world.[43]

Despite his initial reluctance to run, and a similar reluctance from the ex-president's longtime Whig and Liberty enemies to have him as their standard-bearer, the Buffalo convention overcame the hesitations and named Martin Van Buren to head their ticket against Cass and Taylor. He accepted, an action that caused Polk to describe his rival in his diary as "the most fallen man I have ever known."

The son of John Quincy Adams, Charles Francis Adams was the leader of the anti-slavery Massachusetts Whigs. HARPER'S WEEKLY.

Charles Francis Adams, the son of John Quincy, became the party's vice-presidential candidate. With the once reviled "Northern man with Southern principles" and the son of one of the longest-standing opponents of the South yoked together, the consequences of the decision to annex Texas, and the fallout from doing so, had reached their denouement.[44]

THE FREE SOILERS FOCUSED THEIR CAMPAIGN on resisting slavery's further expansion into any territory now free, that is, California, New Mexico, and the rest of the Mexican Cession. Repeating that they had no intention of interfering with slavery where it already existed, they added that "we cannot sanction its extension, directly or indirectly, where it does not exist." That was the crux of their campaign. "The principles of Free Soil are the only ones at issue in the contest for President." In that battle, "there is no middle course, you are for slavery or you are against it." John Van Buren was particularly active on behalf of his father from the August meeting on. His basic campaign speech rang all of the elements of the by now well internalized theme: the southern conspiracy to extend slavery into new territory, which had led, in turn, to the annexation of Texas and then the war with Mexico.[45]

The regular Democrats behind Cass, and the Whigs, in their turn, fought back, emphasizing both the traditional lines of political controversy and the dangerous radicalism that the Free Soilers represented. The Cass Democrats spent a great deal of effort identifying the Van Buren bloc as the betrayers of the party, not a group trying to recover the party's soul, as they claimed to be. They were "a sectional faction arrayed against the democracy of the Union" for their own parochial purposes. Place and revenge, not principle, was their motivation. "If they cannot be everything," William Marcy angrily suggested, "they are determined that no democrat shall be anything."[46]

Among the Whigs, similar hostility to the third party reigned. Many of their leaders in the North, no matter how hostile they were toward the South and slavery, and despite their commitment to the Wilmot Proviso, refused to join the Free Soil movement, clinging instead to their traditional associations and loyalties. Both William Henry Seward and Congressman Lincoln, for example, actively pushed Taylor's candidacy, ridiculed the Free Soilers, and argued, somewhat disingenuously, that the Whigs were more likely to achieve restrictions on the extension of slavery than were the Free Soilers—thereby making a partisan argument to attract sectional support. Most of all, they reminded Whig audiences of Van Buren's Democratic background, a heritage that made him anathema to Whig voters, even those who supported the Wilmot Proviso. Could the latter "be brought to trust him whom they never trusted before, on account of his present betrayal of his old friends and supporters?" To ask the question was to answer it. It was clear that the imperatives of party commitment still reigned supreme with these men.[47]

As with the leadership, so it was with their followers. The revolt against Polk originated among established political leaders. But, as their protests spread and became widely articulated in newspapers, at party rallies, and at other meetings of the faithful, numbers of committed party members, both Democrats and Whigs, were drawn in against the parties' candidates, usually following, as they did so, the lead of their local leaders. There were not enough of them, though. By the time the voters cast their ballots that November, it was obvious that the Free Soilers were not going to win the presidency (if they had ever expected to). Partisan influences, "the tyranny of the old parties," once more demonstrated their power by keeping most voters in their usual party homes on election day. As one Democrat put it, "I have so strong a repugnance to see the Whigs . . . elect General Taylor, that I am resolved to give my vote to General Cass." Although, he went on, he preferred Van Buren because of what he stood for in the election, between Cass and the Whig candidate, the likely winners, he did not hesitate. Cass was "with us on all those issues that have divided parties for years past." That should now be the most important matter to all Democrats as the election approached. Rank-and-file Whig voters reacted in similar fashion.[48]

As a result of such widely held attitudes, most Democrats and Whigs voted in 1848 as they normally did, supporting the candidates of their party when they went to the polls, much to the relief of each coalition's leadership. The two major parties together received just under 90 percent of the popular votes cast for president that autumn, each of them drawing votes from their supporters on both sides of the sectional divide as they had done in the past.[49]

On the other side of the electoral ledger, although badly hurt by such traditional party thinking and the behavior at the polls that followed from it, the Free Soilers did gain enough support in a number of strategic places to be able to claim some influence on the outcome of the election. New York State gave Van Buren more than 25 percent of its popular vote, for example, his highest total in any state. It was enough so that Cass lost the largest state in the Union, one that the Democrats had narrowly won four years before—and needed now. On the other hand, the Free Soil vote, largely drawn from Whig voters in Ohio and Indiana, coupled with the refusal of other Whigs to come to the polls at all to vote for a slaveholder and a general, probably gave those states to Cass. The important thing was, when the electoral smoke had cleared across the country, the Whig candidate, the Louisiana slaveholder Zachary Taylor, with no political experience, and his reputation primarily resting on his victorious leadership of American military forces in the war against Mexico, would be the nation's new president.[50]

"The Peace and Repose of the Union"

What did all of this political turmoil add up to as the election results were announced? The Free Soilers had engaged in a bold, disruptive action in 1848. What had they accomplished? If the purpose of the Van Burenite revolt was to punish the Polk-led Democratic Party even if that meant helping a Whig slaveholder gain the presidency, they were successful. To reiterate an earlier central point, until now, the northern blocs of each of the major parties sought to work with their southern colleagues to further their many common policy interests. As a result, once there had been, if not total tolerance of sectional differences, at least a strong sense of realism concerning them, coupled with a tendency to leave things alone in the interest of the larger goals of the Democrats and Whigs. But now a critical group of northern Democrats, heretofore marked by their willingness to submit to southern crankiness and give in to that section's often difficult-to-meet demands in the interest of party harmony, had become extremely disenchanted with their party's leaders and, as noted, mutinous. They had lived by a partisan code that had now become problematic for them. Their upset was real, their reactions forceful, their determination clear. And, as they dealt with their situation and pursued their restorationist goals, sectional impulses became more important among them than they had ever been in the partisan era before the outbreak of the conflict over Texas annexation.

As James K. Polk left office in early 1849, observers of the nation's political scene could discern some ominous cracks in the various processes of national unity that had characterized and shaped the United States to this point. The warfare originating in the Texas issue had become so bitter as to undermine the belief among Democrats that reciprocity would always be followed in party, and perhaps national, affairs. Sparring between sectional spokesmen was constant. As each side had pushed, the other had pushed back; as one of them routinely constructed negative images of the other section and persistently questioned the motives and honesty of its leaders, notions of amity, tolerance, and common unities became quite strained.

Ominously, the sensitivities revealed in these constant expressions of hostility seemed to be more widespread and to be creating much more turmoil and contentiousness than had earlier outbursts of North-versus-South hostility. The evidence suggested to some political activists that a sense of difference that had always been present was, for the first time, hardening into enduring confrontation. To those who felt that way, it seemed clear that the Texas matter, and what followed thereafter, had scarred the normal structure and understandings of national politics. In consequence, political parties, and the imperatives they espoused, seemed to a number of observers to be less dominant than they had been.[51]

BEYOND THE NOISY AND BITTER RHETORIC, changes in the way that politically involved Americans acted had occurred as well. In itself, Van Buren's running for president on a third-party ticket, whatever the provocation, suggests that sectional issues and activity were more prominent than they had been for a generation past. But there were other shifts in political behavior as well. The inability of Congress to organize the Oregon Territory for so long because its members were hamstrung by the persistent articulation, and reality, of sectional animosities and the inability to find common ground certainly underlined that some sort of weakening of partisan leaders' capacity to manage matters was taking place.

A similar result rising out of all of this tumult was that southerners' distemper in the face of the attacks on them and their rights in the territories now moved from rhetorical flourishes toward something more concrete. While remaining frustratingly conscious of the fact that "the South is not united and will not be united to resist the assaults of the North until it should be eternally too late," some of the section's leaders began to look, once more, toward forging political unity among the slave states—cutting across partisan lines as they did so.[52]

John C. Calhoun, as always, had articulated this idea earlier than most and took the lead in the Senate in seeking to build a permanent slave-state coalition through his many speeches and letters warning southerners of the dangers they faced and, most critically, by the introduction of measures denying Congress's right to restrict slavery in the territories. Finally, in reaction to a New York congressman's resolution to abolish the slave trade in the District of Columbia, introduced when Congress reconvened after Taylor's election, Calhoun moved beyond statements of resistance and called a caucus of southern congressmen to meet in January 1849 in the Capitol to consider their situation and find an effective means of working together against the danger that they faced. His "Southern Address," prepared for the meeting, called on them to form, at last, a coalition of southerners, both Whigs and Democrats, to act together in their section's defense.[53]

Despite all that had been occurring that had led to the demands that southerners now come together as a united bloc, the meeting was not the success hoped for. The numbers were not there. The southern Whigs who attended were determined to put the brakes on any Calhoun-led cross-partisan movements, while many of the southern Democrats proved to be still very hesitant about pushing the sectional-unity political idea too far. As a result, support for his Southern Address fell far short of the South Carolinian's hopes, with only forty-eight slave-state congressmen, of the 121 then serving in the House and Senate, willing to sign it. "We have done what we could here to unite the South on some common ground," Calhoun ruefully wrote from Washington after the meeting adjourned, but "our success has not been nearly as complete as we at one time hoped it would be."[54]

Nevertheless, to repeat, despite Calhoun's chagrin, something was in the air that could not be simply dismissed. The fact that the meeting took place and attracted widespread attention in both North and South did add something to the raising of the intensity of sectional concerns as the 1840s drew to a close, despite the limitations experienced and the failure to move as far forward as Calhoun and his southern-rights allies thought necessary. The rumblings about Texas and the fallout from them were more clearly part of the political landscape than such sectional angst had been for some time.

Two major questions remained as these currents settled into the nation's soil: First, did the apparently jelling sectional tensions reach beyond the most politically active Americans to include and mobilize the body of the nation's voters as well? The size of the Free Soil vote and the failure of southern Democrats to respond to appeals during the campaign that they support the slaveowner Taylor indicated that the answer was no, not yet. Whatever the force of the increased sectional rumblings, and the potential that they appeared to have for further development, the nation's political terrain had not yet shifted as much as it might have, given the range and intensity of the sectional uproar over Texas and its aftermath. Despite claims that sectional prejudices were spreading more widely in the general population, "we cannot shut our eyes to the fact," one congressman suggested, "that there is very often to be found a vast difference [in outlook] between the Representative and those who send him here." The legislators, he went on, too often were too quick to disturb "the peace and repose of the union." Their constituents, in contrast, were much less involved in such tendencies and less prone to do so.[55]

That evaluation seems to cover the situation present in the late forties. Partisan realities had always been an effective counterweight to whatever sectional impulses were present in America, and they remained so. The events of these years had significantly challenged the primacy of parties and their ways. But the continued commitment to them and the unity displayed amid the recent sectional uproar still constituted much more than a "facade," as one historian has labeled it, covering over more critical elements in the nation's political equation.[56]

THE SECOND QUESTION raised an old issue once more, one that remained no less pertinent despite its age and familiarity. Regardless of its failure to sweep the political field in the late 1840s, and the potency of the partisan imperative, was this sectional confrontation different? Did it, unlike earlier outbursts of North-versus-South bitterness in the political arena, have more staying power than usual? Had Texas created the possibility of a different direction in the future? Was Free Soil, which had grown out of the annexation controversy, not just an episode but, rather, a directional marker to a primarily sectional future in the United States, as some contemporaries believed? Had, in fact, the long shadow of the Texas controversy, whatever its apparent limitations, been able to reach well beyond the constraints that had always heretofore so effectively limited the reach and power of sectional differences in the usual run of American political life?

7

"THEIR HEINOUS SIN"

The Long Shadow of Texas

"I AM AWARE," JOHN VAN BUREN TOLD THE MASS MEETING of the Barnburners in the upstate New York town of Herkimer in October 1847, "that a fierce political storm is raging—that the political sea was rolling mountains high."[1] And so it was, had been for some time, and would continue to do. The political class and their constituents had become cognizant, as never before, at least since Thomas Jefferson's "firebell in the night" warning over Missouri in 1819, of the harsh realities of the nation's sectional divisions and of the serious potential that those divisions could have for great, and perhaps more long lasting and destabilizing, mischief.

Matters were about to shift significantly, however. Between the winter of 1848–49 and the spring of 1854, the unfinished business growing out of territorial expansion flamed up once more, but was then quieted by the enactment of congressional compromise measures that political leaders argued should finally close the books on the issue and allow them to redirect their concerns back to the familiar policy arguments that had traditionally aligned northern and southern Whigs against Democrats, with each coalition drawing support from all sections of the country, in a confrontation not primarily shaped by sectional sensitivities and prejudices.

Restoring Peace

During 1848 and 1849, prolonged debates in Congress over formally organizing, as federal territories, Oregon and the other new areas

The son of Martin Van Buren, John was a fiery orator and shrewd politician.
LIBRARY OF CONGRESS.

recently added to the United States repeatedly ended in the failure to accomplish that purpose. Neither northern nor southern congressmen would give way in their sectional war against each other. Attempts at a compromise solution to deal with the Wilmot Proviso were defeated, and the temper of the representatives and senators grew harsher as Congress remained tied up in knots. Each side filled the air with threats against their enemies, denunciations of the injustices they had to endure, and the injuries inflicted on them by the unacceptable demands of the other side. Congressmen committed to the Free Soil perspective frequently assailed the Democrats for "their heinous sin in annexing Texas," as the source of their current sectional woes. It was an action "projected by southern men avowedly to preserve the preponderance of the slave states" in the Union. It had been "a southern measure."[2]

Southerners responded in kind, quick to defend themselves and their interests against the attacks on them. They and their section had done nothing wrong. The South, in fact, was the one on the defensive due to the "wanton and unconstitutional aggression" on its "rights" by its northern enemies. Such attacks and counterattacks suggested how charged and harsh the atmosphere had become. Many political activists were in despair as a result. Writing to his brother from Washington, the usually moderate Georgia Whig congressman Alexander Stephens noted that he was convinced "that there never will again be harmony and peace between the two great sections of the Union."[3]

Congress finally managed to break through the difficulties it faced and enact an Oregon territorial bill in the summer of 1848. Given its location in the far Northwest, and the many people from the free states who had already settled in the region, some of the southern congressmen and their constituents accepted that slavery would never go there. They eased up, therefore, on their resistance to its organization as a federal territory closed to slavery. (Senator Calhoun, predictably, disagreed with the bill and actively fought against its passage.)[4]

The rest of the recently acquired lands in the Southwest still remained in organizational limbo, but that problem, too, was on its way to being worked out. Legislators were certainly indicating that they had had enough. Their unsuccessful efforts to end the controversy over the Mexican Cession provoked more and more impatient complaints that its members had been discussing slavery until "*that* topic is well nigh exhausted." It had been "the one perpetual theme" that congressmen had had to confront repeatedly. There had been too much, the critics went on, of such sectional obsession. "I hope that the Southern caucus is morally paralyzed," an Ohio Whig wrote. "I look on Calhoun and [the anti-slavery Joshua] Giddings as alike fanatics and disturbers, albeit at opposite extremes. Depend on it, no good can come from ultra courses." "Our true policy," a Democratic congressman summed up, "is to repudiate the slave question as a political issue" and stop its constant manipulation by those using it for their own purposes.[5]

When the Thirty-first Congress convened in December 1849 to hear the new president's State of the Union address, therefore, it contained enough members who wanted to end their stalemate over the unorganized territory. Even with a troublesome beginning when the House could not elect its Speaker, they came together to pass a series of compromise proposals over a very difficult nine-month session. Congress admitted California as a free state, left the future of slavery in the rest of the acquired lands up to the decision of the people living in the newly created territories of New Mexico and Utah (that is, by popular sovereignty, as it was labeled), settled Texas's disputed boundary with New Mexico, ended the slave trade in the District of Columbia, as many northerners had demanded, and enacted a strengthened fugitive slave law, as pressed by southern slaveholders.[6]

Passing these measures was not easy. There were bumps in the road, disappointments and frustrations along the way, stretching through the heat of a Washington summer when Congress usually closed down. Sectional tensions remained very high. Much fighting occurred over the various provisions debated, the heated rhetoric of the past few years continued to be voiced, and there was a great deal of divisive behavior when matters came to a vote. The debates echoed the usual range of North-South disagreements that had become so much a part of the nation's political discourse since the mid-forties. Ultimately, however, under the skilled leadership first of Henry Clay and then, and particularly, of Stephen A. Douglas, Congress managed to pull together and pass the various measures into law. A long, wearing episode now seemed to be, at last, behind the congressmen and their constituents.[7]

ALTHOUGH THE COMPROMISE EFFORTS WERE SUCCESSFUL, the hostility engendered by the battle over slavery extension did not immediately disappear. People on both sides of the sectional divide continued to find matters to agitate and constantly vented their feelings about them throughout 1851 and into 1852. As was usually the case with legislative solutions where neither side had gotten all that it wanted, spokesmen from both North and South voiced much heartburning about what Congress had done. Some of them wanted to continue the battle over the territories until they won their point, either the application of the Wilmot Proviso to the Mexican Cession, or the acceptance of the Calhoun thesis that the federal government had no power to exclude slaveholders from bringing their property into new federal territories.[8]

Calhoun had died at the end of March 1850, but he left behind a loyal group of followers, the so-called southern-rights men, who thought as he did and carried on his efforts to protect and expand slavery, since it was, in their constantly reiterated view, constitutionally protected. Their understanding of what had happened in American politics since 1844 continued to differ markedly from the perspective of the Van Burenites and their Free Soil allies. Calhounites believed and relentlessly argued the familiar theme that it was their section that was under attack and being treated unfairly. They demanded that the laws just passed dealing with the territories be repudiated because they were not, in fact, a compromise but, rather, quite prejudicial to their section's interests. California was lost to them, and there were no guarantees that slavery could ever go into New Mexico or Utah. This was not an acceptable situation.[9]

Their political tactics were also familiar. Another attempt to unite southerners behind a sectionally aggressive (or defensive) program led to the southern-rights advocates calling a convention at Nashville, Tennessee, in June 1850. They tried, once again, when the meeting convened, to carry through Calhoun's dream of defending the South by creating an undivided phalanx of his sectional colleagues despite the usual divisions caused by the pulls of party loyalty. (The attempt came to very little, to be sure. Nevertheless, it demonstrated the tenacious determination of some southerners to pursue their sectional goals above all other matters before them.)[10]

There was restlessness, as well, among other southern Democrats who had not usually been friendly to Calhoun's ideas, and some efforts among them to repudiate the compromise measures. They felt the increased pressure from the Calhounites and from their own constituents as the battle over the territories became as prolonged as it did and the arguments offered became so divisive and vicious. Many southern Whigs were also unhappy about what had been happening during the territorial debates. They generally accepted the compromise measures but believed that their northern party colleagues had been too harsh in their condemnation of slavery during the battles in Congress despite the political needs of their partisan associates in the South. Unfortunately, that rhetorical hostility continued even after the legislation had passed. The southern bloc wanted such sectional sniping to end, by whatever means possible, and the recognition by all Whigs that territorial compromises were necessary for the sake of the Union and had to be supported.[11]

In the North, at the same time, uncompromising Free Soilers remained active, denouncing the fugitive slave law in particular, while lamenting anew the potential extension of slavery into former Mexican territory, a potential made increasingly possible, they pointed out, by the popular-sovereignty formula for deciding the issue. They were much reduced in numbers by significant defections of their supporters as the territorial settlement was worked out. But in a number of state legislatures where they could do so, they entered into coalitions with either Democrats or Whigs who were sympathetic to them to elect United States senators who would, when they got to Congress, presumably continue to agitate against the further extension of slavery and find a way to repeal the fugitive slave law.[12]

SUCH EXPRESSIONS OF UNHAPPINESS reflected some of the normal trajectories of political discourse in the United States, where one side's triumph was usually seen as another's loss, and, as well, the continued imprint of the battles that had erupted in the mid-forties. Ultimately, however, the resistance to the settlement was brought under control—some would argue, papered over—and the expressions of discontent eased. Pro-compromise Democrats and Whigs in the South temporarily joined together to defend the measures passed in 1850 against the dissidents and their threats (including some calls for disunion, if necessary to save the South). They won a number of hard-fought state-level elections on the issue that helped materially, at last, to quiet things down. In disgust, a Calhounite Georgia newspaper editor lamented that "our own recent [state] election has taught us that there is a spell in party, a charm in good prices for cotton, and a power in the cry of 'Union,' too strong for the love of right or devotion to principle. The lesson is humiliating."[13]

There were also some efforts made to create a national union party of compromise supporters from both sections, which would, its advocates hoped, be strong enough to defeat outbursts from either edge of the political spectrum against the territorial legislation. At the same time, national party leaders were working hard to accomplish the same end by turning everybody's focus back to earlier partisan concerns and reasserting the dominance of traditional lines of battle between the Whigs and the Democrats. "We go," one editor summed up, "for maintaining the old party lines." He was not alone in his advocacy.[14]

The strategy of these groups demanded the end of the preoccupation with sectional issues, constant arguments along sectional fault lines, and the rousing of sectional sensitivities for electoral purposes and advantages, north or south. "We can understand and appreciate the reasons for preferring another plan to the set of compromise measures," a northern Whig wrote, "for they were not favorites with us; but there must be a point where both good sense and patriotism require that individual preferences should cease to be the subject of vituperation, and that point, we apprehend, has been reached in this instance."[15]

In particular, the compromisers offered a formula, embedded in the platforms that emerged from the national conventions of both parties in 1852 and echoed in state party platforms and legislative resolutions as well, that the issue of slavery extension into new territories had now been settled in the manner effected by Congress, that each party accepted that commitment, and that each would uphold the compromise measures and resist any attempt to reopen the question. Despite continued difficulties, anger, and intense opposition to it by some members of both parties, that "finality" formula seemed to bite in successfully among the politically active in both sections and was widely accepted in the public at large.[16]

The political consequences were quickly felt. Many of the Free Soilers, close allies against southern aggression since Wilmot Proviso days in 1846, now found themselves, for example, once again in different political camps. The Democrats among them generally fell in behind their party's presidential candidate, Franklin Pierce, in 1852. Most of the Whigs similarly supported Winfield Scott as their party's candidate for the presidency, whatever the frequently expressed hesitancies some of them still had about the way political affairs were tending and the refusal by the most disaffected among them to turn out to vote.[17]

For the moment, the events of 1850–52 appeared to have largely restored the political world to its pre-Texas equilibrium, in which national partisanship directed the energies of both political activists and voters. The contrasting tugs of sectional particularism and partisan values had struggled for dominance since 1844. That battle, many of those involved insisted, was now over. As Senator Douglas wrote to a colleague in Illinois, "You will have observed by the papers, that the proceedings of Congress are dull and quiet. There is very little attempt at agitation & excitement upon the vexed question of slavery. All seem to have exhausted their energies last Session and still need rest."[18]

While things had indeed quieted down with national politics again following its normal pursuits, how real was this celebrated stability? The appearance of normality reassured most of those committed to the workings of the existing system. They believed that a critical question about impact and persistence had been answered and that the sectional outburts that continued to be heard were, like earlier moments of such eruptions, neither so widespread nor so sustained as to suggest that a critical issue was capable of overwhelming other matters of political concern. Instead, Democrats again faced Whigs in renewed battles over policies that crossed sectional lines, that is, the old issues of economic development and the way that each party approached governing and defined the power of the national government in the domestic realm. Some skeptics suggested that a number of the old issues that had divided Whigs from Democrats no longer seemed as important as they once had been, but a real sense of the deep policy differences between the parties remained relevant and continued to be articulated in legislative debates and campaigns for office.[19]

Even the New York Democrats managed, albeit grudgingly on the part of many of them, to mend enough of their differences so as to find ways to cooperate with one another once again. After the election of 1848 and the retirement from the presidency of their mortal enemy, "Young Hickory," and then his death a short time afterward, many of the malcontents, including Martin Van Buren, his son John, Benjamin Butler, Samuel J. Tilden, and others, began to edge back toward their party home and continued to do so into the early fifties. This was not surprising, given their deeply internalized partisan values and commitments and the fact that the issues raised within the party by Texas annexation and all that had followed were now settled. (The Van Burens even supported William Marcy for the party's presidential nomination in 1852 as New York State's favorite son.)[20]

With the bulk of the Van Buren Democrats back in their party homes, and with the decline in the sectional uproar around the country, it was possible for many observers to believe that a dangerous political wound had been healed. The angry feelings that had been expressed against the other section after 1844 were now muted, if spoken at all. Senator David Yulee, a Florida Democrat, told Stephen A. Douglas that "I discard all feeling belonging to the late sectional controversy, and I resume the old democratic associations, as they were in the beginning." His was not a solo voice, either among southerners or among other Democrats—or Whigs.[21]

AMID ALL OF THIS apparent restorative good feeling, it was often easy to downplay, or ignore, that there was something else also buried within the system: the continuing fragmenting tensions within both parties, and the existence of sectional sensitivities and anger that would not completely go away. Fierce hostility to the Van Burenite Free Soil defectors was overt among many unreconciled Hunkers (the Hards, as they were now called) in New York, for example, a hostility that was, in turn, reciprocated by the friends of Silas Wright. Similar hostility continued to exist in other states, particularly among southerners, divided between party loyalists on one side and the Calhoun group and their allies on the other, neither fully reconciled to working with the other bloc.[22]

Still, on balance, whatever the apparent slippage from party devotion and the sometimes ragged unity that were present on the scene, and the continuing evidence of heartburn over recent events, the most dangerous and divisive matters that had confronted Americans since the sectional outbursts over Texas in 1844 and thereafter had now quieted down sufficiently, certainly in the public realm, for Americans to return to focusing on other policy matters, "to attend to the business of the nation," as one northern editor put it—which most political activists proceeded to do. For the first time since the Texas controversy had erupted, things were well under control. As the editor of the Richmond *Enquirer* reminded his readers: "Never has the country been so exempt from sectional disturbance. Never were the abolitionists so powerless, so discredited in public esteem. . . . Universal peace pervades the country."[23]

"A Hell of a Storm"

In 1849, Horace Greeley referred on the floor of the House of Representatives to "an immense, an almost total revolution in the northern public opinion [that] has been wrought within a few years past, by the annexation of Texas and the resistance on this floor to the right of petition."[24] That revolution had not yet occurred when Greeley spoke out. Northern public opinion remained more divided than he suggested—and continued to be so well into the 1850s. Traditional partisan commitments continued to be the main shaper of that public opinion, as they had been for so long. But, in the years after 1854, the consequences of the renewed outburst of sectional conflict would, for the first time, more nearly approximate Greeley's description.

What happened was the rise of an issue that severely affected—in fact, threatened—the dominance of both national parties and, second, the powerful reinvigoration of the forces released by the Texas controversy and what had followed from it. The teetering balance between the groups in conflict would finally spill over and change the nation's political trajectory. Sectional politics would come to the top once again and this time stay there. A sectionalized northern public opinion, hostile to the South, would become more widespread and more sustained than ever known before, as opposition to perceived aggression by slaveholders broadened and jelled into a new political movement.

Senator Douglas, who chaired the Committee on the Territories in the upper house of Congress, was a committed expansionist and dedicated to the rising power and continued prosperity of the West within the American nation. His immediate interest as the Thirty-third Congress convened in December 1853 was to organize the vast Nebraska area west of the Mississippi River into a federal territory. It was a region that was part of the Louisiana Purchase, and, since it lay north of the 36° 30' line, slavery was forbidden there under the Missouri Compromise. To Douglas, however, that ban was obsolete, and he drew up a bill in light of the recent legislation of 1850 concerning the territories.[25]

Douglas argued, when he introduced the Nebraska bill, that the territorial laws passed in 1850 had superseded those passed in 1820 by imprinting popular sovereignty at the center of national policy in the territories. Some of his Democratic colleagues, such as Lewis Cass, the party's presidential nominee in 1848, had championed popular sovereignty as a useful way of dealing with the issue of slavery's expansion. To Cass and the others who agreed with him, including Douglas, popular sovereignty had become the mainstream Democrats' alternative to the Wilmot Proviso and to Calhoun's doctrine. Douglas, in particular, had been pushing this notion for some time, and he expected his fellow Democrats to fall in behind his bill as reflecting good Jacksonian party doctrine.[26]

But something momentous happened. As Douglas manuevered his proposal, soon relabeled the Kansas-Nebraska bill, through Congress, he constantly had to deal with pressures from some of his southern Democratic colleagues interested in nailing down firm guarantees of the right of slaveholders to go, with their property, anywhere in federal territory as they pleased. Douglas was willing to go along with them because he needed the southerners' support to get the bill through and because of his strong belief that local power, i.e., popular sovereignty, rather than congressional mandates, should decide most matters in the new territories, even those concerning slavery.[27]

When Douglas agreed, under the political pressure, to include in the bill a clause explicitly repealing the limitations established on slavery in the Kansas-Nebraska area by the Missouri Compromise legislation, he allegedly commented that his action in doing so "will raise a hell of a storm." He was right. "No southern warrior," William Freehling has cogently argued, "could complain about the Kansas-Nebraska bill" as it emerged from Douglas's pen. Northern warriors could—and would—quite vehemently and loudly.[28]

GENERATIONS OF HISTORIANS have recounted in great detail what then happened. When the Nebraska bill was first introduced, popular opposition to it was muted, but, as it moved through Congress, Douglas's effort precipitated an intense uproar throughout the North, stimulated by the publication of a pamphlet, *The Appeal of the Independent Democrats,* which appeared in early 1854, originally in an anti-slavery newspaper, as Douglas was beginning to shepherd his bill through the legislative process. The *Appeal* was widely distributed in the North and almost immediately had the effect its authors desired. In it, they tellingly referred to and condemned the Illinois senator's, and the South's, "gross violation of a sacred pledge"—that is, the Missouri Compromise limits on slave territory—pointing to the Nebraska bill's origins as part of the aggressive slave power's "atrocious plot," the section's long-standing determination to expand the reach of its power aggressively and to have its own way in the federal territories, regardless of earlier agreements—in short, to let no one stand in its way.[29]

The *Appeal* was a powerful piece of propaganda, making a strong case about what was happening to unsettle the American nation, as well as pointing to who was responsible for the brewing crisis. It was accompanied by a tide of protest rallies throughout the North, stoked in part by those long opposed to the Democratic Party but also because of a spontaneous reaction by many who had rarely before been politically involved to any great degree, now outraged by what Senator Douglas had done. The Kansas-Nebraska bill, as described by the "Independent Democrats" and their allies, touched a very sensitive nerve in the North, the consequences from which refused to die down. As Salmon P. Chase, one of the pamphlet's authors, underscored in a subsequent speech in the Senate, the country had been at peace. Now it was no longer. Why? "It is *Slavery* that renews the strife," he argued. "It is Slavery that again wants room. It is Slavery with its insatiable demand for more slave territory and more slave states."[30]

Strong resolutions of condemnation passed by the protest meetings (accompanied, at times, by the much denounced Douglas being hanged in effigy) and state legislative resolutions against "so flagrant an act of injustice" followed, all designed to "awaken the people of Connecticut [and elsewhere] to the aggressive character of slavery as political power." Organizational initiatives taken at the protest meetings and in other venues soon coalesced into what was, at first, labeled the anti-Nebraska movement. Douglas's "hell of a storm" was well under way.[31]

How one deals with an emerging issue is rooted in past experience, long-standing beliefs and commitments, and the needs of politics at a given moment. So it was with both Senator Douglas and those who opposed him. The problem with the Illinois senator's bill, no matter how much he argued that it reflected Democratic expansionist orthodoxy and the party's commitment to local control of an area's affairs, was that it reawakened, with a fury, dangerous echoes from the past. First, Douglas was applying the notion of popular sovereignty to a region where slavery had always been banned under the Missouri Compromise passed almost thirty-five years earlier. He had engaged in an action that, in Kenneth Stampp's words, succeeded in "recklessly unsettling existing sectional adjustments," adjustments that were widely accepted and taken for granted as settled policy. In doing so, he was, once again, in the eyes of his opponents, denying northern whites, who had no wish to live among blacks, few or many, free or slave, their right to take up desirable land on the western frontier.[32]

Second, what was striking was how all of this was framed by events of a decade before. The 1854 crisis eerily echoed 1844. To the bill's opponents, none of what Douglas was engaged in was accidental. Since the beginning in the Texas controversy, through to the present attempt to dominate the Nebraska area, territorial matters, they argued, had always had "the marks of concert of action and of a deliberate plan." The long, torturous passage of the bill through Congress underlined to northerners that the South was on the march again, its intentions and determination clear, its plans well thought out, its northern minions doing its bidding. Slaveowners were, once again, asserting their control of affairs in the territories in order to get their way. In so doing, they confirmed what had been seen ten years before: that southerners would not abide by their agreements, accept what was appropriate, or recognize the legitimate concerns of others. They remained determined, instead, to force their will and aggrandize their section at the expense of the other parts of the Union.[33]

The consequences of that belief quickly became clear. As Francis P. Blair summed up, "the whole work was done by the Southern planters operating through their automaton." President Pierce, in supporting the initiative, clearly seemed to be also under the domination of southerners when it came to territorial policy. As a result, recent events "have done much to dissipate our confidence in southern honor," one protest meeting declared, "and forced us to the unpleasant conclusion, that the obligations of plighted faith and the force of sacred compacts are of no avail when the insatiate demands of slavery require their sacrifice." In the minds and expressions of many in the North, the Texas matter had returned with a vengeance.[34]

Southerners, faced with the uproar that Douglas had set off, denied the charges thrown at them and insisted that they were entitled to equal treatment in the territories, something that the restrictions of the Missouri Compromise denied to them. The latter "insults the South . . . brands us with inferiority, and shuts us within prison bounds." As a result, the North had "almost monopolized all that is really valuable of our public domain. Is this a just plan? Can it be defended?" It could be, and was, as the debate continued. "A great deal has been said," a Pennsylvania congressman responded to the southerners, "about equality of rights between the North and the South. Why was that not thought of when Texas was annexed?—that vast territory, all dedicated to the interests of slavery."[35]

"Old Political Landmarks Disappeared"

Long afterward, James G. Blaine wrote in his memoirs that in 1854 "old political landmarks disappeared, and party prejudices of three generations were swept aside in a day." It did not happen quite that fast, but the storm against Douglas's bill was rapid, intense, and far-reaching in its implications. The events of early 1854 energized and gave new life and force to long-held, but usually contained suspicions and attitudes. Day after day, the Kansas bill, "conceived in bad faith and repudiation," dominated congressional attention, accompanied by a range of insults, denunciations, and recriminations hurled across the aisles. It seemed clear to many of the protesters that an organized pro-northern movement had become necessary. As anti-Nebraska meetings roared their opposition to what Douglas was doing, shrewd political activists, mostly Whigs, began to build an anti-slavery-extension coalition under various names, ultimately settling on the name Republican.[36]

In their early stages, the Republicans were not a fully formed political party but, rather, a determined congeries of anti-Nebraska protest groups, albeit the membership included some familiar names, two among them being Preston King and David Wilmot. But, beginning as a pressure group focusing on an immediate matter, some of its leaders were determined to go further—to create a powerful and sustained alliance that would compete effectively at the polls and overthrow the southern-dominated Democratic Party and its unacceptable policies, once and for all.[37]

THEY WERE AIDED IN THEIR QUEST because events played into their hands and pushed their challenge forward. Although the national parties had regained much of their earlier position in the political world by 1853, despite the constant turmoil challenging them and the ragged edges in their situation, their restoration did not last long.

A radical Van Buren supporter, Preston King took the lead in Congress in trying to prevent slavery's expansion. LIBRARY OF CONGRESS.

When Douglas moved to bring the Nebraska bill before the new Congress in late 1853, the nation was already into a period of severe political turmoil—the first stages of a major political realignment that severely impacted events and significantly shaped the future direction that American political life would take.[38]

The United States was being shaken by an explosion of new issues, particularly the angry reaction of many to the rush of immigrants into the eastern seaboard cities, and the religious and cultural baggage they brought with them. Anti-immigrant, anti-Catholic, and various education and temperance reform movements, which had been simmering for some time, suddenly blossomed and then mixed together at the local level into a formidable protest force determined to recapture and reform the nation. "When the scum of European society, ejected by its rotten institutions," one pamphlet summed up, "or cast up by the surges of revolution, floats to our shores and demands immediate baptism to the high honor of American citizenship, there arise questions worthy of our maturest consideration." And, they swiftly concluded, new political outlets as well.[39]

The surge of nativism hurt the old parties severely because, on this issue, they had "been found wanting." They appeared, to many voters, to be either indifferent to or unable or unwilling to deal with an issue that was seen as a crisis for the nation by a growing number of Americans. Political action outside the Whig and Democratic orbits, therefore, was necessary, and engaged in. At first, public reactions caused a great splintering of parties at the local and state levels, culminating eventually in the rise of the Know Nothing Party, embodying themes set off by the Catholic migration and the failure of the established parties to do anything about this rising danger to the United States and its values.[40]

Initially, in the first stages of the electoral realignment, the Know Nothing Party proved to be a formidable alternative in the northern states to the anti-slavery-extension groups beginning to coalesce into the Republican Party. Many voters seemed more attracted to the former when they went to the polls in local and state elections in 1853 and 1854. In both years, many Whigs and Democrats defected to the nativist parties, and the latter, in their turn coalescing into a national party, also drew support from new voters pulled into politics by their determination to confront the immigrant-Catholic menace.[41]

THE ELECTORAL UPHEAVAL OF 1853–54 was particularly overwhelming in the free states. When the electorate left the polls on election day, they had significantly weakened the grip of the old parties to an unexpected degree. At the national level, in 1854, the Democrats lost sixty-six of the ninety-one northern seats they had held in the federal House of Representatives in the previous Congress. The party was now in the minority in the House. Their traditional Whig enemies held on to only fifty-six seats. Both of their newly emerging opponents, the anti-Nebraska coalition, at that point competing under various names, and the nativists, benefited from the rout of the old parties at all levels, but the returns seemed to give great impetus, in particular, to the rising Know Nothings. They drew enough support in the Northeast to win seats in several state legislatures, gaining a massive majority in Massachusetts and the governorship there. They won fifty-two seats in the national House of Representatives, while the northern sectionalist parties, the anti-Nebraska, Republican, and People's parties, won forty-five.[42]

Many observers, including leaders of the emerging Republican coalition, thought the nativist appeal was strong enough so that the Know Nothings would become the dominant second party against the Democrats. As one Whig leader argued, "this election has demonstrated that, by a majority, Roman Catholicism is feared more than American Slavery." Stephen A. Douglas agreed. As Congress finally passed the Kansas-Nebraska bill and turned to other matters, its author was sanguine that these other issues would now replace the territorial matter at the forefront of people's minds. As he told a Democratic editor, "the Nebraska fight is over, and Know Nothingism has taken its place as the chief issue in the future."[43]

He was an optimist—and once again, unusually for such a shrewd political activist, wrong.

"An Immense, An Almost Total Revolution"

The Know Nothing surge did not attain the political heights expected of it. What happened instead was a powerful stimulation of the sectional impulse already present, which planted it into the nation's political soil with a power and reach previously unknown. In the presidential election of 1856, the Republican Party, with its anti-slavery-extension appeal, continued to compete with the Know Nothings' powerfully expressed nativism and hatred of Catholiciam for the anti-Democratic vote in the northern states. But the Republicans were in luck politically. They were already becoming something more than just one of the opposition parties as events, and their leaders' compelling explanation of why things were occurring as they were, convinced their audience that they best understood the dangers that the nation now faced and what had to be done to confront them.[44]

What made this possible was that much of what was occurring in national politics unfolded unexpectedly to the Republicans' advantage, adding greatly to their attraction to northern voters. It began with the surge of events in 1856, most particularly what came to be called (by Republicans) "the crime against Kansas" and the fallout from that. The notion of an aggressive slave power, already on Republican lips, was reenergized beyond anything seen before, to become their effective rallying cry against their opponents. As a result, over the next four years, the Know Nothings fell behind as former Whigs and Free Soilers, as well as once loyal Democrats, joined together in the North in the face of the South's repeated misdeeds and continued assault on the rights and interests of the other area of the nation.[45]

From the beginning, popular sovereignty had shown a most violent and destructive character on the plains of Kansas. A bloody struggle for control of the territory had broken out there between slave-state and free-state advocates. It had become a testing ground of each side's dermination to win out. Nothing seemed to be out of bounds in this battle for supremacy. Northerners and southerners gunned each other down, individually and in groups, burned houses, destroyed property, and did all else that they could to drive their sectional enemies from Kansas. The successive governors of the territory seemed helpless to do anything about it without help from the national government, but the Democratic administration in Washington dithered.[46]

The violence was carefully tracked and emblazoned in heated headlines in newspapers and speeches in the eastern states in order to assail and discredit the other side. Northern editors reported that Missouri "border ruffians" rode over into the area and added to the bloody confrontation. The free-state town of Lawrence was attacked ("sacked," in Republican rhetoric); southern settlers were shot dead in their turn ("massacred" in slave-state parlance, by wild-eyed abolitionists). Senator Henry Wilson of Massachusetts summed up the case against the South and Douglas in terms that, with appropriate adjustments, characterized the tone of both sides as the situation on the plains deteriorated. "Kansas lies bleeding at your feet today, a conquered, a subdued Territory. You have invaded it; you have conquered it; you have warned out its people; you have murdered them; you have plundered them; you have battered down their dwellings with cannon."[47]

And if anything demonstrated all that had been going on since 1844 in the Democratic Party, with great effect beyond it as well, it was the evidence before everyone of how the South was trying to steal Kansas, with both the Pierce and Buchanan administrations, and their congressional allies, willing to help them do so. The Democracy, "This southern sectional party," it was claimed, "has gone so far south that it has even lost sight of the 'North Star.'" Or, on the other side of the debate, in rebuttal, how much anti-slavery groups were determined to deny the South its constitutional rights in the territory.[48]

EVENTS KEPT MOVING ON in the Republicans' direction. Senator Charles Sumner of Massachusetts, an uncompromising anti-slavery advocate with a tart tongue reminiscent of John Quincy Adams but even more biting, roared out against events in the western territories in a number of speeches, the last of which was stingingly entitled "The Crime Against Kansas." He flayed the South and its out-of-control leaders in Congress for their single-minded aggression on behalf of an evil cause in words that were hot, extreme, and highly personal. Some days later, Congressman Preston Brooks of South Carolina answered the charges made by the "criminal aggressor" Sumner by coming into the Senate chamber and, with little warning, brutally beating the Massachusetts senator with a cane.[49]

There was an uproar once more in the North as Republican newspapers and speechmakers invoked harsh images of southerners again demonstrating their uncompromising determination to have all things go their way in the territories and to brook no opposition and let no one interfere, even if that meant resorting to the most extreme violence against their opponents. Citizens' meetings, spontaneous

One of the leading anti-slavery opponents of annexation, Charles Sumner of Massachusetts became a victim and symbol of the "aggressive slavocracy." LIBRARY OF CONGRESS.

and otherwise, once again passed resolutions, this time against Brooks and the forces behind him. How could any northerner, Republicans asked, remain complacent about such aggression and the threats to their rights underscored by Brook's action and his section's enthusiastic support for it?[50]

On the other side, southern editors largely celebrated Brooks's action as a necessary thing to do in order to protect themselves from the kind of northern aggression against them that Sumner personified. A number of southern spokesmen added the thought that there were other northern leaders who deserved the same treatment Sumner had received. A few were more cautious, even condemning the South Carolinian's action, but the much louder voices of those who joyfully supported him were what northerners heard from the South. Things did not improve when "Bully Brooks," having resigned from the House of Representatives, returned to South Carolina to be triumphantly reelected to his seat. As Michael Morrison has written, "popular sovereignty had not provided a common ground but a battleground."[51]

THE EVENTS OF 1856 strikingly and decisively confirmed the Republican message. From then on, "Bleeding Kansas" and "Bleeding Sumner" became highly emotional catchwords, extensively and effectively used by the Republicans to describe the rampaging South. But that was not the end of their political good fortune. Incidents favoring them continued to occur. The Supreme Court's decision in the Dred Scott case early in 1857, under the leadership of its southern-born chief justice, Roger B. Taney, caused the sectionalist argument against southern aggression to bite more and more deeply into the political soil of the northern states. Taney's "shocking" opinion, denying the federal government's authority to limit the extension of slavery into United States territory, was to Republicans a "bold perversion of the Constitution." They saw it as the latest "in a chain of sinister events beginning with the annexation of Texas and including the war with Mexico, the passage of the fugitive slave act of 1850, and the adoption of the Kansas-Nebraska Act." Each was, to them, "part of a conspiracy promoted by the Southern slave power and assisted by its Northern doughface allies."[52]

The Republicans were quick to take advantage of the failure of Douglas's celebrated popular-sovereignty formula, both on the ground in Kansas and in the courts, and the impending further expansion of slavery into free territory as a result. And they did so in the strongest, and by now quite familiar, terms. The South's aggression in 1854 and thereafter—the violation of the Missouri Compromise, followed by the activities by southerners in the West, in Congress, and on the Supreme Court to ensure that Kansas became a slave state—reawakened echoes from a decade before. From Tyler, Calhoun, and Polk to Douglas, the new, pro-Southern president, James Buchanan, and the pro-slavery Lecompton legislature in Kansas seemed like a very short road to many northerners.[53]

Abraham Lincoln made the point well in his "House Divided" speech in 1858. Although direct and absolute evidence of a connection—that is, a pro-slavery conspiracy—was not present, he said,

> When we see a lot of framed timbers, different portions of which we know have been gotten out at different times and places and by different workmen—Stephen, Franklin, Roger and James, for instance—and when we see these timbers joined together . . . or, if a single piece be lacking, we can see the place in the frame exactly fitted and prepared to yet bring such a piece in—in such a case we find it impossible not to believe that Stephen and Franklin and Roger and James all understood one another from the beginning and all worked upon a common plan or draft drawn up before the first lick was struck.[54]

The South's aggressive plot began "in relation to the admission of Texas"; the joint resolution bringing her into the Union was "a most gross, palpable, direct violation of the Constitution." But the Democrats had gone along with it. They did so then, and acted in similar ways at other moments since, because, as Lincoln had underscored, the Democratic Party had become a slave-power-dominated organization, no longer the national coalition that it claimed to be.[55]

THE REPUBLICANS WON over a third of the nation's popular vote in the three-way presidential race in 1856, finishing second to the Democrats. The strength of this coalition of anti-southern groups of mixed antecedents was clearly on the rise, and it was becoming more and more effective as matters continued to go its way. The Know

Nothings remained, but in a weaker state, internally divided between their northern and southern wings. Everything seemed to be going in one direction. The dam holding back sectional outbursts had been breached once more, but with evidence of a significant difference this time. The Free Soil Party had been a temporary one; the Republican Party was turning out to be more solidly rooted, thanks largely to the continuing uproar in Kansas and the violent fallout from it in Washington. Political parties still existed as important forces in the nation, but their dimensions and nature had shifted. One of them was now a sectional movement, with little support in the South.[56]

Southerners were not inert as the northern political revolution against them drew more and more support and grew in fury. They reacted violently to the case being made against them. To them, it was the same issue as in the Texas crisis: the refusal of northerners to accept slaveholders' constitutional right to take their property into federal territory. In response, some began, once more, to push for sectional political unity. This time, they claimed, there was a significant difference from earlier times. When the Kansas battle erupted, one southern-rights editor argued that "it has been the misfortune of the South. . . . that its own people have been divided in every crisis or peril to its institutions, but now for the first time they are thoroughly and cordially united."[57]

Others, in their response to the continuing northern political uproar, argued that the unity of the national Democratic Party, rather than sectional unity, would best serve the South's interests. The northern Democrats, these men kept reminding their colleagues, "at the sacrifice of popularity at home," had "manfully battled for the constitutional rights of the South," and their record made it clear that they would continue to do so. No one could make similar claims about any Republican's commitment to bisectional cooperation.[58]

In fact, in the mid- and late fifties, the national Democratic Party still appeared strong, including in the northern states. They maintained the support of their traditional constituencies. Many of the Barnburners, for example, who had been such a major force in the initial unloosing of the anti-southern frame of mind that now defined the Republicans, had stayed with the Democracy even in the face of the controversies unleashed by Douglas's bill. But this strength and support was not what it once had been. As the renewed southern aggression intensified and Republicans attracted more and more northerners to their ranks, Democratic defections increased. Former Barnburners, such as Benjamin Butler, and their allies in other states, Gideon Welles, Hannibal Hamlin, and Francis P. Blair, at first hesitant, now left their Jacksonian home and came over to the new party. Others of them, Martin Van Buren, for one, were retired from politics entirely, or, as in the case of his son John, no longer active in that arena. (Both of them remained loyal, in this new sectional crisis, to their Democratic home, however.)[59]

Nevertheless, despite the leakage from its ranks, the Democracy remained a substantial political force, led by Stephen A. Douglas with his loyal following throughout both the northern and southern states. There was a problem, though. The party's northern wing was becoming less important than it had been. Its congressional bloc, for example, was more and more dominated by the party's southern wing as popular elections in the North replaced sitting Democrats or refused to elect new ones in their place when they retired. In 1845, at the meeting of Polk's first Congress, 43 of the 137 Democratic representives were from the slave states, 94 from the North. In the House that debated the Kansas constitution in 1858, there were 76 southern Democrats of the party's total of 130, only 54 from the non-slave states.[60]

This demonstration of the South's increasing, and now dominant, power within the nation's traditional majority party, and of the section's leaders' willingness to use that power, as they had been doing and continued to do, for their own parochial purposes added much fuel to the fire that was raging against the aggressive slavocracy among northerners, continually stoked as it was by the Republicans in their campaigns for office. "The Texas scheme for the aggrandizement of the slave power," one Republican congressman charged, had led in one direction. "From that time to this, the tendency of that party [the Democrats] to sectionalism has been constant; its strength in the slave States steadily increasing; and the decadence in the free States equally steady and uniform." The result was clear to see: "The power of the Democratic party is in the South. Gentlemen of the Democratic party in the North must follow [a] southern [h]ead."[61]

The Revolt of Stephen A. Douglas

Things continued to go from bad to worse, and began to solidify in the latter condition. Violence had diminished in Kansas under the firm hand of a new territorial governor. But there were other ways to win out. Certainly, "neither side was willing," as Kenneth Stampp has written, "to leave the outcome [there] altogether to chance."[62] In the turmoil of the past few years, free-state advocates had boycotted local elections in protest against the violence and the ineffective way that the Pierce administration had handled it—or refused to. Those favoring slavery, determined to make Kansas a slave state, took advantage of the boycott. Elected to a constitutional convention in Lecompton by a minority of the area's residents, pro-slavery advocates drew up a constitution that, among other provisions, permitted slave labor in the new state. Then they engaged in a series of political manipulations of election procedures to move the document forward, which provoked another uproar.[63]

It had been understood that the people of Kansas had to ratify, by popular referendum, any constitution drawn up by the convention. The free-state population in the territory was clearly larger than that supporting slavery. So the slave-state activists in control in the territorial capital at Lecompton deliberately manipulated the requirement for a popular vote on the document they had drawn up and moved to submit their constitution directly to Washington for final approval by Congress, whatever the actual weakness of their situation on the ground in Kansas.[64]

President Buchanan had appointed Robert J. Walker, of all people, as the fourth governor of the troubled territory. Even he had enough when he saw what was going on and the refusal of the administration to do much about it despite his pleas. He was convinced that Kansas would never be a slave state and warned the president that the manipulations that had produced a pro-slavery constitution should not be accepted, given Kansas's free-state majority. Southerners in Kansas and Congress denounced him roundly, and Buchanan, following his pro-southern instincts and his own preferences, went along with the Lecomptonites and decided to send the submitted constitution to Congress, whatever its provenance or legitimacy, for acceptance. He did so in early February 1858.[65]

Kenneth Stampp rightly labels the Lecompton constitution episode "politics as farce."[66] But beyond that, all of this deceit and slippery dealing was familiar and, once again, distressing to those who had to contend with it. Memories of the past and all that had happened to cripple northern interests remained clear and sharp. To angry Republicans and a good many appalled northern Democrats, the southerners, led by the Lecompton "assembly of usurpers," were trying to seize another territory by using political muscle, trickery, and deceit, not to mention violence, to get their own way. Even a number of southern Democrats were startled by the effontry of their colleagues and the administration. "The South," one of them wrote, "seems to be in a great hurry to injure her friends in the North, and help her enemies to the power to break her own head."[67]

The rhetoric was followed by a great deal of anti-southern action. Protest meetings against the Lecompton Constitution similar in style and intensity to those of 1854 against the Nebraska bill were called together in the northern states to vent popular anger and pass resolutions against accepting the document. It "was the embodiment and consummation of a series of violent, usurping and fraudulent acts." This course was also followed, and the charge echoed, by a number of state legislatures in the free states similarly directed against "the alarming aggressions of the slave power."[68]

Such denunciations were not all that dramatized the issue among northerners. What followed as the protests built up into a firestorm also echoed earlier moments in the Texas controversy. The culmination of the widening war over Kansas, and the Buchanan administration's behavior in response to it, was another revolt of one of the party's most prominent leaders, this time Stephen A. Douglas, accompanied by some of his Democratic colleagues, against their party's president and the policies he was pursuing in the western territories.[69]

"No statesman of the North," the editor of the Richmond *Enquirer* wrote in mid-1858, "and very few at the South, have defended the rights of slaveholders more warmly and effectively . . . than has Stephen A. Douglas."[70] Then the world caved in. The Illinois senator was no Barnburner but rather had always been a mainstream Democrat, tolerant of slavery, or indifferent to it, and, above all, committed to letting it alone. That characterization, of course, also once described Martin Van Buren. Douglas now confronted the same situation that the New York leader and his supporters had faced as the Texas episode unfolded. Southerners were undermining them by using the Democratic Party in a most unacceptable and surely destructive way, solely as their instrument on behalf of their particular interests without regard to party balances, rules, and traditional understandings or to the consequences of their behavior for the party's, or for the nation's, fortunes. In addition to everything else, the southerners' overweening behavior had destroyed Van Buren's presidential ambitions and now threatened to do the same to Douglas's similar expectation of his party's nomination in 1860 and then his victory, with the support of northern voters on election day.

As with Van Buren ten years before, Douglas had had enough. He had tried for a decade to find a formula, consistent with the Democratic Party's values, to end the angry confrontation over slavery in the territories that had erupted over Texas annexation and continued thereafter. For his pains, Douglas had met with a devastating storm of opposition, both from Republicans and from members of his own party. But, whatever the hostile uproar against popular sovereignty being extended into Kansas, he had believed that it would work if carried out in an appropriate manner, not through violence and denial of a real consideration of how the people of the territory felt. The actions of the Buchanan administration completely undercut him. Expansion, coupled with popular sovereignty, was the right policy to follow, but not in the way it had been allowed to play out in Kansas.

Faced with this extraordinary corruption, as he saw it, of the popular-sovereignty principle, "a mode of submission that is a mockery and an insult," and the threat that it posed to his presidential ambitions, and despite great pressure from his party colleagues to go along with the administration's decision, Douglas startled the political world by defying his former southern allies and Buchanan's demand for party unity on the bill. He came out against Kansas's admission to the Union under the Lecompton Constitution, given the way it had been crafted and then submitted. A bruising fight not unexpectedly broke out between Douglas and the administration, again echoing familiar themes and anger from ten years before.[71]

In his bitter and uncompromising speeches defending his actions, Douglas denounced what was happening because of the administration's Kansas policy in terms familiar to any Van Burenite. Against the true meaning of Jacksonian Democracy, against the pledges party leaders had made as to the right of the people of Kansas to freely choose what they wanted in reference to slavery, the administration had caved in to the southern aggressors. Polk, at least, had been a southerner himself. Buchanan, from Pennsylvania, had by his actions revealed the truth of the old Free Soil, and now Republican, charge that northern Democrats were "doughfaces," that is, "northern men with southern principles," always submissive to southern demands—at least those associated with the administration were. Douglas would not compromise his principles for such men, or for any other reason that he could see. Working with Republican senators and representatives—"stranger political bedfellows no one had ever seen"—and the few Democratic congressmen willing to join him in defying the administration, Douglas vigorously labored to defeat the Kansas statehood bill.[72]

President Buchanan and his supporters reacted to Douglas's revolt in ways familiar to those with memories of the Polk administration: They wielded the power of federal patronage in order to punish the recalcitrant Illinois senator, particularly to weaken him in his own state. Beyond that, the president's men began to work actively to prevent his reelection to the Senate by the Illinois state legislature in 1858 and then instigated his removal by the Democratic caucus from his power base as chairman of the Senate Committee on the Territories. All of these events badly divided the party in the North into two bitter factions, each determined to subdue, or destroy, the other. "It has become apparent," Douglas wrote in early 1858, "that the administration is more anxious for my distruction [*sic*] than they are for the harmony and unity of the Democratic party."[73]

"The Domineering and Aggressive Spirit of a Portion of the South"

The last word on all that had occurred after 1854 belongs to Preston King, once a loyal Van Buren lieutenant and a close friend of Silas Wright, now, in the late 1850s, a Republican senator from New York. Lecompton revealed, he said, that "the organization of the Democratic party has fallen irretrievably under the control of nullifiers and slave propagandists."[74] He had said similar things, a decade and more earlier, in response to the Texas controversy. The result of that belief—and condition—had been that two of the party's most important leaders since the 1830s, Van Buren and now Douglas, both noted for their deep partisan loyalties, as well as for their very cooperative attitude toward their southern colleagues, had mutinied against the actions of the latter and the way that southerners, indifferent to consequences and to the nature of the Democracy, demanded and got control of the party and used it for sectarian purposes.

In response, demands for northern sectional unity against southern aggression more and more became the rhetorical order of the day. The reading of the events that had occurred in 1854 and thereafter, and the accumulation of anger as a result, all building, in turn, on a foundation originally established in the Texas controversy, had had a significant impact on northern public opinion, well beyond its roots of a decade before. "The anti-slavery sentiment of the North has become," one congressman argued, "a religious sentiment, and is now particularly powerful, growing out of the domineering and aggressive spirit of a portion of the South." As Michael Holt has written, "the intensity of northern anger at slave power aggressiveness and the aid it gave Republicans cannot be exaggerated. Northerners felt a profound need for a party that championed the North."[75]

There continued to be, at the same time, resistance to allowing such sectional pressures to sweep away old guidelines, a resistance strongly pushed by many leaders of the Democratic Party in the free states. Many elements of the Jacksonian political world survived and remained vigorous. Party members voices were still heard in the political arena; they still offered other issues for debate and took policy positions that separated them from the successors to the Whigs. The partisan imperative continued to influence the way that people acted. Many of them still resisted, with great vigor, any further sectionalizing of American politics, either by their fellow northerners or by southerners, as an unacceptable direction for the nation to take. They wanted to "turn from the constant jealousies of the North toward the South, and the South toward the North," and return to the more important task before them, of furthering "national achievement."[76]

Their message was heartfelt and familiar, and it had worked in the past. Yet clearly much had changed. The Kansas-Nebraska bill, "that great crime against the nation's peace," and what had followed in its wake had "convulsed" public opinion and politics to new heights of sectional frenzy.[77] That convulsion was still under way as Douglas took the field in opposition to what had been done to his creation. American politics toward the end of the 1850s was a mixture of sectional and partisan concerns competing for dominance, with the significant fact being that, unlike a decade before, the latter were slipping fast in their hold on the politically involved.

Martin Van Buren still survived in retirement, and Stephen A. Douglas remained a formidable, if badly wounded, political figure, determined to remain a Democrat and bring the party back to its senses and its correct course. But their experiences over a dozen and more years suggested how much their party, and the United States, had moved a long and dangerous way from the hopes, understandings, and expectations of the Jacksonian era, particularly in the weakening of those elements that they had pressed forward so hard in order to overcome or contain the destabilizing sectional impulses present in their society.

8

CONCLUSION

"An Element of Overwhelming Ruin to the Republic"

THE REST WAS ANTICLIMAX, for the nation's political pathway was now indelibly marked. "For my own part, Mr. President and Senators," George Pugh, the staunch Ohio Democrat, told his colleagues in late 1856, "I desire and hope that the sectional contest in which we have indulged for almost three years will soon be hushed and forgotten. . . . Let us turn from the constant jealousies of the North toward the South, and the South toward the North, to proceed in that path of national achievement which now invites our care."[1]

Such statements had been commonplace throughout the sectional uproars of the forties and early fifties as political leaders sought to calm the latest outburst between northerners and southerners. But it was now too late. Pugh would find no solace in the events leading to Douglas's revolt in 1857, and the following years would see even more sectional battling over the territories and the rights and wrongs avowed by each side. The war between Douglas and the Buchanan administration continued. The Illinois senator used all of his powerful rhetorical gifts and political skills against the president and his southern antagonists, in retribution for all that they had done to force Kansas to become a slave state. He faced a hard race for reelection in 1858 against a tough, shrewd, and rhetorically gifted opponent, Abraham Lincoln. In his campaign Douglas not only made his opposition to Buchanan's Kansas policy even sharper than it had been but further infuriated southern leaders because of his development of an argument that, if followed, threatened to keep slaveowners and their property out of Kansas and other territories despite the restrictions against any attempt to do so put forth by the Supreme Court in the Dred Scott decision.[2]

The controversy badly fractured and grievously weakened the bisectional Democratic Party. Party members loyal to President Buchanan tried to maintain a cross-sectional perspective (a pro-southern one, their enemies would have argued) and preserve the political world's traditional party-centered framework against the rising tide of sectionalism. They continued to demand loyalty, in the sharpest terms, to the party's national leader, the president, and his policies. But to many northern Democrats that effort now entailed paying too high a price in order to placate the ravenous, demanding slaveholders.

With the Democrats in disarray, the sectional chasm continued to widen. Hair-trigger sensitivities were even more the order of the day, while the roars of outrage from both sides became even louder than they had been in the recent past. As northern anger over the situation in the territories grew, southerners became more and more fearful and aggressively defensive toward outsiders, convinced, as some of them always had been, that they were unfairly and unconstitutionally under attack by those who were determined to destroy their system. When John Brown, one of the violent men of Kansas, led his raid on the federal armory at Harper's Ferry, Virginia, in 1859 as the first step in a plan to foment a slave uprising, many southerners believed that their worst fears were now confirmed: that the behavior of Douglas and the Republicans, directed against their interests, encouraged men like Brown to threaten their rights and their continued existance as a society.

It would soon be over. The Democrats split in two during the presidential election of 1860, and Douglas, the nominee of one of the two party conventions held that year, was bitterly forsaken by the furious southern bloc and their allies, the northern Buchanan loyalists. They ran their own candidate, John Breckinridge, named by another meeting of party faithful. Abraham Lincoln then led the Republicans to victory over the divided Democracy and the remnants of the Whig party (and some Know Nothings), now labeled Constitutional Unionists. This sectionally driven election was quickly followed, as had been threatened so often in recent years, by the secession of seven slave states and then civil war.

MUCH HAD HAPPENED to cause this final blow. At bedrock was, of course, the existence of slavery in one part of the nation as the fulcrum of its economic and social systems—a reality that some outside of the South bitterly opposed, and others were uncomfortable about but accepted as necessary within an array of understandings in regard to reciprocal behavior and the balances between different interests in their pluralist nation. They did so because their main focus was on other matters, because they needed southern political support, and because most of them were indifferent to slavery as a moral issue. Sectional confrontations did occur. Each of those that broke out before Texas left some mark on American politics. Nevertheless, what David Potter has called the "constant exploitation of sectional tensions for purposes of arousing the voters" had had indifferent success into the early and mid-forties. The outbursts were symptons of underlying tendencies, not causal impulses shaping what was to come. Their force sputtered out over time except in the minds of those intransigent groups in the North and South who were eager to keep the sectional fires burning.[3]

The sectional impulse reappeared with great force in 1844, and this time the political situation began to change, ultimately in most dramatic fashion. Expansion into Texas did not originate as primarily a sectional issue, but it became one, accompanied by much anger and shouting. Still, it might have been expected to follow the existing pattern of great uproar along sectional fault lines, at least in parts of the political world, to be then followed by a calming of the passions unleashed and a return to normalcy. It did, to some degree, as the ever resiliant political parties took hold again across sectional lines. Critically, however, the controversy unexpectedly became the pivot on which events subsequently turned in a different direction from formerly, a turn that proved to be persistent, and dangerous. It took some time for that to happen, to be sure, but once on the scene the annexation experience never totally disappeared from view. Texas set the stage for the opening of a Pandora's box and the arousal, to new heights, of destabilizing passions that, if never totally dormant, had previously always been effectively controlled by the nation's political system and its partisan-dominated way of carrying on public business.

Annexation's consequences unfolded not only during the controversy itself, with its element of southern territorial aggressiveness, but, most especially, in combination with an unexpected and significant fallout from it, when the many strands unleashed by the emergence of Texas as a major theme in American politics, and the consequent political overturn of 1844, came together in the first days of the Polk presidency. The administration's actions, beginning with the manner in which the new president handled Tyler's final attempt to foreclose the Texas matter, allowing annexation to go forward under Milton Brown's formula despite expectations that he would act otherwise, became entangled in the difficult and still unsettled politics of the Democratic Party, ultimately to be viewed as a massive assault on an important group of party members and President Polk's deliberate rupturing of the consensus of unwritten understanding by which the Democratic Party, and beyond that American politics more generally, lived.[4]

Much more followed from that initial situation. By the end of the Polk era in 1849, a great deal had happened to place the acquisition of Texas in a new light. What occurred in 1844–45 remained alive in the minds, discourse, and behavior of the losers in the battle. First of all, it was the focus of a continuing and evolving northern anger against what was seen as slavery's unacceptable overreach. Sectional opposition to annexation was originally rooted among those deeply hostile to slavery and determined to prevent its further extension. To these anti-slavery advocates who had opposed Tyler's plans from the first, Texas annexation was, as it always would be, "an element of overwhelming ruin to the republic."[5]

But the anger and frustration that these men continued to express was only one part of the emerging landscape. Whatever their determination, anti-slavery advocates had not been strong enough, by themselves, to challenge the South with much success in the years before Texas. Anti-slavery sentiment may have been more widespread among Americans, particularly those living in the free-labor North, than was always apparent in the world of political parties and elections. But movements to end slavery had been limited in popular support and impact and remained so until such sentiment became part of larger concerns—in this case, the unacceptable ambitions of the slave power.

This shift began to occur between 1844 and 1848, as a persistent sense of sectional wrongs pushed further into the center of affairs, coupled, as it became, with a powerful perception of betrayal among pivotal groups in the North. Those who had opposed slavery for so long suddenly began to pick up allies in unexpected places, from among the disaffected 54° 40' men, as well as from other angry dissidents determined to challenge what they deemed to be unacceptable. As a result, anger against the South now extended well beyond abolitionists, anti-slavery Whigs, and a few hostile Democrats, to include a larger number of political activists, especially among some of those Democrats who had long been defenders of the slave states, ultimately to be joined, in their outlook and intense hostility, by many of the voters who supported them in their home districts on election day.

THE CRITICAL TURNING POINT embedded in the Texas crisis was the powerful loss of faith it engendered among these latter elements due to the way that others—meaning southerners—had acted. The Van Buren Democrats and all that they stood for, those men who had been, and continued to believe that they were, the heart and core of the Democratic Party, felt that their party had been hijacked by those who would corrupt it on behalf of "Mr. Calhoun's sectional minority policy." They were appalled, and the consequences were severe. Their unhappy feelings surfaced, not just once but, rather, several times, and raised each time intensely expressed, dismaying questions about the future direction of American politics and society. As the Connecticut Democratic leader Gideon Welles subsequently wrote, as all of this hostility built up during the Polk years, "confidence and united zeal never again prevailed, and parties subsequently took a sectional or personal character."[6]

WELLES'S COMMENT WENT TOO FAR. The sectional impulses that had been unleashed were effectively brought back under control in 1850, and for a time thereafter confidence returned. "The country was enjoying a remarkable state of repose," a Maine congressman recalled; "the waves of agitation, which in former years had rolled over the country, had abated their fury, and ceased to disturb the peace or threaten the perpetuity of the Union."[7] But that welcome condition (to most) survived only briefly. When, in 1854 and the years following, memories of Texas were again brought to the surface of public affairs by the Kansas-Nebraska undertaking and the even more intense fallout from it, political revolution moved into high gear. The country found that it had moved very far along the road toward the sectionalizing of its politics, both rhetorically and behaviorally.

The surge of sectional anger associated with the Texas controversy crystallized, focused, structured, and then anchored what had previously been inchoate and ephemeral. Americans found that annexation and its fallout had created a perspective, an attitude, among many of them that was to have significant impact after it was reawakened in Kansas, in the Senate, by the Supreme Court, and in the actions of Presidents Pierce and Buchanan. When similar-appearing matters came to the center of the political stage, memories of Texas infused what subsequently happened with certain fears, outlooks that approached the edge of paranoia, and deeply held understandings about how the political process was being misused. At such moments Texas became a benchmark against which to measure and assess the nature and direction of the events coming before the American people. Most of all, it suggested, again and again, too many dark and evil political doings designed to secure southern interests unfairly at the expense of the North's legitimate concerns. For the good of the nation and those legitimate interests, southern overreach had to be stopped.

Looking back, as happens in most historical episodes, the impact of contingency on what happened in the Texas controversy was profound—most strikingly, the obviously unexpected deaths of three major political figures: President Harrison, which brought into office the ardent expansionist John Tyler; then Abel Upshur, which brought into office the ardent sectionalist John C. Calhoun; and, finally, Silas Wright, which led the Van Buren bloc to cross the line from fuming opposition to President Polk into outright rebellion against southern domination. Nevertheless, the presence of such happenstance did not cause anyone to hesitate in the way he reacted and what he did. Northern political leaders did not believe that all that was going on was accidental or unintended, and they were uninterested in notions of the force of contingencies that no one could have foreseen on their fortunes. To them, there was more to events than that.

WHICH RETURNS THE SEARCH for understanding, once more, to the spectacular political failure found in this affair. Successful political parties, and the systems in which they are embedded, are bounded by a range of understandings, the accommodation of different pressures through careful balancing acts among the groups involved, willing submission by their members to agreements made, and an acceptance of compromise about personnel and policies as a normal and necessary approach to political life and to governing. Trust that everyone will live up to what has been worked out and agreed to is the fulcrum on which much that makes the system functional turns. That necessary trust was lost among the ruling Democrats in these years. Their northern bloc's sense of betrayal and the loss of confidence in the good faith and intentions of others within the system became overwhelming, remained so, and were constantly reinforced when new initiatives in the territories and in Washington continued to evoke sharp memories filtered through the lens of the Texas episode.

Although complete sectional unity was never achieved in the upheaval of the mid- and late fifties, either in the North or the South, as this intense realignment bit in, the balance of forces shaping political life clearly shifted very far toward the sectional impulse. To its opponents in the North, the Pierce and Buchanan Democrats had become the "southern sectional party," having lost their soul and purpose in weak-kneed submission to the slave power.[8] To its enemies in the South, the growing Republican coalition was bent on destroying the slave states, while their former northern Democratic allies had assaulted them unfairly and then betrayed them. In this situation, effective containment of the sectional impulse on either side of Mason and Dixon's line became all but impossible, with the violent results that followed from that failure.

All of this brings focus, once again, to Texas and all that was connected with it in the years after 1844. The episode that erupted then can be likened to the proverbial piece of string that when pulled began to unravel, if slowly at first, the ball of which it was part—in this case, the existing partisan political order—until little was left of its original shape. Or, to change the metaphor, Texas annexation turned out to be another sudden, resounding fire bell in the night, one that rang longer and louder, and ultimately with more effect, than any that had preceded it.

NOTES

Preface

1. Washington *National Intelligencer,* June 8, 1847.

2. *Congressional Globe,* 28th Cong., 2d Sess., 351.

3. Kenneth M. Stampp, *America in 1857: A Nation on the Brink* (New York, 1990).

4. Justin H. Smith, *The Annexation of Texas* (New York, 1911); Frederick Merk (with the collaboration of Lois Bannister Merk), *Manifest Destiny and Mission in American History: A Reexamination* (New York, 1965); idem, *Fruits of Propaganda in the Tyler Administration* (Cambridge, Mass., 1971); idem, *Slavery and the Annexation of Texas* (New York, 1972); Charles G. Sellers, *James K. Polk: Continentalist, 1843–1846* (Princeton, 1966); David M. Pletcher, *The Diplomacy of Annexation: Texas, Oregon, and the Mexican War* (Columbia, Mo., 1973); Charles G. Sellers, *The Market Revolution: Jacksonian America, 1815–1846* (New York, 1991); Michael F. Holt, *The Rise and Fall of the American Whig Party: Jacksonian Politics and the Onset of the Civil War* (New York, 1999); Michael A. Morrison, *Slavery and the American West: The Eclipse of Manifest Destiny and the Coming of the Civil War* (Chapel Hill, 1997).

5. Dixon H. Lewis to Richard K. Cralle, March 19, 1844, in Robert L. Meriwether et al., eds., *The Papers of John C. Calhoun* (Columbia, S.C., 1959–2003, 27: 879.

Prologue

1. This session took place on February 27. The events are described in J. Y. Bryan, "Texas by a Nose," *Southwest Review* 55 (Spring 1970): 65–174. The quotation is from Justin H. Smith, *The Annexation of Texas* (New York, 1911), 345.

2. Tyler's message is in James D. Richardson, comp., *A Compilation of the Messages and Papers of the Presidents* (Washington, 1905), 4:334–52; his call for a joint resolution is at 343–45.

3. James Shields to Sidney Breese, February 19, 1845, Sidney Breese Papers, Illinois State Historical Society; Adams's remark, written in his diary, is quoted in Smith, *Annexation of Texas,* 221.

4. See Smith, *Annexation of Texas*, Chapter 16.

5. Ibid., 344–46.

6. David M. Pletcher, *The Diplomacy of Annexation: Texas, Oregon, and the Mexican War* (Columbia, Mo., 1973), 180–82; Michael F. Holt, *The Rise and Fall of the American Whig Party: Jacksonian Politics and the Onset of the Civil War* (New York, 1999), 221.

7. *Congressional Globe,* 28th Cong., 2d Sess., 371–72.

8. Andrew Jackson to Francis P. Blair Sr., April 10, 1845, quoted in Michael A. Morrison, *Slavery and the American West: The Eclipse of Manifest Destiny and the Coming of the Civil War* (Chapel Hill, 1997), 38.

9. Richmond *Enquirer,* March 3, 1845. There was still one more congressional action necessary. In December 1845, the two houses accepted the state constitution submitted to them by the Texans and formally admitted the territory into the Union as the twenty-eighth state. See Smith, *Annexation of Texas,* 466–68.

Chapter 1

1. On Austin, see Gregg Cantrell, *Stephen F. Austin, Empresario of Texas* (New Haven, 1999).

2. A recent introduction to Texas's history is Randolph B. Campbell, *Gone to Texas: A History of the Lone Star State* (New York, 2003).

3. Randolph B. Campbell, *An Empire for Slavery: The Peculiar Institution in Texas, 1821–1865* (Baton Rouge, 1989), Chapters 1 and 2.

4. On economic conditions generally, and about the panic, see Douglas C. North, *The Economic Growth of the United States, 1790–1860* (Englewood Cliffs, N.J., 1961); Paul Wallace Gates, *The Farmer's Age: Agriculture, 1815–1860* (New York, 1960); Peter Temin, *The Jacksonian Economy* (New York, 1969); Reginald C. McGrane, *The Panic of 1837: Some Financial Problems of the Jacksonian Era* (Chicago, 1924).

5. James D. Richardson, comp., *A Compilation of the Messages and Papers of the Presidents* (Washington, 1905), 3:268.

6. On Texas's activities, see Justin H. Smith, *The Annexation of Texas* (New York, 1911), Chapters 3 and 4. The quoted words are from "To the Citizens of the United States of the North," an address issued by the General Council of Texas, October 26, 1835, rpt. in New Orleans *Bulletin,* November 14, 1835.

7. The seven new western states admitted between 1815 and 1836 were Indiana, Alabama, Mississippi, Illinois, Missouri, Michigan, and Arkansas.

8. David M. Pletcher, *The Diplomacy of Annexation: Texas, Oregon, and the Mexican War* (Columbia, Mo., 1973), 70–72. Among the Americans who went to fight were a group of Tennessee volunteers led by Davy Crockett, who died at the Alamo.

9. On America's expansionist impulse, see William Appleman Williams, *The Roots of the Modern American Empire: A Study in the Growth and Shaping of Social Consciousness in a Marketplace Society* (New York, 1969); Albert Weinberg, *Manifest Destiny: A Study of Nationalist Expansionism in American History* (Baltimore, 1935); Charles Vevier, "American Continentalism: An Idea of Expansion," *American Historical Review* 65 (January 1960), 323–35; Frederick Merk (with the collaboration of Lois Bannister Merk), *Manifest Destiny and Mission in American History: A Reinterpretation* (New York, 1965).

10. Pletcher, *Diplomacy of Annexation,* 70.

11. Elgin Williams, *The Animating Pursuits of Speculation: Land Traffic in the Annexation of Texas* (New York, 1968) begins the discussion of this topic.

12. In addition to the works cited in note 9, see also Reginald Horsman, *Race and Manifest Destiny* (Cambridge, Mass., 1981) and Thomas Hietala, *Manifest Design: Anxious Aggrandizement in Late Jacksonian America* (Ithaca, 1985).

13. This was John Quincy Adams's position, expressed in 1838, quoted in Lynn Hudson Parsons, *John Quincy Adams* (Madison, 1998), 231.

14. Pletcher, *Diplomacy of Annexation,* 72ff. describes these matters in succinct form. A more extended if somewhat outdated treatment is George L. Rives, *The United States and Mexico, 1821–1848,* 2 vols. (New York, 1913).

15. On Adams, in addition to Parsons's book, see also Samuel Flagg Bemis, *John Quincy Adams and the Union* (New York, 1956) and Leonard Richards, *The Life and Times of Congressman John Quincy Adams* (New York, 1986).

16. John Caldwell Calhoun to Mrs. Thomas G. Clemson, April 22, in J. Franklin Jameson, ed., *The Correspondence of John C. Calhoun,* Annual Report of the American Historical Association for 1899, vol. 2 (Washington, 1900), 513. Adams's attitudes toward and relationship with anti-slavery forces are well covered in the various biographies cited in note 15.

17. On these men, see James Brewer Stewart, *William Lloyd Garrison and the Challenge of Emancipation* (Arlington Heights, Ill., 1992); Robert H. Abzug, *Passionate Liberator: Theodore Dwight Weld and the Dilemma of Reform* (New York, 1980); Merton L. Dillon, *Benjamin Lundy and the Struggle for Negro Freedom* (Urbana, 1966); and Hugh Davis, *Joshua Leavitt, Evangelical Abolitionist* (Baton Rouge, 1990).

18. In addition to the biographies listed in note 17, see also Betty Fladeland, *James G. Birney: Slaveholder to Abolitionist* (Ithaca, 1955).

19. Much of this activity was being stimulated by Democratic Party members such as Thomas Ritchie of Virginia. See Donald B. Cole, *Martin Van Buren and the American Political System* (Princeton, 1984), 203.

20. Pletcher, *Diplomacy of Annexation,* 73–74.

21. On the Treaty of 1819, see Samuel Flagg Bemis, *John Quincy Adams and the Foundations of American Foreign Policy* (New York, 1949).

22. Donald B. Cole, *The Presidency of Andrew Jackson* (Lawrence, Kans., 1993), 130–33; Bradford Perkins, *The Creation of a Republican Empire* (New York, 1993), 179.

23. Richardson, *Messages and Papers* 3:268; Cole, *Presidency of Jackson,* 266–67.

24. On Van Buren, see, in addition to Cole's book cited in note 19, John Niven, *Martin Van Buren and the Romantic Age of American Politics* (New York, 1983). My description of Van Buren's frame of mind is drawn from these biographies and from Joel H. Silbey, *Martin Van Buren and the Emergence of American Popular Politics* (Lanham, Md., 2002).

25. Major L. Wilson, *The Presidency of Martin Van Buren* (Lawrence, Kans., 1984), 149–52.

26. Ibid.

27. All of the biographies well describe Van Buren's dealing with the Panic of 1837; for example, Silbey, *Van Buren,* 115–23. Also see James C. Curtis, *The Fox at Bay: Martin Van Buren and the Presidency, 1837–1841* (Lexington, Ky., 1970), passim.

28. Wilson, *Presidency of Van Buren,* 157–63; Curtis, *Fox at Bay,* 152ff.

29. Pletcher, *Diplomacy of Annexation,* 72–84.

30. Richard P. McCormick, *The Second American Party System: Party Formation in the Jacksonian Era* (Chapel Hill, 1966) traces the origins of the national parties; Joel H. Silbey, *The American Political Nation, 1838–1893* (Stanford, 1991) describes the party period at high tide. Horace Greeley, "The Grounds of Difference Between the Contending Parties," *Whig Almanac, 1843* (New York, 1843) spells out the wide policy gap separating Whigs from Democrats.

31. This intense rhetorical quality in the political world is discussed in Silbey, *American Political Nation,* Chapter 5. The quotation is in ibid., 75.

32. As revealed in the title of this article, and the discussion of the phenomenon therein: Joel H. Silbey, "'To One or Another of These Parties Every Man Belongs': The American Political Experience from Andrew Jackson to the Civil War," in Byron E. Shafer and Anthony J. Badger, eds., *Contesting Democracy: Substance and Structure in American Political History* (Lawrence, Kans., 2001), 65–92.

33. Washington *Globe,* August 11, 1838; Milledgeville (Ga.) *Federal Union,* January 30, 1849.

34. Quoted in Silbey, *American Political Nation,* 88.

35. There is an enormous literature tracing the sectional element in American life going back at least to Frederick Jackson Turner, *The Significance of Sections in American History* (New York, 1932) and coming up to, most recently, Don E. Fehrenbacher, completed and ed. Ward M. McAfee, *The Slaveholding Republic: An Account of the United States Government's Relations to Slavery* (New York, 2001).

36. The best introduction to nineteenth-century southern thought about slavery, society, and politics is William Freehling, *The Road to Disunion: Secessionists at Bay, 1776–1854* (New York, 1990). See also James Oakes, *Slavery and Freedom: An Interpretation of the Old South* (New York, 1990).

37. A useful examination of this outlook is William J. Cooper, *The South and the Politics of Slavery, 1828–1856* (Baton Rouge, 1978).

38. Richmond *Whig,* April 7, 1835.

39. There are many biographies of Calhoun, most recently John Niven, *John C. Calhoun and the Price of Union* (Baton Rouge, 1988) and Irving H. Bartlett, *John C. Calhoun: A Biography* (New York, 1993).

40. James Brewer Stewart, *Holy Warriors: The Abolitionists and American Slavery* (New York, 1976) is a well-done, succinct examination of the movement.

41. Daniel Walker Howe, *The Political Culture of the American Whigs* (Chicago, 1979) and Michael F. Holt, *The Rise and Fall of the American Whig Party: Jacksonian Politics and the Onset of the Civil War* (New York, 1999) discuss the northern Whigs.

42. Glover Moore, *The Missouri Controversy, 1819–1821* (Lexington, Ky., 1953) and Leonard L. Richards, *The Slave Power: The Free North and Southern Domination* (Baton Rouge, 2000) describe the Missouri flare-up.

43. Freehling, *Road to Disunion,* 308–52 ably analyzes the gag-rule battle.

44. John Quincy Adams, for example, tormented his southern colleagues in the House of Representatives by repeatedly trying to bring to the floor abolitionist petitions despite the rule. Some of the southerners moved to censure him for his efforts. See Parsons, *Adams,* 224–29.

45. Cleveland *Plain Dealer,* May 5, 1845.

46. James K. Polk to William R. Rucker, February 22, 1836, in Herbert Weaver, et al., eds., *Correspondence of James K. Polk* (Nashville, 1969–), 3:511.

47. Holt, *Rise and Fall of Whig Party,* 252.

48. Philadelphia *Pennsylvanian,* February 5, 1845.

49. Mobile *Register,* November 12, 1842.

50. On Jefferson, see, most recently, Robert W. Tucker and David C. Hendrickson, *Empire of Liberty: The Statecraft of Thomas Jefferson* (New York, 1990).

51. *Congressional Globe,* 28th Cong., 2d Sess., Appendix, 227; George W. Dallas to Rody Patterson et. al., January 1, 1844, George W. Dallas Papers, Historical Society of Pennsylvania.

52. Columbus *Ohio State Journal,* March 16, 1842; Howe, *Political Culture of American Whigs,* 143.

53. Michael A. Morrison, "'New Territory versus No Territory': The Whig Party and the Politics of Western Expansion, 1846–1848," *Western Historical Quarterly* 23 (February 1992), 43; Henry Clay to John Jordan Crittenden, December 5, 1843, in Mrs. Chapman Coleman, *Life of John J. Crittenden with Selections from his Correspondence* (Philadelphia, 1873), 1:209; Daniel Webster to Abijah Bigelow et al., January 23, 1844, in Charles M. Wiltse, ed., *The Papers of Daniel Webster* (Hanover, N.H., 1974–89), 6:20.

54. To be sure, there were some dissenters from their party's position among both the Whigs and Democrats. That, however, while complicating the argument somewhat, does not detract from the main point that there were clear differences present between the bulk of the members of each coalition on the issue.

Chapter 2

1. The basic books on which to build an understanding of Tyler and his administration begin with Robert Seager II, *And Tyler Too: A Biography of John and Julia Gardiner Tyler* (New York, 1963) and Norma L. Peterson, *The Presidencies of William Henry Harrison and John Tyler* (Lawrence, Kans., 1989). William Freehling, *The Road to Disunion: Secessionists at Bay, 1776–1854* (New York, 1990), 355ff. and Michael Holt, *The Rise and Fall of the American Whig Party: Jacksonian Politics and the Onset of the Civil War* (New York, 199), Chapter 6 each add a great deal of insight as well.

2. On the Whig victory in the election of 1840 behind Harrison and Tyler, see Robert L. Gunderson, *The Log Cabin Campaign* (Lexington, Ky., 1957) and Holt, *Rise and Fall of Whig Party,* 101–13.

3. George R. Poage, *Henry Clay and the Whig Party* (Chapel Hill, 1936), Robert V. Remini, *Henry Clay, Statesman for the Union* (New York, 1991), 561ff. and Holt, *Rise and Fall of Whig Party,* 127ff. deal with the first Whig administration, the transition to Tyler, and the problems that followed.

4. All of this is discussed in the books cited in note 3.

5. Holt, *Rise and Fall of Whig Party,* 137.

6. The corporal's guard consisted of a few Virginians such as Thomas Gilmer and Henry Wise, as well as stray congressmen from other states. Tyler's position is well discussed in the sources referred to in note 1.

7. In addition to those works already cited, see also Frederick Merk (with the collaboration of Lois Bannister Merk), *Fruits of Propaganda in the Tyler Administra-*

tion (Cambridge, Mass., 1971) and their *Slavery and the Annexation of Texas* (New York, 1972).

8. Edward Crapol, "John Tyler and the Pursuit of National Destiny," *Journal of the Early Republic* 17 (Fall 1997): 467–91; the quotation is at 484–85. William Freehling does a fine job of discussing Upshur's ideology and plans, referring to him as "the zealot ultimately most responsible for pushing President Tyler and the nation toward annexation." *Road to Disunion,* 357; see also 357ff. The standard biography of the secretary of state is Claude H. Hall, *Abel Parker Upshur, Conservative Virginian* (Madison, 1963).

9. Among the many works on Tyler already cited, especially see Peterson, *Presidencies of Harrison and Tyler,* 206ff. Tyler wanted, she writes, "to use a simple 'benefit to the nation' theme in annexation propaganda" (209).

10. James D. Richardson, comp., *A Compilation of the Messages and Papers of the Presidents* (Washington, 1905), 4:324, 355; U.S. Congress, 28th Cong., 1st Sess., House of Representatives, *Documents*, #260, 4.

11. Merk, *Slavery and the Annexation of Texas,* 201ff.; U.S. Congress, 28th Cong., 1st Sess., House of Representatives, *Documents,* #189; ibid., Senate, *Documents,* #215.

12. Robert J. Walker to Andrew Jackson, January 8, 1844, in John Spencer Bassett, ed., *The Correspondence of Andrew Jackson* (Washington, 1926–35), 6:255; William M. Meigs, *The Life of Charles Jared Ingersoll* (Philadelphia, 1897), 257ff.

13. James Shenton, *Robert John Walker: A Politician from Jackson to Lincoln* (New York, 1961) is the standard scholarly biography. There is also a great deal about him in Merk, *Fruits of Propaganda.*

14. David M. Pletcher, *The Diplomacy of Annexation: Texas, Oregon and the Mexican War* (Columbia, Mo., 1973), 140. The letter is reprinted in Merk, *Fruits of Propaganda,* 221–52.

15. See Reginald Horsman, *Race and Manifest Destiny* (Cambridge, Mass., 1981), 215–17.

16. Merk, *Fruits of Propaganda,* 123; *United States Democratic Review* 16 (December 1845), 162; Andrew Jackson to Thomas Hart Benton, May 14, 1844, in Bassett, *Correspondence of Jackson* 6:293. Also see the speech of Senator James Buchanan, June 8, 1844, in John Bassett Moore, ed., *The Works of James Buchanan, Comprising His Speeches, State Papers, and Private Correspondence* (Philadelphia, 1908–11), 6:5–44.

17. Lynn H. Parsons, *John Quincy Adams* (Madison, 1998), 255, 261; Pletcher, *Diplomacy of Annexation,* 115–16.

18. Ibid. The quotation is in Justin H. Smith, *The Annexation of Texas* (New York, 1911), 132.

19. The treaty negotiations, first under Upshur, then under Calhoun, were conducted in secret. Pletcher refers to Tyler's desire to "avoid open discussion of annexation during the early months of 1843." Pletcher, *Diplomacy of Annexation,* 116.

20. Pletcher discusses the seizure of Monterey in ibid., 100–101.

21. On American-British relations in the early 1840s, in addition to Pletcher, see Howard Jones, *To the Webster-Ashburton Treaty . . . 1783–1843* (Chapel Hill, 1977) and Frederick Merk, *The Oregon Question: Essays in Anglo-American Diplomacy and Politics* (Cambridge, Mass., 1967). Ingersoll's quotation can be found in his published and widely distributed statement, "Mr. C. J. Ingersoll's View of the Texas Question" (Washington, 1844), 11.

22. In addition to the books cited in note 21, also see Robert Remini, *Daniel Webster: The Man and His Time* (New York, 1997), the most recent of many studies of Webster.

23. Moore, *Works of Buchanan* 6:44. See also Sam W. Haynes, "Anglophobia and the Annexation of Texas: The Quest for National Security," in Sam W. Haynes and Christopher Morris, eds., *Manifest Destiny and Empire: American Antebellum Expansion* (College Station, 1997), 115–45.

24. Philadelphia *Pennsylvanian,* June 29, 1844.

25. "Ingersoll's View," 14; *Congressional Globe,* 28th Cong., 1st Sess., Appendix, 775; George Bancroft to Martin Van Buren, May 23, 1844, in "Van Buren–Bancroft Correspondence," Massachusetts Historical Society *Proceedings* 42 (1908–9), 428.

26. Pletcher, *Diplomacy of Annexation,* 135–36; Peterson, *Presidencies of Harrison and Tyler,* 202–3.

27. Peterson, *Presidencies of Harrison and Tyler,* 211ff.

28. All of Calhoun's biographers expend a great deal of effort discussing his persistent fears about the South's situation within the nation. See, most recently, Irving Bartlett, *John C. Calhoun: A Biography* (New York, 1993), Chapter 17. The most extensive study of him is the quite old but still insightful Charles M. Wiltse, *John Calhoun,* 3 vols. (Indianapolis, 1944–51). The final volume, *John C. Calhoun: Sectionalist, 1840–1850,* is the most relevant to the concerns being considered here. The southern political context in which Calhoun operated, and which he tried so hard to shape, is the subject of Freehling, *Road to Disunion,* especially Parts 5 and 6.

29. This is drawn from the books cited in note 28. See also Joel H. Silbey, "John C. Calhoun and the Limits of Southern Congressional Unity, 1841–1850," *Historian* 30 (November 1967): 58–71.

30. Smith, *Annexation of Texas,* 221ff.

31. The Pakenham letter is John C. Calhoun to Richard Pakenham, April 18, 1844, in Robert L. Meriwether et al., eds., *The Papers of John C. Calhoun* (Columbia, S.C., 1959–2003), 18:273–81. The North Carolinian's comment is quoted in Marc A. Kruman, *Parties and Politics in North Carolina, 1836–1865* (Chapel Hill, 1983), 110.

32. John C. Calhoun to Richard Pakenham, April 27, 1844, in Meriwether et al., *Papers of Calhoun* 18:299ff; James Gadsen to Calhoun, May 3, 1844, in J. Franklin Jameson, ed., *The Correspondence of John C. Calhoun,* Annual Report of the American Historical Association for 1899, vol. 2 (Washington, 1900), 952–53.

33. Andrew Jackson to Francis P. Blair, May 11, 1844, in Bassett, *Correspondence of Jackson* 6:287.

34. On Duff Green in London, see Freehling, *Road to Disunion,* 385–87 and Peterson, *Presidencies of Harrison and Tyler,* 178ff. Thomas Hart Benton's comment is in his memoirs, *Thirty Years' View . . . ,* (New York, 1854–56), 2:581.

35. Frederick Merk (with the collaboration of Lois Bannister Merk), *The Monroe Doctrine and American Expansion, 1843–1849* (New York, 1966), 18–20; Peterson, *Presidencies of Harrison and Tyler,* 178–79.

36. The internal difficulties facing the Democrats in the early 1840s is the subject of James C. N. Paul, *Rift in the Democracy* (Philadelphia, 1951). On the Whig troubles under Tyler, see Holt, *Rise and Fall of Whig Party,* 122ff. On the gag-rule problem for the South, see Freehling, *Road to Disunion,* 349–52.

37. Abel P. Upshur to John C. Calhoun, August 14, 1843, quoted in Merk, *Slavery and Annexation,* 20.

38. On reactions to the letter, see Benton, *Thirty Years' View* 2:589ff. and Smith, *Annexation of Texas,* 202ff.

39. Calhoun himself wrote, "I have succeeded by *a bold unhesitating course* [italics added] to secure Annexation." Calhoun to Mrs. Thomas G. Clemson, May 22, 1845, in Jameson, *Correspondence of Calhoun,* 657.

40. *Congressional Globe,* 28th Cong., 1st Sess., Appendix, 699. According to one of his biographers, Senator Benton "roared for three days" in the Senate's secret session on the Texas treaty. Elbert B. Smith, *Magnificent Missourian: The Life of Thomas Hart Benton* (Philadelphia, 1958), 195. Francis P. Blair to Andrew Jackson, July 7, 1844, in Bassett, *Correspondence of Jackson* 6:300.

41. Eric Foner, "The Wilmot Proviso Revisited," *Journal of American History* 56 (September 1969): 267–79; Silas Wright to John L. Russell, May 15, 1844, in Ransom H. Gillet, *The Life and Times of Silas Wright* (Albany, 1874), 2:1518. Also see William B. Lewis to Andrew Jackson, April 26, 1844, in Bassett, *Correspondence of Jackson* 6:280n.

42. Philadelphia *Pennsylvanian,* December 13, 1844. The Tappan episode is discussed and placed in context in Daniel Feller, "A Brother in Arms: Benjamin Tappan and the Antislavery Democracy," *Journal of American History* 88 (June 2001), 48–74.

43. On southern reactions, see Freehling, *Road to Disunion,* 413ff.; on northern reactions, see, among others, Feller, "Tappan," 66.

44. Allan Nevins, ed., *The Diary of John Quincy Adams, 1794–1845* (New York, 1951), entry of April 22, 1844, 569.

45. As one South Carolinian wrote to Calhoun, in words echoing much that other southerners voiced throughout the battle: "I think the possession of Texas as a British colony would be a just cause of war, and if the non-slaveholding States oppose its admission upon the ground of its strengthening the slaveholding interests, etc., we will be bound in self respect and self preservation to join Texas with or without the Union." Francis W. Pickens to John C. Calhoun, November 24, 1843, in Chauncey S. Boucher and Robert P. Brooks, eds., *Correspondence Addressed to John C. Calhoun, 1837–1849,* Annual Report of the American Historical Association for 1929 (Washington, 1930), 191.

46. See, for example, "Letter of Hon. Levi Woodbury on the Annexation of Texas" (Washington, 1844) and the speech of James Buchanan in May 1844, in Moore, *Works of Buchanan* 6:44.

47. On Clay and the Whig position, see Holt, *Rise and Fall of Whig Party,* 168ff.; U.S. Congress, 28th Cong., 1st Sess., Senate, *Documents*, #166, #402, #61.

48. Holt, *Rise and Fall of Whig Party,* 176–83; Freehling, *Road to Disunion,* 426ff.

49. Holt, *Rise and Fall of Whig Party,* 177.

50. Adams is quoted in Leonard Richards, "The Jacksonians and Slavery," in Lewis Perry and Michael Fellman, eds., *Anti-Slavery Reconsidered* (Baton Rouge, 1979), 99–118. See also Samuel Flagg Bemis, *John Quincy Adams and the Union* (New York, 1956), 357.

51. Richard H. Brown, "The Missouri Crisis, Slavery, and the Politics of Jacksonianism," *South Atlantic Quarterly* 65 (Winter 1966), 55–72; Leonard Richards, *The Life and Times of Congressman John Quincy Adams* (New York, 1986). For different perspectives on the northern Democrats, see John McFaul, "Expediency

and Morality: Jacksonianism and Slavery," *Journal of American History* 62 (June 1975), 24–39; Joel H. Silbey, "'There Are Other Questions Besides That of Slavery Merely': The Democratic Party and Anti-Slavery Politics," in Alan Kraut, ed., *Crusaders and Compromisers: Essays of the Relationship of the Antislavery Struggle to the Antebellum Party System* (Westport, Conn., 1983), 143–75.

52. This is the argument of Silbey, "'There Are Other Questions,'" passim. As the editor of the the *United States Democratic Review* wrote in April 1844, so far as slavery is concerned, that "is not a federal or national, but a local question" (14: 429).

53. Francis P. Blair to Martin Van Buren, March 18, 1844, quoted in William E. Smith, *The Francis Preston Blair Family in Politics* (New York, 1933), 1:151–52.

54. *Congressional Globe,* 28th Cong., 1st Sess., 652.

55. The seven Democratic senators who voted *no* were, in addition to Wright and Benton, Niles of Connecticut and Fairfield of Maine, Benton's Missouri colleague Lewis Atherton, and Allen and Tappan of Ohio: two from New England, two from the Old Northwest, and one from a border slave state.

56. New York *Tribune,* June 11, 13, 1844.

57. Richardson, *Messages and Papers* 4:327.

Chapter 3

1. John Tyler's message to Congress, repeating the arguments in favor of annexation and calling for further action, was sent two days after the treaty was defeated. See James D. Richardson, comp., *A Compilation of the Messages and Papers of the Presidents, 1789–1902* (Washinton, 1905), 4:323–27.

2. Charles G. Sellers Jr., "Election of 1844," in Arthur M. Schlesinger Jr. and Fred Israel, eds., *History of American Presidential Elections* (New York, 1971, 2002), 2:745–861 presents an excellent overview of the run-up to the campaign and what then followed and superbly analyzes the outcome.

3. James C. N. Paul, *Rift in the Democracy* (Philadelphia, 1951) remains a good introduction to the Democrats' travails in the early forties. It should be supplemented by more recent biographies of Martin Van Buren and James K. Polk. On the former, see John C. Niven, *Martin Van Buren: The Romantic Age of American Politics* (New York, 1983) and Donald B. Cole, *Martin Van Buren and the American Political System* (Princeton, 1984); on the latter, see Charles Grier Sellers Jr., *James K. Polk, Continentalist, 1843–1846* (Princeton, 1966) and Thomas M. Leonard, *James K. Polk: A Clear and Unquestionable Destiny* (Wilmington, 2001). The Whigs are well covered in Michael Holt, *The Rise and Fall of the American Whig Party: Jacksonian Politics and the Onset of the Civil War* (New York, 1999) and Robert Remini, *Henry Clay: Statesman for the Union* (New York, 1991).

4. On the traditional issue agendas of the two parties, see, in addition to the citations in notes 2 and 3, Joel H. Silbey, *The American Political Nation, 1838–1893* (Stanford, 1991), Chapter 4.

5. See Niven, *Van Buren* and Remini, *Clay.*

6. My understanding of the mood and expectations of the parties is drawn from the sources in note 3. Calhoun's efforts in 1844 are covered in Irving H. Bartlett, *John C. Calhoun: A Biography* (New York, 1993), Chapter 16.

7. Norma L. Peterson, *The Presidencies of William Henry Harrison and John Tyler* (Lawrence, Kans., 1989), 224ff.; Holt, *Rise and Fall of Whig Party,* 164ff.

8. Aileen Kraditor, "The Liberty and Free Soil Parties," in Arthur M. Schlesinger Jr. and Fred L. Israel, eds., *History of U.S. Political Parties* (New York, 1973), 741–882 is a brief general introduction to the Liberty Party. See also, more recently, Vernon L. Volpe, *Forlorn Hope of Freedom: The Liberty Party in the Old Northwest* (Kent, Ohio, 1990) and John R. McKivigan, ed., *Abolitionism and American Politics and Government* (New York, 1999).

9. Charleston *Mercury,* quoted in the Philadelphia *Pennsylvanian,* July 10, 1843.

10. On the Whigs, see Holt, *Rise and Fall of Whig Party*.

11. Remini, *Clay*, 644–46 covers the convention. The party's statement of principles is printed in Kirk H. Porter and Donald Bruce Johnson, comps., *National Party Platforms, 1840–1964* (Urbana, 1967), 8–9.

11. Quoted in Holt, *Rise and Fall of American Whig Party,* 162.

13. Sellers, *Polk, Continentalist,* 14.

14. Quoted in Sellers, "Election of 1844," 751.

15. Silbey, *Van Buren,* 162–64 briefly sums up the case made against the ex-president.

16. Hendrick B. Wright to James Buchanan, May 1, 1844, and Simon Cameron to Buchanan, January 23, 1844, James Buchanan Papers, Historical Society of Pennsylvania. See also Andrew Johnson to Robert Reynolds, September 9, 1843, and Johnson to A.O.P. Nicholson, February 12, 1844, in Leroy P. Graf et al., *The Papers of Andrew Johnson* (Knoxville, 1957–2000), 1:121, 149; Paul Bergeron, *Antebellum Politics in Tennessee* (Lexington, Ky., 1982), 92.

17. Richard Rush to Charles J. Ingersoll, April 27, 1844, Charles J. Ingersoll Papers, Historical Society of Pennsylvania.

18. The shifting currents within the Democracy are touched on in all of the Van Buren biographies. I have summed up the situation in my *Van Buren,* 162–64. See also Jean E. Friedman, *Revolt of the Conservative Democrats: An Essay in American Political Culture and Political Development, 1837–1844* (Ann Arbor, 1978).

19. William W. Payne to John C. Calhoun, October n.d., 1842, in Robert Meriwether et al., eds., *The Papers of John C. Calhoun* (Columbia, S.C., 1959–2003), 16:482; Edward J. Black to Calhoun, January 8, 1844, in Chauncey S. Boucher and Robert P. Brooks, eds., *Correspondence Addressed to John C. Calhoun, 1837–1849,* Annual Report of the American Historical Association for 1929 (Washington, 1930), 204.

20. See note 18.

21. Robert W. Johannsen, "The Meaning of Manifest Destiny," in Sam W. Haynes and Christopher Morris, eds., *Manifest Destiny and Empire: American Antebellum Expansionism* (College Station, 1997), 7–20. See also the chapter on John L. O'Sullivan and the *Democratic Review* in Edward L. Widmer, *Young America: The Flowering of Democracy in New York City* (New York, 1999), 27–63.

22. The long battle between them for preference is traced in the already cited biographies of each man. John C. Calhoun to James H. Hammond, May 17, 1844, in Meriwether et al., *Papers of Calhoun* 18:534; James Gadsden to Calhoun, January 27, 1844, in J. Franklin Jameson, ed., *The Correspondence of John C. Calhoun*, Annual Report of the American Historical Association for 1899, Vol. 2 (Washington, 1900), 917.

23. Robert M. T. Hunter to John C. Calhoun, October 10, 1843, in Boucher and Brooks, *Correspondence,* 188.

24. Herbert D. A. Donovan, *The Barnburners, . . . 1830–1852* (New York, 1925) still has relevance for understanding what was going on. See also Friedman, *Revolt of Conservative Democrats.* Wright is quoted in Ronald Shaw, *Erie Water West: A History of the Erie Canal, 1792–1854* (Lexington, Ky., 1966), 346.

25. Gideon J. Pillow to James K. Polk, May 24, 1844, Herbert Weaver et al., eds., *Correspondence of James K. Polk* (Nashville, 1969–), 7:151.

26. Sellers, "Election of 1844," 755–57; Niven, *Van Buren,* 512ff., traces Van Buren's rising delegate numbers in the pre-convention period.

27. James L. English to Lewis Cass, May 21, 1844, Lewis Cass Papers, William E. Clements Library, University of Michigan; James J. Faran to William Allen, May 20, 1844, William Allen Papers, Library of Congress; Philadelphia *Pennsylvanian,* February 2, 1844.

28. Silas Wright to Benjamin F. Butler, May 24, 1844, Silas Wright/Benjamin Butler Papers, New York Public Library.

29. Hammet's letter was written in late March and held by Van Buren for almost a month.

30. Niven cogently discusses the letter in his *Van Buren,* 526–30.

31. The entire text of the Hammet letter is conveniently reprinted in Sellers, "Election of 1844," 822–28. The quotation is at 827.

32. Cole, *Van Buren,* 393–95 and Freehling, *Road to Disunion,* 411–13 both discuss some of the reaction. See also Silas Wright to Samuel J. Tilden, April 30, 1844, Samuel J. Tilden Papers, New York Public Library; William J. Brown to Martin Van Buren, April 29, 1844, Martin Van Buren Papers, Columbia University; Hendrick B. Wright to James Buchanan, May 13, 1844, James Buchanan Papers, Historical Society of Pennsylvania.

33. Thomas Ritchie to Howell Cobb, May 23, 1844, in "Three Letters of Thomas Ritchie to Howell Cobb," *John P. Branch Historical Papers of Randolph Macon College* 3 (June 1912): 357. On Ritchie's relationship with Van Buren, see the cited biographies of the latter, and Karen C. Janes, "From Ally to Enemy: Thomas Ritchie and Martin Van Buren, 1835–1848" (M.A. thesis, Cornell University, 1973).

34. Thomas Ritchie to Martin Van Buren, May 5, 1844, in "Unpublished Letters of Thomas Ritchie," *John P. Branch Historical Papers of Randolph Macon College* 3 (June 1911): 251.

35. Job Pierson to James K. Polk, October 15, 1844, in Weaver et al., *Correspondence of Polk* 8:192. Some observers believed then, and others have echoed the notion more recently, that there was some kind of bargain between Clay and Van Buren to issue these letters and remove Texas as an issue from the presidential election. See Remini's cogent discussion of it in *Clay*, 639–40; see also Silbey, *Van Buren,* 173–74.

36. Amos Kendall to Andrew Jackson, August 28, 1844, in Bassett, *Correspondence of Jackson,* 7:316.

37. Silas Wright to Samuel J. Tilden, April 30, 1844, Tilden Papers. On the other hand, Wright was much less hopeful a month later on the day that the convention convened. See Silas Wright to Joel R. Poinsett, May 27, 1844, Joel R. Poinsett Papers, Historical Society of Pennsylvania.

38. Andrew Jackson to Benjamin F. Butler, May 14, 1844, Martin Van Buren Papers, Library of Congress.

39. Niven, *Van Buren,* 535–37 well describes the opening of the convention.

40. See Sellers, *Polk, Continentalist,* 76–85. The proceedings of the convention are reprinted in Sellers, "Election of 1844," 829–52.

41. The balloting is covered in ibid. Van Buren received 127 votes on the second ballot, then 121 and 111 on the third and fourth, reaching a low of 99 on the fifth.

42. The switch to Polk is well covered in Sellers, "Election of 1844," 767–71.

43. Ibid., 773; Robert S. Lambert, "The Democratic National Convention of 1844," *Tennessee Historical Quarterly* 14 (March 1955), 18–19.

44. Cave Johnson to James K. Polk, June 13, 1844, in Weaver et al., *Correspondence of Polk* 7: 248; Silas Wright to Benjamin F. Butler, May 29, 1844, Wright/Butler Letters; Sellers, "Election of 1844," 772–73.

45. George W. Bancroft to E.D. Beach, June 8, 1844, George Bancroft Papers, New York Public Library. In a less celebratory but quite thankful mood, one editor referred to "the deliverance of the party from Van Buren." John W. Forney to James Buchanan, June 11, 1844, Buchanan Papers.

46. John Adams Dix to Azariah Flagg, June 14, 1844, Azariah Flagg Papers, New York Public Library; Silas Wright to Benjamin F. Butler, May 29, 1844, Wright/Butler Letters.

47. William C. Bryant et al. to "Sir," July 17, 1844, printed copy in the Flagg Papers.

48. Ransom H. Gillet, *The Life and Times of Silas Wright* (Albany, 1874), 2:1552–74; George W. Dallas to Henry Muhlenberg, June 5, 1844, George M. Dallas Papers, Historical Society of Pennsylvania.

49. Sellers, "Election of 1844," 784; Holt, *Rise and Fall of Whig Party,* 173.

50. Holt, *Rise and Fall of Whig Party,* 175.

51. As Michael Morrison has written, "the Texas issue, defined and framed by the party's ideology, served to solidify the Democracy" during the campaign. Morrison, "Van Buren and Texas," 697; "The South in Danger. Read Before You Vote. Address of the Democratic Association of Washington, D.C." (Washington, 1844).

52. Sellers, "Election of 1844," 776–78.

53. Ibid., 782. Michael Morrison argues that Democrats "understood expansion to be consistent with the ideological premises of the Democracy and placed annexation within the context of their established policies." Morrison, "Van Buren and Texas," 722–23.

54. William Henry Seward to E. A. Stansbury, September 2, 1844, Salmon P. Chase Papers, Historical Society of Pennsylvania.

55. Freehling, *Road to Disunion,* 436; Holt, *Rise and Fall of Whig Party,* 177ff. The struggle of one prominent southern Whig on the issue is recounted in Thomas E. Schott, *Alexander H. Stephens of Georgia: A Biography* (Baton Rouge, 1996), 59ff.

56. James E. Winston, "Louisiana and the Annexation of Texas," *Louisiana Historical Quarterly* 19 (January 1936), 105; Alexander H. Stephens to James Thomas, May 17, 1844, in Ulrich B. Phillips, ed., *The Correspondence of Robert Toombs, Alexander H. Stephens, and Howell Cobb,* Annual Report of the American Historical Association for 1911 vol. 2, (Washington, 1913), 158.

57. Remini, *Clay,* 659–60.

58. Holt, *Rise and Fall of Whig Party,* 180–83; Freehling, *Road to Disunion,* 435–37.

59. Glyndon G. Van Deusen, *William Henry Seward* (New York, 1967), 102; James Brewer Stewart, *Joshua R. Giddings and the Tactics of Radical Politics* (Cleveland, 1970), 94–97.

60. Philadelphia *Pennsylvanian,* September 11, 1844.

61. The election results are discussed in Sellers, "Election of 1844," 796–98 and Holt, *Rise and Fall of Whig Party,* 196–206. State-by-state returns are listed in Sellers, 861.

62. The new Twenty-ninth Congress would have 143 Democrats and 77 Whigs in the House of Representatives and 31 Democrats and 25 Whigs in the Senate.

63. Both Sellers and Holt discuss the role that Texas played in the result. See Sellers, "Election of 1844," 797–98; Holt, *Rise and Fall of Whig Party,* 200ff. On the impact of the Liberty Party, see Vernon L. Volpe, "The Liberty Party and Polk's Election, 1844," *Historian* 53 (Summer 1991): 691–710.

64. John Fairfield to James K. Polk, September 20, 1844, in Weaver et al., *Correspondence of Polk* 8:100.

65. William G. Shade, *Democratizing the Old Dominion: Virginia and the Second Party System, 1824–1861,* 103.

66. Lee Benson, *The Concept of Jacksonian Democracy: New York as a Test Case* (Princeton, 1961) pioneered in the exploration of the importance of ethnocultural forces in American politics in the 1840s. Holt, *Rise and Fall of Whig Party,* 203–6.

67. Sellers, "Election of 1844," 797–98.

Chapter 4

1. Tyler had been preparing a new message on the issue since October. Norma L. Peterson, *The Presidencies of William Henry Harrison and John Tyler* (Lawrence, Kans., 1989), 250.

2. James D. Richardson, comp., *A Compilation of the Messages and Papers of the Presidents* (Washington, 1905), 4:344.

3. *Congressional Globe,* 28th Cong., 2d Sess., Appendix, 227; New York *Evening Post,* January 23, 1845.

4. Sara E. Lewis, "Digest of Congressional Action on the Annexation of Texas, December 1844 to March 1845," *Southwest Historical Quarterly* 50 (October 1946), 251–68.

5. Peterson, *Presidencies of Harrison and Tyler,* 250–51.

6. New York *Evening Post,* January 23, 1845; Richmond *Enquirer,* January 9, 1845.

7. Silas Wright to John Adams Dix, February 15, 1845, in Ransom H. Gillet, *The Life and Times of Silas Wright* (Albany, 1874), 2:1625; Preston King to Azariah Flagg, January 11, 1845, Azariah Flagg Papers, New York Public Library.

8. Whig senator Willie P. Mangum wrote that "Polk has given a strong impulse to party action on this subject since his arrival." Mangum to William A. Graham, February 21, 1845, in Henry T. Shanks, ed., *The Papers of Willie Persons Mangum* (Raleigh, 1950–56), 4: 271. See also David M. Pletcher, *The Diplomacy of Annexation: Texas, Oregon, and the Mexican War* (Columbia, Mo., 1973), 182–83 and Peterson, *Presidencies of Harrison and Tyler,* 256.

9. Robert Johannsen, *Stephen A. Douglas* (New York, 1973), 157.

10. William W. Freehling, *The Road to Disunion: Secessionists at Bay, 1776–1854* (New York, 1990), 446–47; William Nisbet Chambers, *Old Bullion Benton: Senator from the New West: Thomas Hart Benton, 1782–1858* (Boston, 1956), 277.

11. *Congressional Globe,* 28th Cong., 2d Sess., Appendix, 81.

12. Washington *Globe,* February 20, 1845.

13. *Congressional Globe,* 28th Cong., 2d Sess., Appendix, 122; Holt, *Rise and Fall of Whig Party*, 220.

14. Holt, *Rise and Fall of Whig Party*, 229–21.

15. Ibid.; Freehling, *Road to Disunion,* 441–43.

16. *Congressional Globe,* 28th Cong., 2d Sess., Appendix, 122, 133, 143.

17. New York *Evening Post,* January 24, 1845; Martin Van Buren to John Adams Dix, February 4, 1845, quoted in Martin Lichterman, "John Adams Dix, 1798–1879" (Ph.D. diss., Columbia University, 1952), 140.

18. Freehling, *Road to Disunion,* 440ff.; Johannsen, *Douglas,* 157.

19. Aaron V. Brown to James K. Polk, January 25, 1845, in Herbert Weaver et al., eds., *Correspondence of James K. Polk* (Nashville, 1969–), 9:71; Washington *Globe,* February 27, 1845. The votes are listed and their nature discussed in John R. Collins, "The Mexican War: A Study of Fragmentation," *Journal of the West* 11 (April 1972): 227.

20. Nine Whig senators from the South voted against the joint resolution. Ibid.

21. John Adams Dix to Silas Wright, February 27, 1845, quoted in Richard R. Stenberg, "President Polk and the Annexation of Texas," *Southwestern Social Science Quarterly* 14 (March 1934): 348; Thomas Hart Benton, *Thirty Years' View . . .* (New York, 1854–56), 2:638.

22. James K. Polk to William Haywood, August 9, 1845, in Stenberg, "Polk and Annexation," 345. Certainly the president-elect was kept well informed about the Texas situation as Congress met to deal with it. See Cave Johnson to Polk, December 12, 14, 18, 1844, and Charles J. Ingersoll to Polk, December 12, 1844, all in Weaver et al., *Correspondence of Polk* 8:422, 429, 440, 473.

Chapter 5

1. Justin H. Smith, *The Annexation of Texas* (New York, 1911), 456–60; James D. Richardson, comp., *A Compilation of the Messages and Papers of the Presidents, 1789–1902* (Washington, 1905), 4:386.

2. Kinley J. Brauer, "The Massachusetts State Texas Committee," *Journal of American History* 51 (September 1964), 214–31; see also his *Cotton versus Conscience: Massachusetts Whig Politics and Southwestern Expansion, 1843–1848* (Lexington, Ky., 1967).

3. Philadelphia *Pennsylvanian,* December 18, 1845; Nathan Appleton to Charles Francis Adams et al., November 10, 1845, quoted in Brauer, "Massachusetts State Texas Committee," 225; Smith, *Annexation of Texas,* 467; *United States Democratic Review* 17 (July 1845): 5.

4. Smith, *Annexation of Texas,* 467–58. Florida had been admitted earlier in the year as the twenty-seventh state.

5. On Polk as he entered the presidency, see Charles G. Sellers Jr., *James K. Polk, Continentalist, 1843–1846* (Princeton, 1966).

6. Cave Johnson to James K. Polk, December 18, 1844, in Herbert Weaver et al., eds., *Correspondence of James K. Polk* (Nashville, 1969–), 8:441; Philadelphia *Pennsylvanian,* December 1, 1845; Martin Van Buren to George Bancroft, January 30, 1845, "Van Buren-Bancroft Correspondence," *Massachusetts Historical Society Proceedings* 42 (June 1909): 436.

7. Paul Bergeron, *The Presidency of James K. Polk* (Lawrence, Kans., 1987) nicely covers Polk's term in office.

8. On Polk before his presidency, see Charles G. Sellers Jr., *James K. Polk, Jacksonian, 1795–1843* (Princeton, 1957).

9. Sellers, *Polk, Continentalist,* 4–5, 164ff.

10. By early 1846, one Whig congressman, surveying the Polk administration's first months in office, referred to the 1844 Democratic National Convention as "that Pandora's box, whence originated most of the troubles that now afflict this country." *Congressional Globe,* 29th Cong., 1st Sess., Appendix, 500. On the Whigs' attitude generally as Polk entered office, see Michael F. Holt, *The Rise and Fall of the American Whig Party: Jacksonian Politics and the Onset of the Civil War* (New York, 1999), 232ff.

11. Richardson, *Messages and Papers* 4:377–80.

12. See Bergeron, *Presidency of Polk* and Sellers, *Polk, Continentalist.*

13. David M. Pletcher, *The Diplomacy of Annexation: Texas, Oregon, and the Mexican War* (Columbia, Mo. 1973), passim; Norman A. Graebner, *Empire on the Pacific: A Study in American Continental Expansion* (New York, 1955), passim; Richard Bruce Winders, *Crisis in the Southwest: The United States, Mexico, and the Struggle over Texas* (Wilmington, 2002), passim.

14. "The Twenty-Ninth Congress, Its Men and Measures; Its Professions and Its Principles" (Washington, 1846), rpt. in Joel H. Silbey, ed., *The American Party Battle: Election Campaign Pamphlets, 1828–1876* (Cambridge, Mass., 1999), 1:237; *Congressional Globe,* 29th Cong., 1st Sess., Appendix, 585.

15. James K. Polk to George Bancroft, July 20, 1844, and Polk to Martin Van Buren, July 4, 1845, in Weaver et al., *Correspondence of Polk* 7:372, 9:19.

16. See some of the letters that passed between the New York Democrats and between them and Polk in the transition period leading toward Polk's accession to office: John Adams Dix to Samuel J. Tilden, January 3, 1845, Samuel J. Tilden Papers, New York Public Library; Preston King to Azariah Flagg, February 8, 1845, Azariah Flagg Papers, New York Public Library; Benjamin F. Butler to James K. Polk, November 12, 1844, in Weaver et al., *Correspondence of Polk,* 8:310–11.

17. This is based on the analysis in the biographies of Van Buren: John Niven, *Martin Van Buren: The Romantic Age of American Politics* (New York, 1983), 548ff.; Donald B. Cole, *Martin Van Buren and the American Political System* (Princeton, 1984), 399ff.

18. Aaron V. Brown to James K. Polk, December 29, 1844, in Weaver et al., *Correspondence of Polk,* 8:475.

19. "I am also advised," one of them wrote, "that Wright & VanB will be his advisers in all matters conected with N.Y." John Adams Dix to Samuel J. Tilden, January 3, 1845, Tilden Papers.

20. Silas Wright to James K. Polk, June 2, 1844, and Cave Johnson to Polk, December 18, 26, 1844, in Weaver et al., *Correspondence of Polk* 7:187, 8:441, 467.

21. James K. Polk to Martin Van Buren, January 4, 1845, and Polk to Silas Wright, January 4, 1845, ibid. 9:19, 21; Martin Van Buren to Polk, January 18, 1845, ibid. 9:54–61.

22. John L. O'Sullivan to Samuel J. Tilden, June 3, 1845, Tilden Papers. Joseph Rayback, "Martin Van Buren's Break with James K. Polk: The Record," *New York History* 36 (January 1955): 51–62 is a useful examination of the conflict about to erupt.

23. Sellers, *Polk, Continentalist,* Chapter 5, "The Cabinet and Texas," is an excellent description of Polk's cabinet making. See also Bergeron, *Presidency of Polk,* 23–50.

24. James K. Polk to Silas Wright, December 7, 1844, in Weaver et al., *Correspondence of Polk* 8:410. Wright's refusal and Buchanan's appointment can be followed in Sellers, *Polk, Constitutionalist,* 178–79, 194–96.

25. Sellers, *Polk, Continentalist,* 203–4. The "chess game" remark is in Bergeron, *Presidency of Polk,* 29.

26. The Butler episode is well described in Niven, *Van Buren,* 550ff., among other places.

27. F.F. Marbury to Samuel J. Tilden, February 1, 1846, Tilden Papers; Gouverneur Kemble to James K. Polk, February 25, 1845, in Weaver et al., *Correspondence of Polk*, 9:136.

28. See Martin Van Buren's angry letter to James K. Polk, February 27, 1845, ibid. 9:144.

29. James K. Polk to Andrew Jackson, March 26, 1845, ibid. 9:233; Andrew Jackson to Francis P. Blair, April 9, 1845, in John Spencer Bassett, ed., *The Correspondence of Andrew Jackson* (Washington, 1926–35), 6:396; Milo M. Quaife, ed., *The Diary of James K. Polk During His Presidency, 1845 to 1849* (Chicago, 1910), 1:356–58.

30. John Adams Dix to Azariah Flagg, March 3, 1845, Flagg Papers; John L. O'Sullivan to Samuel J. Tilden, June 3, 1845, Tilden Papers.

31. The party certainly came together effectively in Congress during Polk's first year in office. See Joel H. Silbey, *The Shrine of Party: Congressional Voting Behavior, 1841–1852* (Pittsburgh, 1967), 67ff. See also Azariah Flagg to John W. Lawrence, October 27, 1845, Flagg Papers.

32. James K. Polk to Silas Wright, July 8, 1845, quoted in Sellers, *Polk, Continentalist,* 283.

33. William Dusinberre, *Slavemaster President: The Double Career of James Polk* (New York, 2003).

34. Sellers, *Polk, Continentalist,* 204; Lewis Coryell to John C. Calhoun, May 27, 1845, and Duff Green to Calhoun, June 1, 1845, in Ulrich B. Phillips, ed., *Correspondence Addressed to John C. Calhoun, 1837–1845,* Annual Report of the American Historical Association for 1911, vol. 2 (Washington, 1913), 295, 296.

35. James K. Polk to Benjamin F. Butler, May 5, 1845, in Weaver et al., *Correspondence of Polk* 9: 342.

36. *Polk Diary* 1:104.

37. James K. Polk to Benjamin F. Butler, May 5, 1845, in Weaver et al., *Correspondence of Polk* 9:341. See also James K. Polk to Silas Wright, July 8, 1845, James Polk Papers, Library of Congress; Sellers, *Polk, Continentalist,* 286–87.

38. John L. O'Sullivan to Samuel J. Tilden, June 3, 1845, Tilden Papers.

39. Rayback, "Van Buren's Break with Polk" and Eric Foner, "The Wilmot Proviso Revisited," *Journal of American History* 56 (September 1969): 262–79 discuss the reasons for the Van Burenites' reactions.

40. Foner, "Wilmot Proviso Revisited," passim.

41. See above, Chapter 1.

42. This is the argument of Joel H. Silbey, *Martin Van Buren and the Emergence of American Popular Politics* (Lanham, Md., 2002). Also see above, Chapter 1.

43. The quotation is from Van Buren's meliorating toast at the Jefferson Day Dinner in 1830 when President Jackson and Vice President Calhoun squared off against one another. See Cole, *Van Buren,* 210, among other places. The mutual-forbearance notion is repeatedly discussed in party newspapers. See, for example,

Chicago *Democrat* March 24, 1846; Athens (Ga.) *Southern Banner,* August 5, 1847. See also *Congressional Globe,* 30th Cong., 1st Sess., Appendix, 1183.

44. See, for example, Cleveland *Plain Dealer,* January 15, 1846.

45. As one historian has written, "the Old Republican orthodoxy and the Doctrines of '98 clearly dominated the 'new Democracy' led by James K. Polk as it had the Van Buren generation of Democrats." William G. Shade, *Democratizing the Old Dominion: Virginia and the Second American Party System* (Charlottesville, 1996), 253. The Van Burenites supported the president's stand on the rivers-and-harbors veto, as traditional Democratic ideology dictated that they should.

46. Churchill C. Cambreleng to Joel Poinsett, November 25, 1845, Joel Poinsett Papers, Historical Society of Pennsylvania.

47. Silbey, *Van Buren and Emergence of Popular Politics,* 182ff.

48. At the outset of his administration Polk, whom one historian has called "a skilled political dissimulator," had reportedly told a Van Burenite that he "had acted [in his cabinet making] from misinformation." Freehling, *Road to Disunion,* 447; Samuel J. Tilden to ?, March 4, 1845, Tilden Papers.

49. The sense of estrangement that many of the Van Buren bloc felt is well represented in John Adams Dix to Samuel J. Tilden, December 19, 1845, Tilden Papers.

50. See Pletcher, *Diplomacy of Expansion,* 229ff.

51. Charles Stickney to William Allen, January 19, 1846, William Allen Papers, Library of Congress.

52. Thomas R. Hietala, *Manifest Design: Anxious Aggrandizement in Late Jacksonian America* (Ithaca, 1985) is a useful study that is quite critical of Polk's plans and policies. See also Sellers, *Polk, Continentalist* and Pletcher, *Diplomacy of Annexation*.

53. *Congressional Globe,* 29th Cong., 2d Sess., Appendix, 179.

54. Cleveland *Plain Dealer,* June 16, August 24, 1846.

55. Little Rock *Arkansas Banner,* December 23, 1843; *Congressional Globe,* 28th Cong., 2d Sess., Appendix, 171; John Hope Franklin, "The Southern Expansionists of 1846," *Journal of Southern History* 25 (August 1959), 323–38.

56. Howell Cobb to his wife, June 14, 1846, and John H. Lumpkin to Cobb, November 13, 1846, in Phillips, *Correspondence of Cobb, Toombs, and Stephens,* 81–82, 86.

57. *American Whig Review* 5 (April 1847): 325; *Congressional Globe*, 29th Cong., 2d Sess., 57, 310. John H. Schroeder, *Mr. Polk's War: American Opposition and Dissent, 1846–1848* (Madison, 1973) explores the opposition to the president's war policies. John C. Calhoun, who had returned to the Senate, also vigorously opposed the war. See Niven, *Calhoun,* 335ff.

58. *Congressional Globe,* 29th Cong., 1st Sess., Appendix, 916; 29th Cong., 2d Sess., Appendix, 57, 260, 290, 310, 369. Donald W. Riddle, *Congressman Abraham Lincoln* (Urbana, 1957) examines the behavior of one of Polk's harshest critics in the House of Representatives.

59. John B. Lamar to Howell Cobb, June 24, 1846, in Phillips, *Correspondence of of Cobb, Toombs, and Stephens*, 82.

60. Jonathan H. Earle, "The Undaunted Democracy: Jacksonian Antislavery and Free Soil, 1828–1848" (Ph.D. diss., University of North Carolina, 1996), 361.

61. See, for one example, the extensive discussion of these splits in Walter Ferree, "The New York Democracy: Division and Reunion, 1847–1852" (Ph.D. diss., Univ. of Pennsylvania, 1953).

62. Benjamin Lundy, "The War in Texas, a Review of Facts and Circumstances . . ." (Philadelphia, 1836). The quotation is on the front cover of the pamphlet; Leonard Richards, *The Life and Times of Congressman John Quincy Adams* (New York, 1986).

63. As Thomas Hietala suggests, Polk's handling of the Oregon matter "alienated many northern Democrats and made them more suspicious of their southern counterparts. Like so many other developments after the Baltimore convention, the Oregon settlement seemed a manifestation of a strong prosouthern orientation in the Jacksonian party." Hietala, *Manifest Design,* 238.

64. Leonard L. Richards, *The Slave Power: The Free North and Southern Domination, 1780–1860* (Baton Rouge, 2000) and Don S. Fehrenbacher, completed and ed. Ward M. McAfee, *The Slaveholding Republic: An Account of the United States Government's Relations to Slavery* (New York, 2001) explore the details of this architecture.

65. Freehling, *Road to Disunion,* 403; Benton, *Thirty Years' View,* 638; William L. Henderson to William Allen, February 6, 1846, Allen Papers.

66. Freehling, *Road to Disunion,* 324.

67. See above, Chapter 2.

68. See the discussion of the Democrats and slavery in Chapter 2.

69. Gideon Welles, *Diary,* ed. Howard K. Beale (New York, 1960), 2:387.

70. Although, as Freehling, *Road to Disunion* and Sellers, *Polk: Continentalist* describe throughout their discussions of the Polk administration's behavior on Oregon and other matters, the case was not entirely without enough merit to raise the kind of suspicions that were widespread by mid-1846.

71. David Davis, *The Slave Power Conspiracy and the Paranoid Style* (Baton Rouge, 1969), 61.

72. Morgan A. Dix, comp., *The Memoirs of John Adams Dix* (New York, 1883), 1:205n; Don E. Fehrenbacher, *Chicago Giant: A Biography of "Long John" Wentworth* (New York, 1957), 70.

Chapter 6

1. The Texans were seated in February and March.

2. Although that did not stop such continuing to be expressed in speeches and newspaper editorials.

3. Calhoun's resolutions are printed in U.S. Congress, 30th Cong., 1 Sess., Senate *Miscellaneous Documents,* #8, December 15, 1847.

4. See Michael F. Holt, *The Rise and Fall of the American Whig Party: Jacksonian Politics and the Onset of the Civil War* (New York, 1999) and Kinley J. Brauer, *Cotton versus Conscience: Massachusetts Whig Politics and Southwestern Expansion* (Lexington, Ky., 1967).

5. Albany *Atlas,* September 18, 1846, and November 30, 1848.

6. The background of the Proviso is covered in Chaplain W. Morrison, *Democratic Politics and Sectionalism: The Wilmot Proviso Controversy* (Chapel Hill, 1967), 15ff. See also Charles Going, *David Wilmot, Free Soiler: A Biography of the Great Advocate of the Wilmot Proviso* (New York, 1924).

7. The full text of the amendment reads: "*Provided*, That, as an express and fundamental condition to the acquisition of any territory from the Republic of Mexico by the United States, by virtue of any treaty which may be negotiated

between them, and to the use by the Executive of the moneys herein appropriated, neither slavery nor involuntary servitude shall ever exist in any part of said territory, except for crime, whereof the party shall first be duly convicted."

8. *Congressional Globe,* 29th Cong., 2nd Sess., Appendix, 318; 30th Cong., 1st Sess., Appendix, 1079.

9. See, for example, the speech by the Barnburner leader in the Senate, John A. Dix, in July 1848, ibid., 1182–83.

10. See Morrison, *Democratic Politics and Sectionalism.*

11. See, among other comments, the remarks of Democratic congressmen Strong and Chipman in the *Congressional Globe,* 29th Cong., 2d Sess., Appendix, 320, 323.

12. John Bigelow, ed., *Writings and Speeches of Samuel J. Tilden* (New York, 1885), 2:542.

13. William W. Freehling, *The Road to Disunion: Secessionists at Bay, 1776–1854* (New York, 1990), 462.

14. See the resolutions introduced by Senator Arthur Bagby of Alabama, in U.S. Congress, 30th Cong., 1st Sess., *Senate Miscellaneous Documents,* #35, January 25, 1848.

15. *Congressional Globe,* 29th Cong., 2d Sess., Appendix, 159, 320; Niagara *Democrat* in Albany *Argus,* February 3, 1847; Springfield *Illinois State Register,* April 2, 1847.

16. "Great Speech of the Hon. George Mifflin Dallas upon the Leading Questions of the Day . . ." (Philadelphia, 1847), 14; Philadelphia *Pennsylvanian,* February 15, 1847.

17. Milo M. Quaife, ed., *Diary of James K. Polk During His Presidency from 1845 to 1849 . . .* (Chicago, 1910), 2:305–6, 458–59.

18. A good introduction to this controversy is David M. Potter, completed and ed. Don E. Fehrenbacher, *The Impending Crisis, 1848–1861* (New York, 1976), Chapters 3 and 4.

19. *Congressional Globe,* 30th Cong., 2d Sess., Appendix, 495.

20. Francis P. Blair to Martin Van Buren, December 26, 1846, quoted in Martin Lichterman, "John Adams Dix, 1798–1879" (Ph.D. diss., Columbia University, 1952), 180; *New York Globe,* October 6, 1847.

21. Morrison, *Democratic Politics,* 31ff.; *Congressional Globe,* 30th Cong., 2d Sess., Appendix, 139.

22. One editor summed up that northern Democrats "have evinced a disposition not to surrender national questions and measures for a new and a sectional issue." New York *Globe,* October 14, 1847. See also Michael Morrison, *Slavery and the American West: The Eclipse of Manifest Destiny and the Coming of the Civil War* (Chapel Hill, 1997), 63–65.

23. Albany *State Register,* April 16, 1850.

24. Holt, *Rise and Fall of Whig Party,* 253; Michael Morrison, "'New Territory versus No Territory': The Whig Party and the Politics of Western Expansion, 1846–1848," *Western Historical Quarterly* 23 (February 1992), 25–51.

25. The story of the breakup of the Democratic Party in New York is well told in Walter Ferree, "The New York Democracy: Division and Reunion, 1847–1852," Ph.D. diss., Univ. of Pennsylvania 1953) and Herbert D. A. Donovan, *The Barnburners . . . 1830–1852* (New York, 1925).

26. On Wright's problems, in addition to the works cited in note 25, see also John A. Garraty, *Silas Wright* (New York, 1949).

27. Albany *Atlas,* December 7, 1846; Henry B. Stanton, *Random Recollections* (New York, 1887), 159; Silas Wright to Martin Van Buren, October 14, 1846, quoted in Donovan, *Barnburners,* 76.

28. Morgan Dix, comp., *Memoirs of John Adams Dix* (New York, 1883), 2 vols, I, 227.

29. The Whigs regained control of the House of Representatives in Washington and won governorships in Ohio, North Carolina, and Massachusetts in addition to New York. See Holt, *Rise and Fall of Whig Party,* 208–10, 236ff.

30. As John Niven has written, "divisions over issues had been real enough, but the Barnburners to a man felt the Hunkers had murdered Wright as surely as if they had used a dagger in the dark of night." Niven, *Martin Van Buren: The Romantic Age of American Politics* (New York, 1983), 574. The "regicides" remark is in Azariah Flagg to John A. Dix, August 31, 1847, quoted in Lichterman, "Dix," 195.

31. Quaife, *Diary of Polk* 2:218, 3:153.

32. Albany *Atlas,* June 27, 1848; "Address of the Democratic Members of the Legislature of the State of New York," in Bigelow, *Writing and Speeches of Tilden* 2:562.

33. See "Annexation of Texas," *Massachusetts Historical Society Proceedings* 43 (November 1909): 115, 116; Daniel Feller, "A Brother in Arms: Benjamin Tappan and the Antislavery Democracy," *Journal of American History* 88 (June 2001): 68.

34. Quaife, *Diary of Polk* 4:39, 42.

35. Sellers, *Polk, Continentalist,* 208, 217, 219–20.

36. John L. O'Sullivan to Samuel J. Tilden, April 30, 1848, Samuel J. Tilden Papers, New York Public Library.

37. In addition to Ferree, "New York Democracy" and the biographies of Van Buren, see also Richard Sewell, *Ballots for Freedom: Antislavery Politics in the United States, 1837–1860* (New York, 1976), 152ff., Joseph G. Rayback, *Free Soil: The Election of 1848* (Lexington, Ky., 1970), and Frederick J. Blue, *The Free Soilers: Third Party Politics, 1848–1854* (Urbana, 1973).

38. *United States Democratic Review* 23 (July 1848): 4.

39. See Ferree, "New York Democracy."

40. Oliver C. Gardiner, *The Great Issue; or, The Three Presidential Candidates . . .* (New York, 1848), 104.

41. Benjamin F. Butler to Martin Van Buren, May 29, 1848, in Ferree, "New York Democracy," 180; *Barnburner,* July 29, 1848.

42. The Free Soil platform is printed in Kirk H. Porter and Donald Bruce Johnson, eds., *National Party Platforms, 1840–1964* (Urbana, 1967), 13–14.

43. Few chances were missed to attack the "congenial disunionists of the Van Buren and abolition school," or to characterize John Van Buren as "the leader of these pious disorganizers." Albany *Argus,* November 1, 1848; Philadelphia *Pennsylvanian,* July 24, 1848.

44. Quaife, *Diary of Polk* 4:67.

45. New York *Evening Post,* October 14, 1848; *Barnburner,* August 11, 1848; Ferree, "New York Democracy," 223.

46. Albany *Argus,* November 2, 1848; William L. Marcy to Prosper Wetmore, June 10, 1848, in Ivor D. Spencer, *The Victor and the Spoils: A Life of William L. Marcy* (Providence, 1959), 175.

47. *Congressional Globe,* 30th Cong., 1st Sess., Appendix, 794. On the Whigs generally, see Holt, *Rise and Fall of Whig Party,* Chapter 11.

48. New York *Globe,* November 6, 1848; William Pettit to Gideon Welles, October 28, 1848, Gideon Welles Papers,

49. In addition to Holt's discussion in *Rise and Fall of Whig Party,* see Thomas B. Alexander, "Harbinger of the Collapse of the Second Two-Party System: The Free Soil Party in 1848," in Lloyd Ambrosius, ed., *A Crisis of Republicanism: American Politics During the Civil War Era* (Lincoln, 1990), 17–54.

50. The Democratic vote in New York fell to about half of what it had been four years before; the Whig vote stayed about the same. In Ohio and Indiana, the drop in Whig support was not massive but enough to make a difference. See Holt's chart in *Rise and Fall of Whig Party*, 371.

51. To be sure, party spokesmen were quick to blame "the Kinderhook wire pullers" for the Democrats' loss and to see, as well, the continued relevance of the party instead of believing that there was evidence of a swing away from partisan commitment. *Democratic Review* 23 (December 1848), 482; Albany *Argus,* November 28, 1848.

52. Armistead Burt to Henry W. Conner, February 1, 1847, Henry W. Conner Papers, Library of Congress.

53. Calhoun's activities are well covered in Freehling, *Road to Disunion,* 479ff.

54. John C. Calhoun to Henry W. Conner, February 2, 1849, Conner Papers.

55. *Congressional Globe,* 30th Cong., 2d Sess., Appendix, 189.

56. Charles Grier Sellers Jr., *The Market Revolution: Jacksonian America, 1815–1846* (New York, 19), 425.

Chapter 7

1. Reprinted in Oliver C. Gardiner, *The Great Issue; or, The Three Presidential Candidates . . .* (New York, 1848), 72.

2. *Congressional Globe,* 30th Cong., 2d Sess., Appendix, 236, 231.

3. Charleston *Courier,* March 8, 1850; Alexander H. Stephens to Linton Stephens, January 21, 1850, Alexander H. Stephens Papers, Manhattanville College.

4. The battle over the Oregon territorial settlement is described in David M. Potter, completed and ed. Don E. Fehrenbacher, *The Impending Crisis, 1848–1861* (New York, 1976), 63–76.

5. Thomas B. Stevenson to Caleb B. Smith, February 5, 1849, Caleb B. Smith Papers, Library of Congress; *Congressional Globe,* 30th Cong., 2d Sess., Appendix, 155.

6. Holman Hamilton, *Prologue to Conflict: The Crisis and Compromise of 1850* (New York, 1964); Mark J. Stegmaier, *Texas, New Mexico, and the Compromise of 1850: Boundary Dispute and Sectional Crisis* (Kent, Ohio, 1996); John C. Waugh, *On the Brink of Civil War: The Compromise of 1850 and How It Changed the Course of American History* (Wilmington, 2003).

7. On Douglas, see Robert W. Johannsen, *Stephen A. Douglas* (New York, 1973), Chapters 12 and 13; on Clay, see Robert V. Remini, *Henry Clay: Statesman for the Union* (New York, 1991), Chapter 40.

8. Allan Nevins cogently entitles his chapters on the reaction to the bills passed in 1850 "Southern Acquiescence with Conditions" and "Northern Acquiescence with Reservations." See Nevins, *Ordeal of the Union* (New York, 1947), vol. 1 Chapters 11 and 12.

9. William W. Freehling, *The Road to Disunion: Secessionists at Bay, 1776–1854* (New York, 1990), 509ff.

10. Thelma Jennings, *The Nashville Convention: Southern Movements for Unity* (Memphis, 1980).

11. Michael F. Holt, *The Rise and Fall of the American Whig Party: Jacksonian Politics and the Onset of the Civil War* (New York, 1999), 554, 633.

12. Richard H. Sewell, *Ballots for Freedom: Antislavery Politics in the United States, 1837–1860* (New York, 1976), Chapter 9, "Coalitions," and 231–32.

13. Potter, *Impending Crisis,* 124–30; Columbus *Sentinel* in Charleston *Mercury,* December 16, 1850.

14. Washington *Union,* October 11, 1850; Washington *National Intelligencer,* November 11, 1850; Sam Houston to Robert G. Scott, May 20, 1852, in Amelia W. Williams and Eugene C. Barker, eds., *The Writings of Sam Houston* (Austin, 1938–43), 5:341.

15. Columbus *Ohio State Journal,* November 22, 1850.

16. The "finality" resolutions in the major party platforms are in Kirk H. Porter and Donald B. Johnson, comps., *National Party Platforms, 1840–1964* (Urbana, 1966), 16–18, 20–21.

17. A general overview of the election is in Roy Nichols and Jeannette Nichols, "Election of 1852," in Arthur M. Schlesinger Jr. and Fred L. Israel, eds., *History of American Presidential Elections, 1789–1968* (New York, 1971), 2:921–1003. On the hesitancies and resistance still present, see Holt, *Rise and Fall of Whig Party*, Chapter 20 and Potter, *Impending Crisis*, 231ff.

18. Stephen A. Douglas to Thomas Settle, January 16, 1851, in Robert W. Johannsen, ed., *The Letters of Stephen A. Douglas* (Urbana, 1961), 207.

19. Each national platform reiterated a number of its party's earlier positions on domestic policies such as the tariff and the reach of government power, as did debates in Congress and on the campaign trail.

20. The movements of the Barnburners can best be followed in Walter Ferree, "The New York Democrats: Division and Reunion, 1847–1852" (Ph.D. diss., Univ. of Pennsylvania, 1953).

21. David Yulee to Stephen A. Douglas, February 8, 1853, Stephen A. Douglas Papers, University of Chicago.

22. Roy F. Nichols, *The Democratic Machine, 1850–1854* (New York, 1923) contains many still-useful insights about the tensions within the Democratic Party. Freehling, *Road to Disunion,* 511ff. cogently traces the divisions among southern politicians in the early fifties.

23. Richmond *Enquirer,* August 27, 1851; Springfield *Illinois State Journal,* December 19, 1850.

24. *Congressional Globe,* 30th Cong., 2d Sess., Appendix, 248.

25. Johannsen, *Douglas,* 390–400.

26. Ibid., 400, 405ff. On Cass and popular sovereignty, see Michael Morrison, *Slavery and the American West: The Eclipse of Manifest Destiny and the Coming of the Civil War* (Chapel Hill, 1997), 84–86.

27. Johannsen, *Douglas,* Chapter 17 describes the bill's passage through Congress. See also, for the pressures on Douglas, Roy F. Nichols, "The Kansas-Nebraska Act: A Century of Historiography," *Mississippi Valley Historical Review* 43 (September 1956), 197–212.

28. Douglas's comment is quoted from the memoirs of another senator, Archibald Dixon, in Potter, *Impending Crisis,* 160; Freehling, *Road to Disunion,* 536.

29. Potter, *Impending Crisis,* 163–64; Sewell, *Ballots for Freedom,* 255–57.

30. "Maintain Plighted Faith. Speech of the Honorable Salmon P. Chase . . . Against Repeal of the Missouri Prohibition of Slavery North of 36°, 30'" (Washington, 1854), 4.

31. The quotations are from U.S. Congress, 33d Cong., 1st Sess., *Senate Miscellaneous Documents,* #24 and #62.

32. Kenneth Stampp, *America in 1857: A Nation on the Brink* (New York, 1990), 4. On the racism imbedded in the northern side of the expansion debates, including those over the Wilmot Proviso, see the discussion of this at the appropriate points above in Chapters 1 and 5.

33. New York *Times*, September 25, 1856, quoted in Morrison, *Slavery and the American West,* 169.

34. Blair is quoted in Reginald C. McGrane, *William Allen; A Study in Western Democracy* (Columbus, Ohio, 1925), 136–37; *Congressional Globe,* 33d Cong., 1st Sess., Appendix, 429.

35. *Congressional Globe,* 33d Cong., 1st Sess., Appendix, 557, 1145; 34th Cong., 1st Sess., Appendix, 1067.

36. James G. Blaine, *Twenty Years in Congress: From Lincoln to Garfield . . .* (Norwich, Conn., 1884–86), 1:118; *Congressional Globe,* 34th Cong., 1st Sess., Appendix, 1196. The early uproar that led to the building of an anti-slavery coalition can best be followed in Michael F. Holt, *The Political Crisis of the 1850s* (New York, 1978) and William E. Gienapp, *The Origins of the Republican Party, 1852–1856* (New York, 1987).

37. The further development of the Republican Party after 1854 is the subject of Gienapp, *Origins of the Republican Party.* Its ideological perspective is the subject of Eric Foner, *Free Soil, Free Labor, Free Men: The Ideology of the Republican Party Before the Civil War* (New York, 1970).

38. The electoral realignment of the 1850s is briefly discussed in Joel H. Silbey, *The American Political Nation, 1838–1893* (Stanford, 1991), 156–57 and more fully developed in Holt, *Political Crisis* and Gienapp, *Origins of the Republican Party.*

39. Again, Gienapp and Holt well cover this ground. In the South, the Know Nothing movement, as both authors show, attracted support less for its nativism than because Whigs there saw it as a possible pro-union second national party to challenge the Democrats. See also Holt, *Rise and Fall of Whig Party,* Chapters 23 and 24. The quotation is from "A Few Considerations for Relecting Voters" (New York, 1855), rpt. in Joel H. Silbey, ed., *The American Party Battle: Election Campaign Pamphlets, 1828–1876* (Cambridge, Mass., 1999), 2:57.

40. "A Few Considerations," 69.

41. Holt, *Rise and Fall of Whig Party,* 835–908 has a detailed discussion of the elections of 1853–54.

42. The fragmented state of parties in the House of Representatives led to a great deal of confusion, conflict, and delay when the new Congress met in late 1855, indicating most of all that the forces of northern sectionalism had not yet mastered the landscape. See Joel H. Silbey, "After 'the First Northern Victory': The Republicans Come to Congress, 1855–1856," *Journal of Interdisciplinary History* 20 (Summer 1989): 1–24. The Massachusetts situation is the subject of

John Mulkhearn, *The Know Nothing Party in Massachusetts: The Rise and Fall of a People's Movement* (Boston, 1990).

43. J. W. Taylor to Hamilton Fish, November 11, 1854, quoted in William E. Gienapp, "Nativism and the Creation of a Republican Majority in the North Before the Civil War," *Journal of American History* 72 (December 1985): 531; Stephen A. Douglas to Charles Lanphier, December 12, 1854, in Johannsen, *Letters of Douglas,* 331.

44. Gienapp, *Origins of the Republican Party* well covers the ground through the election of 1856.

45. This is described and analyzed in Holt, *Political Crisis of the 1850s,* Chapter 7.

46. The most recent study of "Bleeding Kansas" is Nicole Etcheson, *Bleeding Kansas: Contested Liberty in the Civil War Era* (Lawrence, Kans., 2004).

47. Holt, *Political Crisis of the 1850s,* 192–94; *Congressional Globe,* 34th Cong., 1st Sess., Appendix, 773.

48. Ibid., 475, 476.

49. The context and substance of Sumner's speech are well covered in David Herbert Donald, *Charles Sumner and the Coming of the Civil War* (New York, 1960), Chapter 11; the "criminal aggressor" remark is in *Congressional Globe,* 34th Cong., 1st Sess, Appendix, 625.

50. William E. Gienapp, "The Crime Against Sumner: The Caning of Charles Sumner and the Rise of the Republican Party," *Civil War History* 25 (September 1979), 218–45; Nevins, *Ordeal of the Union* 2:446–48; Donald, *Sumner,* 298–301.

51. The South's reaction is discussed in Donald, *Sumner,* 297ff.; Avery O. Craven, *The Growth of Southern Nationalism, 1848–1861* (Baton Rouge, 1953), 228–36; Morrison, *Slavery and American West,* 154.

52. Don E. Fehrenbacher, *The Dred Scott Case: Its Significance in American Law and Politics* (New York, 1978); Chicago *Tribune,* April 10, 1857; U.S. Congress, 35th Cong., 1st Sess., *Senate Miscellaneous Documents,* #206; Stampp, *America in 1857,* 105–6.

53. Stampp, *America in 1857,* 104–9.

54. Roy Basler, ed., *The Collected Works of Abraham Lincoln* (New Brunswick, 1953–55), 2:465–66.

55. *Congressional Globe,* 34th Cong., 1st Sess., Appendix, 53; William E. Gienapp, "The Republican Party and the Slave Power," in Robert Abzug and Stephen Maizlish, eds., *New Perspectives on Race and Slavery in America* (Lexington, Ky., 1986), 51–78.

56. Gienapp, *Origins of the Republican Party*, Chapters 12 and 13, detail and analyze the strong condition of the Republicans by 1856.

57. Richmond *Enquirer*, March 2, 1854.

58. Ibid., March 5, 1856; see also Louisville *Democrat,* May 6, 1857, and Milledgeville (Ga.) *Federal Union,* October 10, 1857, among many others.

59. Douglas's party had won the presidential election in 1856 behind James Buchanan and, if losing strength in many parts of the North, still had taken some of the larger states there. On the former Barnburners and their allies in the late fifties, see Foner, *Free Soil,* Chapter 5 and Sewell, *Ballots for Freedom*, 263–64.

60. These numbers are calculated from the returns in Michael J. Dubin, ed., *United States Congressional Elections, 1788–1997* (Jefferson, N.C., 1998).

61. *Congressional Globe,* 34th Cong., 3d Sess., Appendix, 57–58; 35th Cong., 1st Sess., Appendix, 276.

62. Stampp, *America in 1857,* 145.
63. Etcheson, *Bleeding Kansas,* Chapter 7, "Imposing a Constitution Against Their Will."
64. Ibid.
65. Stampp, *America in 1857,* Chapters 6, 10–12.
66. Ibid., 266.
67. *Congressional Globe,* 34th Cong., 1st Sess., Appendix, 203; Louisville *Democrat,* January 7, 1858.
68. U.S. Congress, 35th Cong., 1st Sess., *Senate Miscellaneous Documents*, #206, #232.
69. Johannsen, *Douglas,* 582ff.; Damon Wells, *Stephen Douglas: The Last Years, 1857–1861* (Austin, 1971).
70. Richmond *Enquirer*, July 26, 1858.
71. "Speech of Senator Douglas, of Illinois, on the President's Message Delivered in the Senate of the United States, December 9, 1857" (n.p., n.d.), 15; Johannsen, *Douglas* and Wells, *Douglas: The Last Years* skillfully cover this moment.
72. Potter, *Impending Crisis,* 321.
73. Ibid., 393–95; Stephen A. Douglas to Samuel Treat, February 28, 1858, in Johannsen, *Letters of Douglas,* 418. The most thorough study of the Democratic breakup remains Roy F. Nichols, *The Disruption of the American Democracy* (New York, 1948).
74. *Congressional Globe,* 35th Cong., 1st Sess., 1136.
75. "Admission of Kansas Under the Lecompton Constitution. Speech of Hon. John B. Haskin . . . Against the Admission of Kansas . . . March 10, 1858" (n.p., n. d.), 11; Holt, *Rise and Fall of the American Whig Party,* 981.
76. *Congressional Globe,* 34th Cong., 3d Sess., Appendix, 62.
77. Ibid., 34th Cong., 1st Sess., Appendix, 1069.

Conclusion

1. *Congressional Globe,* 34th Cong., 3d Sess., 62.
2. Events from 1858 to 1861 have been thoroughly explored by many historians. Among the best places to start are David M. Potter, completed and ed. Don E. Fehrenbacher, *The Impending Crisis, 1848–1861* (New York, 1976); Robert Johannsen, *Stephen A. Douglas* (New York, 1973); and Avery O. Craven, *The Growth of Southern Nationalism, 1848–1861* (Baton Rouge, 1953).
3. Potter, *Impending Crisis,* 28.
4. Peter B. Knupfer, *Constitutional Unionism and Sectional Compromise, 1787–1861* (Chapel Hill, 1991) has interesting things to say about notions of compromise and reciprocity in American political culture.
5. *Congressional Globe,* 28th Cong., 2d Sess., Appendix, 351.
6. Ibid., 35th Cong., 1st Sess., Appendix, 277; Gideon Welles, *Diary,* ed. Howard K. Beale (New York, 1960), 2:387.
7. *Congressional Globe,* 34th Cong., 1st Sess., Appendix, 469.
8. Ibid., 35th Cong., 1st Sess., Appendix, 277.

BIBLIOGRAPHIC ESSAY

In writing this book I have drawn largely on contemporary sources: newspapers, the correspondence of public figures, the debates in Congress, and other official documents. In addition, I have relied heavily on the very large body of monographic literature about American expansion, the political scene in the 1840s, and biographies of the main players in the events discussed. The following discussion focuses on a range of the latter material that I found particularly useful as a guide for these who wish to pursue this subject further.

The Expansion Moment

The study of Texas annexation begins with Justin H. Smith's classic, *The Annexation of Texas* (New York, 1911) and David M. Pletcher, *The Diplomacy of Annexation: Texas, Oregon, and the Mexican War* (Columbia, Mo., 1973), which cover the ground admirably. Albert K. Weinberg, *Manifest Destiny: A Study of Nationalist Expansionism in American History* (Baltimore, 1935) is an early but still relevant analysis of the ideological impulses underlining America's expansionist age. More recently, the nation's outward thrust is explored, from often differing perspectives, by William Appleman Williams, *The Roots of Modern American Empire: A Study in the Growth and Shaping of Social Consciousness in a Marketplace Society* (New York, 1969), Richard Van Alstyne, *The Rising American Empire* (New York, 1960), Charles Vevier, "American Continentalism: An Idea of Expansion, 1845–1910," *American Historical Review* 65 (January 1960), 323–35, and Thomas Hietala, *Manifest Design: Anxious Aggrandizement in Late Jacksonian America* (Ithaca, 1985). On its coming to fruition in the 1840s, see, in particular, the works of Frederick Merk, in collaboration with Lois Bannister Merk: *Manifest Destiny and Mission in American History* (New York, 1963); *The Monroe Doctrine and American Expansion, 1843–1849* (New York, 1966); *Fruits of Propaganda in the Tyler Administration* (Cambridge, Mass., 1971); and *Slavery and the Annexation of Texas* (New York, 1972). See also Merk's collection of essays, *The Oregon Question: Essays in Anglo-American Diplomacy and Politics* (Cambridge, Mass., 1967). Norman Graebner, *Empire on the Pacific: A Study in American Continental Expansion* (New York, 1955) and Michael A. Morrison, *Slavery and the American West: The Eclipse of Manifest Destiny and the Coming of the Civil War* (Chapel Hill, 1997) make important contributions to our understanding. The role of speculators in pushing Texas annexation is the subject of Elgin Williams, *The Animating Pursuits of Speculation: Land Traffic in the Annexation of Texas* (New York, new ed., 1968). On racism as a core element in expansionist thinking, see Reginald Horsman, *Race and Manifest Destiny* (Cambridge, Mass., 1981).

America's prickly relations with Great Britain are detailed in Howard Jones, *To the Webster-Ashburton Treaty: A Study in Anglo-American Relations, 1783–1843* (Chapel Hill, 1977), Howard Jones and Donald A. Rakestraw, *Prologue to Manifest Destiny: Anglo-American Relations in the 1840s* (Wilmington, 1997), and Sam W. Haynes, "Anglophobia and the Annexation of Texas," in Sam W. Haynes and Christopher Morris, eds., *Manifest Destiny and Empire: Antebellum American Expansionism* (College Station, 1997), 115–45.

The Political Landscape

The long-range socioeconomic and political context in which the politics of the 1840s occurred are discussed in Charles G. Sellers, *The Market Revolution: Jacksonian America, 1815–1846* (New York, 1991) and John Ashworth, *Slavery, Capitalism, and Politics in the Antebellum Republic*, vol. 1 *Commerce and Compromise, 1820–1850* (Cambridge, Eng., 1995). Understanding the rise and maturing of the two-party system begins with Richard P. McCormick, *The Second American Party System: Party Formation in the Jacksonian Era* (Chapel Hill, 1966). Michael F. Holt, *The Rise and Fall of the American Whig Party: Jacksonian Politics and the Onset of the Civil War* (New York, 1999) is a magisterial history, as is Daniel Walker Howe's cultural-intellectual study of the Whig leadership, *The Political Culture of the American Whigs* (Chicago, 1979). There are no comparable volumes on the Democrats, but see Michael Holt's essay, "The Democratic Party, 1828–1860," in Arthur M. Schlesinger Jr., ed., *History of U.S. Political Parties* (New York, 1973), 1:497–571. A great deal about the party of Jackson, Van Buren, and Polk can be gleaned from the biographies listed below, from studies of popular political attitudes and behavior such as Lee Benson, *The Concept of Jacksonian Democracy: New York as a Test Case* (Princeton, 1961) and Richard Carwardine, *Evangelicals and Politics in Antebellum America* (New York, 1993), and from studies of state politics, which add much material and texture to our understanding. Among the best of these, see William G. Shade, *Democratizing the Old Dominion: Virginia and the Second American Party System, 1824–1861* (Charlottesville, 1996), Marc W. Kruman, *Parties and Politics in North Carolina, 1836–1865* (Baton Rouge, 1983), and Ronald P. Formisano, *The Birth of Mass Political Parties: Michigan, 1827–1861* (Princeton, 1971) and *The Transformation of Political Culture: Massachusetts Parties, 1790s–1840s* (New York, 1983). On Congress and the two-party system, see Thomas B. Alexander, *Sectional Stress and Party Strength: A Computer Analysis of Roll-Call Voting in the United States House of Representatives, 1836–1860* (Nashville, 1967) and Joel H. Silbey, *The Shrine of Party: Congressional Voting Behavior, 1841–1852* (Pittsburgh, 1967). Joel H. Silbey, *The American Political Nation, 1838–1893* (Stanford, 1991) describes the American partisan system as it settled into, and dominated, the landscape.

The situation of the parties in the early 1840s is covered in John Ashworth, *"Agrarians and Aristocrats": Party Political Ideology in the United States, 1837–1846* (London, 1983), William R. Brock, *Parties and Political Conscience: American*

Dilemmas, 1840–1850 (Millwood, N.Y., 1979), and James C.N. Paul, *Rift in the Democracy* (New York, 1961). The travails of the Tyler administration are cogently discussed in Norma Lois Peterson, *The Presidencies of William Henry Harrison and John Tyler* (Lawrence, Kans., 1989) and Robert J. Morgan, *A Whig Embattled: The Presidency Under John Tyler* (Lincoln, 1954).

Biographies

Tyler and his inner circle on Texas are studied in Robert Seager II, *And Tyler Too: A Biography of John and Julia Gardiner Tyler* (New York, 1963), Claude H. Hall, *Abel Parker Upshur: Conservative Virginian* (Madison, 1963), James Shenton, *Robert John Walker: A Politician from Jackson to Lincoln* (New York, 1961), and three biographies of John C. Calhoun: Charles Wiltse's three-volume *John C. Calhoun* (Indianapolis, 1944–51); John Niven, *John C. Calhoun and the Price of Union* (Baton Rouge, 1983); and Irving Bartlett, *John C. Calhoun: A Biography* (New York, 1993). Wiltse's has the fullest coverage of most matters. See also Edward Crapol, "John Tyler and the Pursuit of National Destiny," *Journal of the Early Republic* 17 (Fall 1997): 467–91.

For the Democrats, see, to begin, John Niven, *Martin Van Buren: The Romantic Age of American Politics* (New York, 1983), which is the most detailed biography. It can be supplemented by Donald B. Cole, *Martin Van Buren and the American Political System* (Princeton, 1984) and Joel H. Silbey, *Martin Van Buren and the Emergence of American Popular Politics* (Lanham, Md., 2002). John Garraty, *Silas Wright* (New York, 1949), William N. Chambers, *Old Bullion Benton, Senator from the New West: Thomas Hart Benton, 1782–1858* (Boston, 1956), Philip S. Klein, *President James Buchanan: A Biography* (University Park, Pa., 1962), Frederick M. Binder, *James Buchanan and the American Empire* (Selingsgrove, Pa., 1994), Ivor D. Spencer, *The Victor and the Spoils: A Life of William L. Marcy* (Providence, 1959), Robert Johannsen, *Stephen A. Douglas* (New York, 1973), and Charles Going, *David Wilmot, Free Soiler: A Biography*... (New York, 1924), among many others, consider some of the Democrats involved in the annexation controversy as it unfolded. Two unpublished dissertations of important participants should also be noted: Martin Lichterman, "John Adams Dix, 1798–1879" (Columbia University, 1952) and Ernest Muller, "Preston King: A Political Biography" (Columbia University, 1957). Charles Sellers, *James K. Polk, Jacksonian, 1795–1843* (Princeton, 1957) and *James K. Polk, Continentalist, 1843–1846* (Princeton, 1966) comprise a magnificent biography to the midpoint of "Young Hickory's" administration. Seller's work can be usefully supplemented by the shorter and more recent Sam W. Haynes, *James K. Polk and the Expansionist Impulse* (New York, 1997), William Dusinberre, *Slaveholder President: The Double Career of James Polk* (New York, 2003), and Thomas M. Leonard, *James K. Polk: A Clear and Unquestionable Destiny* (Wilmington, 2001).

On individual Whigs, the best biography of John Quincy Adams in this period remains Samuel F. Bemis, *John Quincy Adams and the Union* (New York, 1956). See also Lynn H. Parsons, *John Quincy Adams* (Madison, 1998) and Leonard Richards, *The Life and Times of Congressman John Quincy Adams* (New York, 1986). On Henry Clay, see George R. Poage, *Henry Clay and the Whig Party* (Chapel Hill, 1936) and Robert Remini, *Henry Clay: Statesman for the Union* (New York, 1991). There are also several biographies of Daniel Webster, the most recent being Robert

Remini, *Daniel Webster: The Man and His Time* (New York, 1997). Other biographies of involved Whigs include Thomas E. Schott, *Alexander H. Stephens of Georgia* (Baton Rouge, 1988), Donald W. Riddle, *Congressman Abraham Lincoln* (Urbana, 1957), David H. Donald, *Lincoln* (New York, 1995), Glyndon G. Van Deusen, *William Henry Seward* (New York, 1967), and the biographical sketches in Howe, *Political Culture of the American Whigs.*

The Rise of Sectional Confrontation

The buildup of anti-slavery sentiment and activities in the northern states is the subject of, among many other works, Richard Sewell, *Ballots for Freedom: Antislavery Politics in the United States, 1837–1860* (New York, 1976), James B. Stewart, *Holy Warriors: The Abolitionists and American Slavery* (New York, 1976) and *Joshua Giddings and the Tactics of Radical Politics* (Cleveland, 1970), and, more recently, John R. McKivigan, *Abolitionism and American Politics and Government* (New York, 1999). The southern sense of its identity, and its danger, is the subject of many books, the best of which is William Freehling, *The Road to Disunion: Secessionists at Bay, 1776–1854* (New York, 1990). There is much material in William Cooper, *The South and the Politics of Slavery, 1828–1856* (Baton Rouge, 1978) and James Oakes, *Slavery and Freedom: An Interpretation of the Old South* (New York, 1990). Leonard Richards, *The Slave Power: The Free North and Southern Domination, 1780–1860* (Baton Rouge, 2000) and Don S. Fehrenbacher, completed and edited by Ward M. McAfee, *The Slaveholding Republic: An Account of the United States Government's Relations to Slavery* (New York, 2001) discuss the perception, and the reality, of the South's great influence over American politics before the Civil War.

The Polk Administration

In addition to what he has said in his biography of Polk, Charles G. Sellers has also written an excellent study, "Election of 1844," in Arthur M. Schlesinger Jr. and Fred L. Israel, eds., *History of American Presidential Elections* (New York, 1971), 2:745–861. Paul Bergeron, *The Presidency of James K. Polk* (Lawrence, Kans., 1987) ably covers "Young Hickory's" years in office. The Wilmot Proviso is the subject of Chaplain Morrison, *Democratic Politics and Sectionalism: The Wilmot Proviso Controversy* (Chapel Hill, 1967). Eric Foner's seminal article, "The Wilmot Proviso Revisited," *Journal of American History* 56 (September 1969), 267–79 should also be consulted. The story of the war with Mexico is told in K. Jack Bauer, *The Mexican War, 1846–1848* (Lincoln, 1974), an excellent military history, and Richard V. Francaviglia and Douglas W. Richmond, eds., *Dueling Eagles: Reinterpreting the U.S.–Mexican War, 1846–1848* (Fort Worth, 2000), which contains essays on military, political, diplomatic, and popular-culture issues.

The opposition to the war is analyzed in John H. Schroeder, *Mr. Polk's War: American Opposition and Dissent, 1846–1848* (Madison, 1973). Also see Kinley J. Brauer, *Cotton versus Conscience: Massachusetts Whig Politics and Southwest Expansion* (Lexington, Ky., 1967). The splintering of the Democratic Party is covered in the biographies of Van Buren listed above, in Herbert D. A. Donovan, *The Barnburners . . . 1830–1852* (New York, 1925), and in the already noted Sewell, *Ballots for Freedom*. See also the excellent unpublished dissertation by Walter Ferree, "The

New York Democracy: Division and Reunion, 1847–1852" (University of Pennsylvania, 1953). The election of 1848 has been particularly well covered by historians; see, among other books, Frederick Blue, *The Free Soilers: Third-Party Politics, 1848–1854* (Urbana, 1973) and Joseph Rayback, *Free Soil: The Election of 1848* (Lexington, Ky., 1970).

The Fallout from Texas.

The 1850s are well covered in Allan Nevins, *Ordeal of the Union* (New York, 4 vols., 1947, 1950), David Potter, completed and edited by Don E. Fehrenbacher, *The Impending Crisis, 1848–1861* (New York, 1976), and Michael Holt, *The Political Crisis of the 1850s* (New York, 1978). The congressional compromise of 1850 is the subject of Holman Hamilton, *Prologue to Conflict: The Crisis and Compromise of 1850* (Lexington, Ky., 1964), Mark Stegmaier, *Texas, New Mexico, and the Compromise of 1850: Boundary Dispute and Sectional Crisis* (Kent, Ohio, 1996), and John Waugh, *On the Brink of Civil War: The Compromise of 1850 . . .* (Wilmington, 2003). The political realignment and the rise of the Republican Party in the mid-1850s is the subject of William Gienapp, *Origins of the Republican Party, 1852–1856* (New York, 1987) and Eric Foner, *Free Soil, Free Labor, Free Men: The Ideology of the Republican Party Before the Civil War* (New York, 1970). See also David Donald's excellent biography of Charles Sumner, *Charles Sumner and the Coming of the Civil War* (New York, 1960). The Democrats are discussed in several books by Roy F. Nichols—*Franklin Pierce: Young Hickory of the Granite Hills* (Philadelphia, 2d ed., 1958), *Blueprints for Leviathan, American Style* (New York, 1963), and *The Disruption of the American Democracy* (New York, 1948)—as well as in Johannsen's biography of Douglas and in Damon Wells, *Stephen A. Douglas: The Last Years, 1857–1861* (Austin, 1971).

Don Fehrenbacher, *The Dred Scott Decision: Its Significance in American Law and Politics* (New York, 1978), Kenneth Stampp, *America in 1857: A Nation on the Brink* (New York, 1990), and Nicole Etcheson, *Bleeding Kansas: Contested Liberty in the Civil War Era* (Lawrence, Kans., 2004) bring the crisis spawned by Texas annexation to its apogee.